2007 SUPPLEMENT

CASES AND MATERIALS

CONSTITUTIONAL LAW

TWELFTH EDITION

by

WILLIAM COHEN
C. Wendell and Edith M. Carlsmith
Professor Emeritus, Stanford Law School

JONATHAN D. VARAT
Professor of Law and Former Dean
University of California, Los Angeles

VIKRAM AMAR
Professor of Law
University of California, Davis

FOUNDATION PRESS

2007

© 2005, 2006 FOUNDATION PRESS
© 2007 By FOUNDATION PRESS
        395 Hudson Street
        New York, NY 10014
        Phone Toll Free 1–877–888–1330
        Fax (212) 367–6799
        foundation–press.com
Printed in the United States of America

ISBN 978-1-59941-191-0

 TEXT IS PRINTED ON 10% POST CONSUMER RECYCLED PAPER

PREFACE

After eleven years without change in the membership of the Supreme Court, two new appointments occurred during the October Term, 2005. Following the retirement of Justice Sandra Day O'Connor and the death of Chief Justice William H. Rehnquist, President George W. Bush, by and with the advice and consent of the Senate, appointed John G. Roberts, Jr. of Maryland as Chief Justice on September 29, 2005, and Samuel A. Alito, of New Jersey as Associate Justice on January 31, 2006.

*

TABLE OF CONTENTS

(**Bold** Indicates Principal Cases)

PART III   GOVERNMENT AND THE INDIVIDUAL: THE PROTECTION OF LIBERTY AND PROPERTY UNDER THE DUE PROCESS AND EQUAL PROTECTION CLAUSES

CHAPTER 9   THE DUE PROCESS, CONTRACT, AND JUST COMPENSATION CLAUSES AND THE REVIEW OF THE REASONABLENESS OF LEGISLATION

CHAPTER 10   THE EQUAL PROTECTION CLAUSE AND THE REVIEW OF THE REASONABLENESS OF LEGISLATION

**CHAPTER 11   DEFINING THE SCOPE OF "LIBERTY" AND
"PROPERTY" PROTECTED BY THE DUE PROCESS
CLAUSE—THE PROCEDURAL DUE PROCESS CASES**

PART IV CONSTITUTIONAL PROTECTION OF EXPRESSION AND CONSCIENCE

CHAPTER 13 GOVERNMENTAL CONTROL OF THE CONTENT OF EXPRESSION

CHAPTER 14 RESTRICTIONS ON TIME, PLACE, OR MANNER OF EXPRESSION

CHAPTER 15 PROTECTION OF PENUMBRAL FIRST AMENDMENT RIGHTS

TABLE OF CASES

Principal cases are in bold type. Non-principal cases are in roman type. References are to Pages.

2007 SUPPLEMENT

CONSTITUTIONAL LAW

*

PART I

THE CONSTITUTION AND THE COURTS: THE JUDICIAL FUNCTION IN CONSTITUTIONAL CASES

CHAPTER 3

THE JURISDICTION OF FEDERAL COURTS IN CONSTITUTIONAL CASES

SECTION 3.   CASES AND CONTROVERSIES AND JUSTICIABILITY

B.   STANDING

2.   STANDING TO ASSERT THE RIGHTS OF THIRD PARTIES

Page 75.   Add after Craig v. Boren:

MASSACHUSETTS v. ENVIRONMENTAL PROTECTION AGENCY, ___ U.S. ___, 127 S.Ct. 1438, 167 L.Ed.2d 248 (2007). The Court ruled 5–4 that the State of Massachusetts had standing to challenge the Federal Environmental Protection Agency's decision not to regulate four particular "greenhouse" gases under the section 202(1)(a) of the Clean Air Act. Writing for the majority,

1

Justice Stevens observed that "[w]hen a State enters the Union, it surrenders certain sovereign prerogatives. Massachusetts cannot invade Rhode Island to force reductions in greenhouse gas emissions, it cannot negotiate an emissions treaty with China or India, and in some circumstances the exercise of its police powers to reduce in-state motor-vehicle emissions might well be pre-empted.... These sovereign prerogatives are now lodged in the Federal Government, and Congress has ordered EPA to protect Massachusetts (among others) by prescribing standards applicable to the 'emission of any air pollutant from any class or classes of new motor vehicle engines, which in [the Administrator's] judgment cause, or contribute to, air pollution which may reasonably be anticipated to endanger public health or welfare.' 42 U.S.C. § 7251(a)(1). Congress has moreover recognized a concomitant procedural right to challenge the rejection of its rulemaking petition as arbitrary and capricious. § 7606(b)(1). Given that procedural right and Massachusetts' stake in protecting its quasi-sovereign interests, the Commonwealth is entitled to special solicitude in our standing analysis."

The majority went on to find the elements of standing to be satisfied because "EPA's steadfast refusal to regulate greenhouse gas emissions presents a risk of harm to Massachusetts that is both 'actual' and 'imminent'.... There is, moreover, a 'substantial likelihood that the judicial relief requested' will prompt EPA to take steps to reduce that risk." As to actual injury, the Court noted that the "widely-shared" nature of climate-change risks "does not minimize Massachusetts' interest in the outcome of this litigation." As for causation, the majority rejected EPA's argument that because the effect of any regulation on the global warming problem would be incremental, the agency's contributions to Massachusetts' injuries are so "insignificant[] ... that the agency cannot be haled into court to answer for them" because this "argument rests on the erroneous assumption that a small incremental step, because it is incremental, can never be attacked in a federal judicial forum. Yet accepting that premise would doom most challenges to regulatory action."

Finally, and relatedly, as to the effectiveness of any remedy to redress Massachusetts' injury, the majority reasoned: "While it may be true that regulating motor-vehicle emissions will not by itself reverse global warming, it by no means follows that we lack jurisdiction to decide whether EPA has a duty to take steps to slow or reduce it.... Because of the enormity of the potential consequences associated with man-made climate change, the fact that the effectiveness of a remedy might be delayed during the (relatively short) time it takes for a new motor-vehicle fleet to replace an older one is essentially irrelevant. Nor is it dispositive that developing countries such as China and India are poised to increase greenhouse gas emissions substantially over the next century: A reduction in domestic emissions would slow the pace of global emissions increases, no matter what happens elsewhere."

The Chief Justice, with Justices Scalia, Thomas and Alito, dissented.

3.   TAXPAYER AND CITIZEN STANDING

Page 76.   Add at end of Note, "Taxpayer Standing":

In Hein v. Freedom From Religion Foundation, Inc., ___ U.S. ___, 127 S.Ct. 2553, ___ L.Ed.2d ___ (2007), the Court rejected by a 5–4 vote standing for taxpayers who challenged on Establishment Clause grounds various conferences, speeches and events organized and sponsored by President George Bush's Administration that allegedly were intended to and did in fact favor religious faith-based providers of social services over secular social service providers. Two Justices, Scalia and Thomas, wrote to say they would overrule *Flast* and eliminate taxpayer standing altogether. Justice Alito, joined by Chief Justice Roberts and Justice Kennedy, wrote an opinion that would preserve *Flast*, but explicitly limit it to spending made pursuant to a Congressional enactment or program that directed the expenditure of funds in the way the plaintiff alleges violates the Establishment Clause. According to these three Justices, where, as in *Hein*, the challenged expenditures were made pursuant not to any directed Act of Congress, but as a matter of Executive discretion under general appropriations to the Executive Branch to fund day-to-day activities, neither *Flast* nor subsequent Court cases applying it support taxpayer standing. Justices Stevens, Souter, Ginsburg and Breyer dissented.

In DaimlerChrysler Corp. v. Cuno, ___ U.S. ___, 126 S.Ct. 1854, 164 L.Ed.2d 589 (2006), state taxpayers brought suit (ultimately removed to federal court) challenging Ohio's grant of property tax exemptions and franchise tax credits to DaimlerChrysler Corp., on the ground that such tax breaks violated the Commerce Clause. The Court ruled that although "*Flast* held out the possibility that 'other specific [constitutional] limitations' " besides the Establishment Clause (invoked in *Flast*) might support taxpayer standing in federal court, alleged violations of the so-called Dormant Commerce Clause doctrine do not bring a case within the *Flast* exception to the general prohibition on taxpayer standing.

*

PART II

Allocation of Governmental Powers: The Nation and the States; The President, The Congress, and The Courts

CHAPTER 4

The Scope of National Power

SECTION 3. THE SCOPE OF NATIONAL POWER TODAY

A. THE COMMERCE POWER

Page 192. Add before Pierce County v. Guillen:

Gonzales v. Raich

545 U.S. 1, 125 S.Ct. 2195, 162 L.Ed.2d 1 (2005).

Justice Stevens delivered the opinion of the Court.

California is one of at least nine States that authorize the use of marijuana for medicinal purposes. The question presented in this case is whether the power vested in Congress by Article I, § 8, of the Constitution "[t]o make all Laws which shall be necessary and proper for carrying into Execution" its authority to "regulate Commerce with foreign Nations, and among the several States" includes the power to prohibit the local cultivation and use of marijuana in compliance with California law.

I

... In 1996, California voters passed Proposition 215, now codified as the Compassionate Use Act of 1996. The proposition was designed to ensure that "seriously ill" residents of the State have access to marijuana for medical purposes, and to encourage Federal and State Governments to take steps towards ensuring the safe and affordable distribution of the drug to patients in need. The Act creates an exemption from criminal prosecution for physicians, as well as for patients and primary caregivers who possess or cultivate marijuana for medicinal purposes with the recommendation or approval of a physician....

Respondents Angel Raich and Diane Monson are ... being treated by licensed, board-certified family practitioners, who have concluded, after prescribing a host of conventional medicines to treat respondents' conditions and to alleviate their associated symptoms, that marijuana is the only drug available that provides effective treatment. Both women have been using marijuana as a medication for several years pursuant to their doctors' recommendation, and both rely heavily on cannabis to function on a daily basis....

Respondent Monson cultivates her own marijuana, and ingests the drug in a variety of ways including smoking and using a vaporizer. Respondent Raich, by contrast, is unable to cultivate her own, and thus relies on two caregivers....

On August 15, 2002, county deputy sheriffs and agents from the federal Drug Enforcement Administration (DEA) came to Monson's home. After a thorough investigation, the county officials concluded that her use of marijuana was entirely lawful as a matter of California law. Nevertheless, after a 3-hour standoff, the federal agents seized and destroyed all six of her cannabis plants.

Respondents thereafter brought this action against the Attorney General of the United States and the head of the DEA seeking injunctive and declaratory relief prohibiting the enforcement of the federal Controlled Substances Act (CSA) [21 U.S.C. § 801 *et seq.*] ... to the extent it prevents them from possessing, obtaining, or manufacturing cannabis for their personal medical use.... Respondents claimed [among other things] that enforcing the CSA against them would violate the Commerce Clause....

. . .

[The Ninth Circuit reversed the district court's denial of respondents' motion for a preliminary injunction.] The Court of Appeals distinguished prior Circuit cases upholding the CSA in the face of Commerce Clause challenges by focusing on what it deemed to be the *"separate and distinct class of activities"* at issue in this case: "the intrastate, noncommercial cultivation and possession of cannabis for personal medical purposes as recommended by a patient's physician pursuant to valid California state law." ...

. . .

The obvious importance of the case prompted our grant of certiorari.... Well-settled law controls our ... [resolution of this case]. The CSA is a valid exercise of federal power, even as applied to the troubling facts of this case. We accordingly vacate the judgment of the Court of Appeals.

II

. . .

... [A]s early as 1906 Congress enacted federal legislation imposing labeling regulations on medications and prohibiting the manufacture or shipment of any adulterated or misbranded drug traveling in interstate commerce....

Marijuana itself was not significantly regulated by the Federal Government until 1937 when accounts of marijuana's addictive qualities and physiological effects, paired with dissatisfaction with enforcement efforts at state and local levels, prompted Congress to pass the Marihuana Tax Act ... [which] did not outlaw the possession or sale of marijuana outright. Rather, it imposed registration and reporting requirements for all individuals importing, producing, selling, or dealing in marijuana, and required the payment of annual taxes in addition to transfer taxes whenever the drug changed hands....

... [I]n 1970, after declaration of the national "war on drugs," federal drug policy underwent a significant transformation.... [Ultimately, that year] ..., prompted by a perceived need to consolidate the growing number of piecemeal drug laws and to enhance federal drug enforcement powers, Congress enacted the Comprehensive Drug Abuse Prevention and Control Act.

Title II of that Act, the CSA, repealed most of the earlier antidrug laws in favor of a comprehensive regime to combat the international and interstate traffic in illicit drugs. The main objectives of the CSA were to conquer drug abuse and to control the legitimate and illegitimate traffic in controlled substances.[20] Congress was particularly concerned with the need to prevent the diversion of drugs from legitimate to illicit channels.

---

20. In particular, Congress made the following findings:

"(1) Many of the drugs included within this subchapter have a useful and legitimate medical purpose and are necessary to maintain the health and general welfare of the American people.

"(2) The illegal importation, manufacture, distribution, and possession and improper use of controlled substances have a substantial and detrimental effect on the health and general welfare of the American people.

"(3) A major portion of the traffic in controlled substances flows through interstate and foreign commerce. Incidents of the traffic which are not an integral part of the interstate or foreign flow, such as manufacture, local distribution, and possession, nonetheless have a substantial and direct effect upon interstate commerce because—

"(A) after manufacture, many controlled substances are transported in interstate commerce,

"(B) controlled substances distributed locally usually have been transported in

To effectuate these goals, Congress devised a closed regulatory system making it unlawful to manufacture, distribute, dispense, or possess any controlled substance except in a manner authorized by the CSA. 21 U.S.C. §§ 841(a)(1), 844(a). The CSA categorizes all controlled substances into five schedules. § 812. The drugs are grouped together based on their accepted medical uses, the potential for abuse, and their psychological and physical effects on the body.... Each schedule is associated with a distinct set of controls regarding the manufacture, distribution, and use of the substances listed therein.... The CSA and its implementing regulations set forth strict requirements regarding registration, labeling and packaging, production quotas, drug security, and recordkeeping....

In enacting the CSA, Congress classified marijuana as a Schedule I drug. 21 U.S.C. § 812(c).... Schedule I drugs are categorized as such because of their high potential for abuse, lack of any accepted medical use, and absence of any accepted safety for use in medically supervised treatment. § 812(b)(1).... By classifying marijuana as a Schedule I drug, as opposed to listing it on a lesser schedule, the manufacture, distribution, or possession of marijuana became a criminal offense, with the sole exception being use of the drug as part of a Food and Drug Administration pre-approved research study. §§ 823(f), 841(a)(1), 844(a); see also United States v. Oakland Cannibis Buyers' Cooperative, 532 U.S. 483, 490 (2001).

... Despite considerable efforts to reschedule marijuana, it remains a Schedule I drug.

III

Respondents ... do not dispute that passage of the CSA, as part of the Comprehensive Drug Abuse Prevention and Control Act, was well within Congress' commerce power.... Nor do they contend that any provision or section of the CSA amounts to an unconstitutional exercise of congressional authority. Rather, respondents' challenge is actually quite limited; they argue that the CSA's categorical prohibition of the manufacture and possession of marijuana as applied to the intrastate manufacture and possession of marijuana for medical purposes pursuant to California law exceeds Congress' authority under the Commerce Clause.

In assessing the validity of congressional regulation, none of our Commerce Clause cases can be viewed in isolation. As charted in considerable detail in United States v. Lopez [514 U.S. 549 (1995)], our understanding of the reach of

interstate commerce immediately before their distribution, and

"(C) controlled substances possessed commonly flow through interstate commerce immediately prior to such possession.

"(4) Local distribution and possession of controlled substances contribute to swelling the interstate traffic in such substances.

"(5) Controlled substances manufactured and distributed intrastate cannot be dif-

ferentiated from controlled substances manufactured and distributed interstate. Thus, it is not feasible to distinguish, in terms of controls, between controlled substances manufactured and distributed interstate and controlled substances manufactured and distributed intrastate.

"(6) Federal control of the intrastate incidents of the traffic in controlled substances is essential to the effective control of the interstate incidents of such traffic." 21 U.S.C. §§ 801(1)–(6).

the Commerce Clause, as well as Congress' assertion of authority thereunder, has evolved over time. . . .

. . .

Our case law firmly establishes Congress' power to regulate purely local activities that are part of an economic "class of activities" that have a substantial effect on interstate commerce. . . . As we stated in [Wickard v. Filburn, 317 U.S. 111, 125], "even if appellee's activity be local and though it may not be regarded as commerce, it may still, whatever its nature, be reached by Congress if it exerts a substantial economic effect on interstate commerce." . . . We have never required Congress to legislate with scientific exactitude. When Congress decides that the " 'total incidence' " of a practice poses a threat to a national market, it may regulate the entire class. . . . In this vein, we have reiterated that when " 'a general regulatory statute bears a substantial relation to commerce, the *de minimis* character of individual instances arising under that statute is of no consequence.' " . . .

Our decision in *Wickard* . . . is of particular relevance. In *Wickard*, we upheld the application of regulations promulgated under the Agricultural Adjustment Act [AAA] of 1938 . . . which were designed to control the volume of wheat moving in interstate and foreign commerce in order to avoid surpluses and consequent abnormally low prices. The regulations established an allotment of 11.1 acres for Filburn's 1941 wheat crop, but he sowed 23 acres, intending to use the excess by consuming it on his own farm. Filburn argued that even though we had sustained Congress' power to regulate the production of goods for commerce, that power did not authorize "federal regulation [of] production not intended in any part for commerce but wholly for consumption on the farm." *Wickard*, 317 U.S. at 188. Justice Jackson's opinion for a unanimous Court rejected this submission. He wrote:

"The effect of the statute before us is to restrict the amount which may be produced for market and the extent as well to which one may forestall resort to the market by producing to meet his own needs. That appellee's own contribution to the demand for wheat may be trivial by itself is not enough to remove him from the scope of federal regulation where, as here, his contribution, taken together with that of many others similarly situated, is far from trivial." *Id.*, at 127–128.

Wickard thus establishes that Congress can regulate purely intrastate activity that is not itself "commercial," in that it is not produced for sale, if it concludes that failure to regulate that class of activity would undercut the regulation of the interstate market in that commodity.

The similarities between this case and *Wickard* are striking. Like the farmer in *Wickard*, respondents are cultivating, for home consumption, a fungible commodity for which there is an established, albeit illegal, interstate market. Just as the Agricultural Adjustment Act was designed "to control the volume [of wheat] moving in interstate and foreign commerce in order to avoid surpluses . . ." and consequently control the market price . . . a primary purpose of the CSA is to control the supply and demand of controlled substances in both lawful and unlawful drug markets. See [n. 20] *supra*. In *Wickard*, we had no difficulty concluding that Congress had a rational basis for believing that, when viewed in the aggregate, leaving home-consumed wheat outside the regulatory scheme would have a substantial influence on price and market conditions. Here too, Congress had a rational basis for concluding that leaving home-consumed marijuana outside federal control would similarly affect price and market conditions.

More concretely, one concern prompting inclusion of wheat grown for home consumption in the 1938 Act was that rising market prices could draw such wheat into the interstate market, resulting in lower market prices.... The parallel concern making it appropriate to include marijuana grown for home consumption in the CSA is the likelihood that the high demand in the interstate market will draw such marijuana into that market.... In both cases, the regulation is squarely within Congress' commerce power because production of the commodity meant for home consumption, be it wheat or marijuana, has a substantial effect on supply and demand in the national market for that commodity.[29]

Nonetheless, respondents suggest that *Wickard* differs from this case in three respects: (1) the Agricultural Adjustment Act, unlike the CSA, exempted small farming operations; (2) *Wickard* involved a "quintessential economic activity"—a commercial farm—whereas respondents do not sell marijuana; and (3) the *Wickard* record made it clear that the aggregate production of wheat for use on farms had a significant impact on market prices. Those differences, though factually accurate, do not diminish the precedential force of this Court's reasoning.

The fact that ... [Filburn's] own impact on the market was "trivial by itself" was not a sufficient reason for removing him from the scope of federal regulation.... That the Secretary of Agriculture elected to exempt even smaller farms from regulation does not speak to his power to regulate all those whose aggregated production was significant, nor did that fact play any role in the Court's analysis. Moreover, even though ... [Filburn] was indeed a commercial farmer, the activity he was engaged in—the cultivation of wheat for home consumption—was not treated by the Court as part of his commercial farming operation. And while it is true that the record in the *Wickard* case itself established the causal connection between the production for local use and the national market, we have before us findings by Congress to the same effect.

Findings in the introductory sections of the CSA explain why Congress deemed it appropriate to encompass local activities within the scope of the CSA. See n. 20, *supra*.... Respondents nonetheless insist that the CSA cannot be constitutionally applied to their activities because Congress did not make a specific finding that the intrastate cultivation and possession of marijuana for medical purposes based on the recommendation of a physician would substantially affect the larger interstate marijuana market. Be that as it may, we have never required Congress to make particularized findings in order to legislate, see *Lopez*, 514 U.S. at 562, Perez [v. United States], 402 U.S. at 156, absent a special concern such as the protection of free speech.... While congressional

---

29. To be sure, the wheat market is a lawful market that Congress sought to protect and stabilize, whereas the marijuana market is an unlawful market that Congress sought to eradicate. This difference, however, is of no constitutional import. It has long been settled that Congress' power to regulate commerce includes the power to prohibit commerce in a particular commodity....

findings are certainly helpful in reviewing the substance of a congressional statutory scheme, particularly when the connection to commerce is not self-evident, and while we will consider congressional findings in our analysis when they are available, the absence of particularized findings does not call into question Congress' authority to legislate.

In assessing the scope of Congress' authority under the Commerce Clause, we stress that the task before us is a modest one. We need not determine whether respondents' activities, taken in the aggregate, substantially affect interstate commerce in fact, but only whether a "rational basis" exists for so concluding. *Lopez*, 514 U.S. at 557.... Given the enforcement difficulties that attend distinguishing between marijuana cultivated locally and marijuana grown elsewhere ... and concerns about diversion into illicit channels, ... we have no difficulty concluding that Congress had a rational basis for believing that failure to regulate the intrastate manufacture and possession of marijuana would leave a gaping hole in the CSA. Thus, as in *Wickard*, when it enacted comprehensive legislation to regulate the interstate market in a fungible commodity, Congress was acting well within its authority to "make all Laws which shall be necessary and proper" to "regulate Commerce ... among the several States." U.S. Const., Art. I, § 8. That the regulation ensnares some purely intrastate activity is of no moment. As we have done many times before, we refuse to excise individual components of that larger scheme.

IV

To support their contrary submission, respondents rely heavily on two of our more recent Commerce Clause cases. In their myopic focus, they overlook the larger context of modern-era Commerce Clause jurisprudence preserved by those cases. Moreover, even in the narrow prism of respondents' creation, they read those cases far too broadly.

Those two cases, of course, are *Lopez* ... and [United States v. Morrison, 529 U.S 598 (2000)]. As an initial matter, the statutory challenges at issue in those cases were markedly different from the challenge respondents pursue in the case at hand. Here, respondents ask us to excise individual applications of a concededly valid statutory scheme. In contrast, in both *Lopez* and *Morrison*, the parties asserted that a particular statute or provision fell outside Congress' commerce power in its entirety. This distinction is pivotal for we have often reiterated that "[w]here the class of activities is regulated and that class is within the reach of federal power, the courts have no power 'to excise, as trivial, individual instances' of the class." ...

At issue in *Lopez* ... was the validity of the Gun-Free School Zones Act of 1990, which was a brief, single-subject statute making it a crime for an individual to possess a gun in a school zone.... Distinguishing our earlier cases holding that comprehensive regulatory statutes may be validly applied to local conduct that does not, when viewed in isolation, have a significant impact on interstate commerce, we held the statute invalid. We explained:

"Section 922(q) [, the Act,] is a criminal statute that by its terms has nothing to do with 'commerce' or any sort of economic enterprise, however broadly one might define those terms. Section 922(q) is not an essential part of a larger regulation of economic activity, in which the regulatory scheme could be undercut unless the intrastate activity were regulated. It cannot, therefore, be sustained under our cases upholding regulations of activities that arise out of or are connected with a commercial transaction, which viewed in the aggregate, substantially affects interstate commerce." 514 U.S. at 561.

The statutory scheme [here] is at the opposite end of the regulatory spectrum. [T]he CSA ... was a lengthy and detailed statute creating a comprehensive framework for regulating the production, distribution, and possession of five classes of "controlled substances." ...

... [The] classification [of marijuana as a Schedule I substance], unlike the discrete prohibition established by the Gun–Free School Zones Act of 1990, was merely one of many "essential part[s] of a larger regulation of economic activity, in which the regulatory scheme could be undercut unless the intrastate activity were regulated." *Lopez*, 514 U.S. at 561.[34] Our opinion in *Lopez* casts no doubt on the validity of such a program.

Nor does this Court's holding in *Morrison* .... The Violence Against Women Act of 1994 ... created a federal civil remedy for the victims of gender-motivated crimes of violence.... The remedy was enforceable in both state and federal courts, and generally depended on proof of the violation of a state law. Despite congressional findings that such crimes had an adverse impact on interstate commerce, we held the statute unconstitutional because, like the statute in *Lopez*, it did not regulate economic activity. We concluded that "the noneconomic, criminal nature of the conduct at issue was central to our decision" in *Lopez*, and that our prior cases had identified a clear pattern of analysis: " 'Where economic activity substantially affects interstate commerce, legislation regulating that activity will be sustained.' " ...

Unlike those at issue in *Lopez* and *Morrison*, the activities regulated by the CSA are quintessentially economic. "Economics" refers to "the production, distribution, and consumption of commodities." Webster's Third New International Dictionary 720 (1966). The CSA is a statute that regulates the production, distribution, and consumption of commodities for which there is an established, and lucrative, interstate market. Prohibiting the intrastate possession or manufacture of an article of commerce is a rational (and commonly utilized) means of regulating commerce in that product....

The Court of Appeals was able to conclude otherwise only by isolating a "separate and distinct" class of activities that it held to be beyond the reach of federal power, defined as "the intrastate, noncommercial cultivation, possession and use of marijuana for personal medical purposes on the advice of a physician and in accordance with state law." ... The court characterized this class as "different in kind from drug trafficking." ... The differences between the members of a class so defined and the principal traffickers in Schedule I substances might be sufficient to justify a policy decision exempting the narrower class from the coverage of the CSA. The question, however, is whether Congress' contrary policy judgment, *i.e.*, its decision to include this

---

34. The principal dissent asserts that by "[s]eizing upon our language in *Lopez*", i.e., giving effect to our well-established case law, Congress will now have an incentive to legislate broadly. Even putting aside the political checks that would generally curb Con-gress' power to enact a broad and comprehensive scheme for the purpose of targeting purely local activity, there is no suggestion that the CSA constitutes the type of "evasive" legislation the dissent fears, nor could such an argument plausibly be made....

narrower "class of activities" within the larger regulatory scheme, was constitutionally deficient. We have no difficulty concluding that Congress acted rationally. . . .

. . .

. . . [It cannot] serve as an "objective marke[r]" or "objective facto[r]" to arbitrarily narrow the relevant class as the dissenters suggest. . . . More fundamentally, if, as the principal dissent contends, the personal cultivation, possession, and use of marijuana for medicinal purposes is beyond the " 'outer limits' of Congress' Commerce Clause authority," . . . it must also be true that such personal use of marijuana (or any other homegrown drug) for recreational purposes is also beyond those " 'outer limits,' " whether or not a State elects to authorize or even regulate such use. . . . One need not have a degree in economics to understand why a nationwide exemption for the vast quantity of marijuana (or other drugs) locally cultivated for personal use (which presumably would include use by friends, neighbors, and family members) may have a substantial impact on the interstate market for this extraordinarily popular substance. . . .

Second, limiting the activity to marijuana possession and cultivation "in accordance with state law" cannot serve to place respondents' activities beyond congressional reach. The Supremacy Clause unambiguously provides that if there is any conflict between federal and state law, federal law shall prevail. . . .

. . .

V

. . . The case is remanded for further proceedings consistent with this opinion. . . .

Justice Scalia, concurring in the judgment.

I agree with the Court's holding that the Controlled Substances Act (CSA) may validly be applied to respondents' cultivation, distribution, and possession of marijuana for personal, medicinal use. I write separately because my understanding of the doctrinal foundation on which that holding rests is, if not inconsistent with that of the Court, at least more nuanced.

. . .

I

. . .

As we implicitly acknowledged in *Lopez* . . . , Congress's authority to enact laws necessary and proper for the regulation of interstate commerce is not limited to laws directed against economic activities that have a substantial effect on interstate commerce. Though the conduct in *Lopez* was not economic, the Court nevertheless recognized that it could be regulated as "an essential part of a larger regulation of economic activity, in which the regulatory scheme could be undercut unless the intrastate activity were regulated." . . . This statement referred to those cases permitting the regulation of intrastate activities "which in a substantial way interfere with or obstruct the exercise of the granted power." ...

... The regulation of an intrastate activity may be essential to a comprehensive regulation of interstate commerce even though the intrastate activity does not itself "substantially affect" interstate commerce. Moreover, as the passage from *Lopez* quoted above suggests, Congress may regulate even noneconomic local activity if that regulation is a necessary part of a more general regulation of interstate commerce.... The relevant question is simply whether the means chosen are "reasonably adapted" to the attainment of a legitimate end under the commerce power....

. . .

II

Today's principal dissent objects that, by permitting Congress to regulate activities necessary to effective interstate regulation, the Court reduces *Lopez* and *Morrison* to "little more than a drafting guide." ... I think that criticism unjustified. Unlike the power to regulate activities that have a substantial effect on interstate commerce, the power to enact laws enabling effective regulation of interstate commerce can only be exercised in conjunction with congressional regulation of an interstate market, and it extends only to those measures necessary to make the interstate regulation effective. As *Lopez* itself states, and the Court affirms today, Congress may regulate noneconomic intrastate activities only where the failure to do so "could ... undercut" its regulation of interstate commerce.... This is not a power that threatens to obliterate the line between "what is truly national and what is truly local." ...

Neither ... [*Lopez* nor *Morrison*] involved the power of Congress to exert control over intrastate activities in connection with a more comprehensive scheme of regulation; *Lopez* expressly disclaimed that it was such a case ... and *Morrison* did not even discuss the possibility that it was.... To dismiss this distinction as "superficial and formalistic," ... [as Justice O'Connor's dissent does] is to misunderstand the nature of the Necessary and Proper Clause, which empowers Congress to enact laws in effectuation of its enumerated powers that are not within its authority to enact in isolation. See McCulloch v. Maryland, 4 Wheat. 316, 421–244 (1819).

And there are other restraints upon the Necessary and Proper Clause authority. As Chief Justice Marshall wrote in *McCulloch* ..., even when the end is constitutional and legitimate, the means must be "appropriate" and "plainly adapted" to that end.... Moreover, they may not be otherwise "prohibited" and must be "consistent with the letter and spirit of the constitution." ... These phrases are not merely hortatory. For example, cases such as Printz v. United States, 521 U.S. 898 (1997) and New York v. United States, 505 U.S. 144 (1992), affirm that a law is not " 'proper for carrying into Execution the Commerce Clause' " "[w]hen [it] violates [a constitutional] principle of state sovereignty." ...

III

The application of these principles to the case before us is straightforward. In the CSA, Congress has undertaken to extinguish the interstate market in

Schedule I controlled substances, including marijuana. The Commerce Clause unquestionably permits this. The power to regulate interstate commerce "extends not only to those regulations which aid, foster and protect the commerce, but embraces those which prohibit it." . . . To effectuate its objective, Congress has prohibited almost all intrastate activities related to Schedule I substances— both economic activities (manufacture, distribution, possession with the intent to distribute) and noneconomic activities (simple possession). . . . That simple possession is a noneconomic activity is immaterial to whether it can be prohibited as a necessary part of a larger regulation. . . .

. . . Not only is it impossible to distinguish "controlled substances manufactured and distributed intrastate" from "controlled substances manufactured and distributed interstate," but it hardly makes sense to speak in such terms. Drugs like marijuana are fungible commodities. As the Court explains, marijuana that is grown at home and possessed for personal use is never more than an instant from the interstate market—and this is so whether or not the possession is for medicinal use or lawful use under the laws of a particular State.[3] . . . Congress need not accept on faith that state law will be effective in maintaining a strict division between a lawful market for "medical" marijuana and the more general marijuana market. . . . "To impose on [Congress] the necessity of resorting to means which it cannot control, which another government may furnish or withhold, would render its course precarious, the result of its measures uncertain, and create a dependence on other governments, which might disappoint its most important designs, and is incompatible with the language of the constitution." *McCulloch* . . . .

. . .

Justice O'Connor, with whom the Chief Justice and Justice Thomas join as to all but part III, dissenting.

. . .

This case exemplifies the role of States as laboratories. The States' core police powers have always included authority to define criminal law and to protect the health, safety, and welfare of their citizens. . . . Today the Court sanctions an application of the federal Controlled Substances Act that extinguishes . . . [California's] experiment, without any proof that the personal cultivation, possession, and use of marijuana for medicinal purposes, if economic activity in the first place, has a substantial effect on interstate commerce and is therefore an appropriate subject of federal regulation. In so doing, the Court

---

3. The principal dissent claims that, if this is sufficient to sustain the regulation at issue in this case, then it should also have been sufficient to sustain the regulation at issue in [*Lopez*]. . . . This claim founders upon the shoals of *Lopez* itself, which made clear that the statute there at issue was "not an essential part of a larger regulation of economic activity." . . . On the dissent's view of things, that statement is inexplicable. Of course it is in addition difficult to imagine what intelligible scheme of regulation of the interstate market in guns could have as an appropriate means of effectuation the prohibition of guns within 1000 feet of schools (and nowhere else). The dissent [mentions] a federal law . . . barring licensed dealers from selling guns to minors, . . . but the relationship between the regulatory scheme of which [that statute] is a part (requiring all dealers in firearms that have traveled in interstate commerce to be licensed . . .) and the statute at issue in *Lopez* approaches the nonexistent—which is doubtless why the Government did not attempt to justify the statute on the basis of that relationship.

announces a rule that gives Congress a perverse incentive to legislate broadly pursuant to the Commerce Clause—nestling questionable assertions of its authority into comprehensive regulatory schemes—rather than with precision. That rule and the result it produces in this case are irreconcilable with our decisions in [*Lopez* and *Morrison*]. Accordingly I dissent.

. . .

II

A

What is the relevant conduct subject to Commerce Clause analysis in this case? The Court takes its cues from Congress. . . . The Court's decision rests on two facts about the CSA: (1) Congress chose to enact a single statute providing a comprehensive prohibition on the production, distribution, and possession of all controlled substances, and (2) Congress did not distinguish between various forms of intrastate noncommercial cultivation, possession, and use of marijuana. . . . Today's decision suggests that the federal regulation of local activity is immune to Commerce Clause challenge because Congress chose to act with an ambitious, all-encompassing statute, rather than piecemeal. In my view, allowing Congress to set the terms of the constitutional debate in this way, i.e., by packaging regulation of local activity in broader schemes, is tantamount to removing meaningful limits on the Commerce Clause.

The Court's principal means of distinguishing *Lopez* from this case is to observe that the Gun-Free School Zones Act of 1990 was a "brief, single-subject statute," . . . whereas the CSA is "a lengthy and detailed statute creating a comprehensive framework for regulating the production, distribution, and possession of five classes of 'controlled substances,' ". . . . Thus, according to the Court, it was possible in *Lopez* to evaluate in isolation the constitutionality of criminalizing local activity (there gun possession in school zones), whereas the local activity that the CSA targets (in this case cultivation and possession of marijuana for personal medicinal use) cannot be separated from the general drug control scheme of which it is a part.

Today's decision allows Congress to regulate intrastate activity without check, so long as there is some implication by legislative design that regulating intrastate activity is essential (and the Court appears to equate "essential" with "necessary") to the interstate regulatory scheme. Seizing upon our language in *Lopez* that the statute prohibiting gun possession in school zones was "not an essential part of a larger regulation of economic activity, in which the regulatory scheme could be undercut unless the intrastate activity were regulated," . . . the Court appears to reason that the placement of local activity in a comprehensive scheme confirms that it is essential to that scheme. . . . If the Court is right, then *Lopez* stands for nothing more than a drafting guide: Congress should have described the relevant crime as "transfer or possession of a firearm anywhere in the nation"—thus including commercial and noncommercial activity, and clearly encompassing some activity with assuredly substantial effect on interstate commerce. Had it done so, the majority hints, we would have sustained its authority to regulate possession of firearms in school zones. . . .

I cannot agree that our decision in *Lopez* contemplated such evasive or overbroad legislative strategies with approval. Until today, such arguments have been made only in dissent.... *Lopez* and *Morrison* did not indicate that the constitutionality of federal regulation depends on superficial and formalistic distinctions. Likewise I did not understand our discussion of the role of courts in enforcing outer limits of the Commerce Clause for the sake of maintaining the federalist balance our Constitution requires ... as a signal to Congress to enact legislation that is more extensive and more intrusive into the domain of state power. If the Court always defers to Congress as it does today, little may be left to the notion of enumerated powers.

The hard work for courts ... is to identify objective markers for confining the analysis in Commerce Clause cases. Here, respondents challenge the constitutionality of the CSA as applied to them and those similarly situated. I agree with the Court that we must look beyond respondents' own activities. Otherwise, individual litigants could always exempt themselves from Commerce Clause regulation merely by pointing to the obvious—that their personal activities do not have a substantial effect on interstate commerce.... The task is to identify a mode of analysis that allows Congress to regulate more than nothing (by declining to reduce each case to its litigants) and less than everything (by declining to let Congress set the terms of analysis). The analysis may not be the same in every case, for it depends on the regulatory scheme at issue and the federalism concerns implicated....

A number of objective markers are available to confine the scope of constitutional review here. Both federal and state legislation—including the CSA itself, the California Compassionate Use Act, and other state medical marijuana legislation—recognize that medical and nonmedical (i.e., recreational) uses of drugs are realistically distinct and can be segregated, and regulate them differently.... Moreover, because fundamental structural concerns about dual sovereignty animate our Commerce Clause cases, it is relevant that this case involves the interplay of federal and state regulation in areas of criminal law and social policy, where "States lay claim by right of history and expertise." ... California, like other States, has drawn on its reserved powers to distinguish the regulation of medicinal marijuana. To ascertain whether Congress' encroachment is constitutionally justified in this case, then, I would focus here on the personal cultivation, possession, and use of marijuana for medicinal purposes.

B

Having thus defined the relevant conduct, we must determine whether, under our precedents, the conduct is economic and, in the aggregate, substantially affects interstate commerce. Even if intrastate cultivation and possession of marijuana for one's own medicinal use can properly be characterized as economic, and I question whether it can, it has not been shown that such activity substantially affects interstate commerce. Similarly, it is neither self-evident nor demonstrated that regulating such activity is necessary to the interstate drug control scheme.

The Court's definition of economic activity is breathtaking. It defines as economic any activity involving the production, distribution, and consumption of commodities. And it appears to reason that when an interstate market for a commodity exists, regulating the intrastate manufacture or possession of that commodity is constitutional either because that intrastate activity is itself economic, or because regulating it is a rational part of regulating its market. Putting to one side the problem endemic to the Court's opinion—the shift in focus from the activity at issue in this case to the entirety of what the CSA regulates, see *Lopez* ... ("depending on the level of generality, any activity can be looked upon as commercial")—the Court's definition of economic activity for purposes of Commerce Clause jurisprudence threatens to sweep all of productive human activity into federal regulatory reach.

... It will not do to say that Congress may regulate noncommercial activity simply because it may have an effect on the demand for commercial goods, or because the noncommercial endeavor can, in some sense, substitute for commercial activity. Most commercial goods or services have some sort of privately producible analogue. Home care substitutes for daycare. Charades games substitute for movie tickets. Backyard or windowsill gardening substitutes for going to the supermarket. To draw the line wherever private activity affects the demand for market goods is to draw no line at all, and to declare everything economic. We have already [explicitly] rejected [in *Lopez*] the result that would follow—a federal police power....

In *Lopez* and *Morrison*, we suggested that economic activity usually relates directly to commercial activity.... The homegrown cultivation and personal possession and use of marijuana for medicinal purposes has no apparent commercial character. Everyone agrees that the marijuana at issue in this case was never in the stream of commerce, and neither were the supplies for growing it. (Marijuana is highly unusual among the substances subject to the CSA in that it can be cultivated without any materials that have traveled in interstate commerce.) *Lopez* makes clear that possession is not itself commercial activity.... And respondents have not come into possession by means of any commercial transaction; they have simply grown, in their own homes, marijuana for their own use, without acquiring, buying, selling, or bartering a thing of value....

The Court suggests that *Wickard*, which we have identified as "perhaps the most far reaching example of Commerce Clause authority over intrastate activity," ... established federal regulatory power over any home consumption of a commodity for which a national market exists. I disagree. In contrast to the CSA's limitless assertion of power, Congress provided an exemption within the AAA for small producers [in *Wickard*].... *Wickard*, then, did not extend Commerce Clause authority to something as modest as the home cook's herb garden. This is not to say that Congress may never regulate small quantities of commodities possessed or produced for personal use, or to deny that it sometimes needs to enact a zero tolerance regime for such commodities. It is merely to say that *Wickard* did not hold or imply that small-scale production of commodities is always economic, and automatically within Congress' reach.

Even assuming that economic activity is at issue in this case, the Government has made no showing in fact that the possession and use of homegrown marijuana for medical purposes, in California or elsewhere, has a substantial effect on interstate commerce. Similarly, the Government has not shown that regulating such activity is necessary to an interstate regulatory scheme....

That is why characterizing this as a case about the Necessary and Proper Clause does not change the analysis significantly.... [If it did] then we could have surmised in *Lopez* that guns in school zones are "never more than an instant from the interstate market" in guns already subject to extensive federal regulation, ... recast *Lopez* as a Necessary and Proper Clause case, and thereby upheld the Gun-Free School Zones Act of 1990. (According to the Court's and the concurrence's logic, for example, the *Lopez* [C]ourt should have reasoned that the prohibition on gun possession in school zones could be an appropriate means of effectuating a related [statutory] prohibition [that currently makes criminal the] ... "sell[ing]" or "deliver[ing]" firearms or ammunition to "any individual who the licensee knows or has reasonable cause to believe is less than eighteen years of age." ...)

There is simply no evidence that homegrown medicinal marijuana users constitute, in the aggregate, a sizable enough class to have a discernable, let alone substantial, impact on the national illicit drug market—or otherwise to threaten the CSA regime.... And here, in part because common sense suggests that medical marijuana users may be limited in number and that California's Compassionate Use Act and similar state legislation may well isolate activities relating to medicinal marijuana from the illicit market, the effect of those activities on interstate drug traffic is not self-evidently substantial.

In this regard, again, this case is readily distinguishable from *Wickard*. To decide whether the Secretary could regulate local wheat farming, the Court looked to "the actual effects of the activity in question upon interstate commerce." ... Critically, the Court was able to consider "actual effects" because the parties had "stipulated a summary of the economics of the wheat industry." ... With real numbers at hand, the *Wickard* Court could easily conclude that "a factor of such volume and variability as home-consumed wheat would have a substantial influence on price and market conditions" nationwide....

. . .

[The findings in the present case do not suffice.] In particular, the CSA's introductory declarations are too vague and unspecific to demonstrate that the federal statutory scheme will be undermined if Congress cannot exert power over individuals like respondents. The declarations are not even specific to marijuana ... The California Compassionate Use Act exempts from other state drug laws patients and their caregivers "who posses[s] or cultivat[e] marijuana for the personal medical purposes of the patient upon the written or oral recommendation of a physician" to treat a list of serious medical conditions.... The Act specifies that it should not be construed to supersede legislation prohibiting persons from engaging in acts dangerous to others, or to condone the diversion of marijuana for nonmedical purposes.... We generally assume States enforce their laws ... and have no reason to think otherwise here.

The Government has not overcome empirical doubt that the number of Californians engaged in personal cultivation, possession, and use of medical marijuana, or the amount of marijuana they produce, is enough to threaten the federal regime. Nor has it shown that Compassionate Use Act marijuana users have been or are realistically likely to be responsible for the drug's seeping into the market in a significant way....

III

. . . If I were a California citizen, I would not have voted for the medical marijuana ballot initiative; if I were a California legislator I would not have supported the Compassionate Use Act. But whatever the wisdom of California's experiment with medical marijuana, the federalism principles that have driven our Commerce Clause cases require that room for experiment be protected in this case. For these reasons I dissent.

Justice Thomas, dissenting.

. . . If Congress can regulate this under the Commerce Clause, then it can regulate virtually anything—and the Federal Government is no longer one of limited and enumerated powers.

. . .

II

B

. . .

. . . [I]t is implausible that this Court could set aside entire portions of the United States Code as outside Congress' power in *Lopez* and *Morrison*, but it cannot engage in the more restrained practice of invalidating particular applications of the CSA that are beyond Congress' power. This Court has regularly entertained as-applied challenges under constitutional provisions. . . . There is no reason why, when Congress exceeds the scope of commerce power, courts may not invalidate Congress' overreaching on a case-by-case basis. . . .

. . .

CHAPTER 5

STATE SOVEREIGNTY AND FEDERAL REGULATION

SECTION 2. ENFORCEMENT OF FEDERAL RIGHTS IN SUITS AGAINST STATE OFFICERS: THE ELEVENTH AMENDMENT

Page 268. Add to end of Note, "Congressional Power to Authorize Suits Against States in Federal Court":

In **CENTRAL VIRGINIA COMMUNITY COLLEGE v. KATZ**, 546 U.S. 356, 126 S.Ct. 990, 163 L.Ed.2d 945 (2006), the Court, 5–4 (with Justice O'Connor, soon to leave the bench, in the majority), held that although "statements in both the majority and the dissenting opinions" in *Seminole Tribe of Florida v. Florida* "reflected an assumption that the holding in that case would apply" to state amenability to suit under the Bankruptcy Clause, Art. I, § 8, cl. 4, which empowers Congress to establish "uniform Laws on the subject of Bankruptcies throughout the United States," that assumption "was erroneous." The majority reasoned that the Bankruptcy Clause's history and rationale, as well as the legislation proposed and enacted under it immediately after ratification, suggest the Clause was more than an ordinary grant of authority to Congress; it was also a subordination of state sovereign immunity. According to the Court, the "ineluctable conclusion . . . is that States agreed in the plan of the Convention not to assert any sovereign immunity defense they might have had in proceedings brought pursuant to 'laws on the subject of Bankruptcies.'"

CHAPTER 6

THE SCOPE OF STATE POWER

SECTION 4. IMPLIED RESTRICTIONS OF THE COMMERCE CLAUSE—PRODUCTION AND TRADE

B. REQUIRING BUSINESS OPERATIONS TO BE PERFORMED IN THE HOME STATE

Page 312. Add after C & A Carbone v. Town of Clarkstown:

UNITED HAULERS ASSOCIATION, INC. v. ONEIDA–HERKIMER SOLID WASTE MANAGEMENT AUTHORITY, __ U.S. __, 127 S.Ct. 1786, 167 L.Ed.2d 655 (2007). The Court found *Carbone* inapplicable to a flow control ordinance that directed waste to a public, rather than a private, facility. Writing for himself and Justices Scalia, Souter, Ginsburg and Breyer, the Chief Justice reasoned that "[c]ompelling reasons justify treating these laws differently from laws favoring particular private businesses over their competitors. 'Conceptually, of course, any notion of discrimination assumes a comparison of substantially similar entities.' . . . But States and municipalities are not private businesses-far from it. Unlike private enterprise, government is vested with the responsibility of protecting the health, safety, and welfare of its citizens. . . . These important responsibilities set state and local government apart from a typical private business. . . . Given these differences, it does not make sense to regard laws favoring local government and laws favoring private industry with equal skepticism. As our local processing cases demonstrate, when a law favors in-state business over out-of-state competition, rigorous scrutiny is appropriate because the law is often the product of 'simple economic protectionism.' . . . Laws favoring local government, by contrast, may be directed toward any number of legitimate goals unrelated to protectionism. Here the flow control ordinances enable the Counties to pursue particular policies with respect to the handling and treatment of waste generated in the Counties, while allocating the costs of those policies on citizens and businesses according to the volume of waste they generate. . . ."

The majority also expressed concern about a slippery slope if public and private favoritism were considered identically for doctrinal purposes: "The contrary approach of treating public and private entities the same under the dormant Commerce Clause would lead to unprecedented and unbounded interference by the courts with state and local government. The dormant Commerce Clause is not a roving license for federal courts to decide what activities are appropriate for state and local government to undertake, and what activities must be the province of private market competition. . . ."

Finally, the Court noted implicitly that Congress has ultimate control over dormant Commerce Clause outcomes: "We should be particularly hesitant to interfere with the Counties' efforts under the guise of the Commerce Clause because '[w]aste disposal is both typically and traditionally a local government function.' ... Congress itself has recognized local government's vital role in waste management, making clear that 'collection and disposal of solid wastes should continue to be primarily the function of State, regional, and local agencies.' ... We may or may not agree with that approach, but nothing in the Commerce Clause vests the responsibility for that policy judgment with the Federal Judiciary."

Justices Scalia and Thomas each wrote separately to make clear their rejection of the entire dormant, or "negative," Commerce Clause doctrine altogether. Justice Alito, in an opinion joined by Justice Stevens and Justice Kennedy, dissented on the ground that *Carbone* controlled.

SECTION 5. EFFECT OF OTHER CONSTITUTIONAL PROVISIONS ON STATE REGULATORY POWER

B. THE TWENTY-FIRST AMENDMENT

Page 371. Add before Brown–Forman Distillers Corp. v. New York State Liquor Authority:

GRANHOLM v. HEALD, 544 U.S. 460, 125 S.Ct. 1885, 161 L.Ed.2d 796 (2005). The Court applied *Bacchus* to invalidate laws from Michigan and New York that allowed in-state, but not out-of-state, wineries to make sales to consumers directly, rather than through wholesale and retail distributors. Rejecting the argument made by the States that the Twenty-First Amendment authorized or permitted this kind of discrimination against interstate commerce, and that *Bacchus* ought to be overruled or limited, the five-member majority (Justices Kennedy, Scalia, Souter, Ginsburg and Breyer) read Section 2 of the Twenty-First Amendment as conferring upon states only that authority which Congress had tried to confer by passing the Wilson Act and the Webb-Kenyon Act prior to the adoption of the Twenty-First Amendment. Because nothing in either of these Acts purported to give states freedom to discriminate against out-of-state alcohol producers in violation of Commerce Clause norms, neither, said the Court, did Section 2 of the Amendment.

CHAPTER 7

Separation of Powers

SECTION 1. The President's Power to Determine National Policy

A. In General

Page 398. Add before Section B. International Relations:

HAMDAN v. RUMSFELD, ___ U.S. ___, 126 S.Ct. 2749, 165 L.Ed.2d 723 (2006). The Court held 5–4 that the President's planned structure and procedures for military tribunals to try alleged terrorists being held after September 11, 2001 in Guantanamo Bay, Cuba (in this case Osama Bin Laden's alleged bodyguard) violated the limitations on military tribunals Congress had imposed in the Uniform Code of Military Justice, as well as certain provisions of the Geneva Conventions. In the course of doing so, the Court observed: "Whether or not the President has independent power, absent congressional authorization, to convene military commissions, he may not disregard limitations that Congress has, in proper exercise of its own war powers, placed on his powers. See *Youngstown Sheet & Tube Co. v. Sawyer*, 343 U.S. 579, 637 (1952) (Jackson, J., concurring). The Government does not argue otherwise."

Government and the Individual: The Protection of Liberty and Property Under the Due Process and Equal Protection Clauses

CHAPTER 9

The Due Process, Contract, and Just Compensation Clauses and the Review of the Reasonableness of Legislation

SECTION 1.   ECONOMIC REGULATORY LEGISLATION

A.   THE RISE AND FALL OF DUE PROCESS

Page 536. Add footnote a. to end of Note, "Due Process Limitations on State Punitive Damages Awards":

a. In Philip Morris USA v. Williams, ___ U.S. ___, 127 S.Ct. 1057 (2007), the Court decided that "the fundamental due process concerns to which our punitive damages cases refer—risks of arbitrariness, uncertainty and lack of notice"—forbid the use of punitive damages awards "to punish a defendant for injury that it inflicts upon nonparties or those whom they directly represent, *i.e.*, injury that it inflicts upon those who are, essentially, strangers to the litigation." Accordingly, although a jury may consider harm to nonparties "to show that the conduct that harmed the plaintiff also posed a substantial risk of harm to the general public, and so was particularly reprehensible . . . , a jury may not go further than this and use a punitive damages verdict to punish a defendant directly on account of harms it is alleged to have visited on nonparties." The Due Process Clause thus requires States to instruct juries in such a way as "to provide assurance that that juries are not asking the wrong question, *i.e.*, seeking, not simply to determine reprehensibility, but also to punish for harm caused strangers."

C.   THE JUST COMPENSATION CLAUSE OF THE FIFTH AMENDMENT—WHAT DOES IT ADD TO DUE PROCESS?

Page 552.   Add at end of Introduction:

The Court in Kelo v. City of New London, ___ U.S. ___, 125 S.Ct. 2655, 162 L.Ed.2d 439 (2005), once more held the "public use" requirement satisfied, this time in a comprehensive opinion addressed exclusively to that question. Four Justices again dissented, although, unlike *Brown*, Justice Kennedy joined the majority and Justice O'Connor dissented. The City, suffering from decreasing population and economic distress, including an unemployment rate nearly double that of the State, sought to capitalize on the pharmaceutical company Pfizer's plans to build a $300 million research facility on a site adjacent to 90 acres in the City's Fort Trumbull area by adopting an economic revitalization plan for the adjacent property. At the City's request, a private nonprofit entity (NLDC) formulated an integrated economic development plan to transform the adjacent property into a "small urban village" with a waterfront conference hotel, shops and restaurants; commercial and recreational marinas; a pedestrian "riverwalk"; 80 new residences "organized into an urban neighborhood and linked by public walkway to the remainder of the development, including the [existing] state park"; a Coast Guard museum; research and development office space close to the Pfizer facility; and parking or retail services for visitors or in support of the marina, which was to be renovated. The State and the City approved the redevelopment plan, and the City authorized NLDC to implement it and to exercise the City's eminent domain power if necessary to acquire the property. Most of the property was acquired by negotiation but the owners of 15 properties—4 sought for office space and 11 for park or marina support— objected, claiming in a state court action that their properties, which were not alleged to be blighted or in poor condition, could not be taken for the purpose of private economic development without violating the "public use" requirement. A divided Connecticut Supreme Court rejected their claim, and the Supreme Court affirmed.

For the majority, Justice Stevens wrote in part:

"Two polar propositions are perfectly clear. On the one hand, it has long been accepted that the sovereign may not take the property of A for the sole purpose of transferring it to another private party B, even though A is paid just compensation. On the other hand, it is equally clear that a State may transfer property from one private party to another if future 'use by the public' is the purpose of the taking; the condemnation of land for a railroad with common-carrier duties is a familiar example. Neither of these propositions, however, determines the disposition of this case. As for the first proposition, the City would no doubt be forbidden from taking petitioners' land for the purpose of conferring a private benefit on a particular private party.... Nor would the City be allowed to take property under the mere pretext of a public purpose, when its actual purpose was to bestow a private benefit. The takings before us, however, would be executed pursuant to a 'carefully considered' development plan. 268 Conn., at 54.... The trial judge and all the members of the Supreme Court of Connecticut agreed that there was no evidence of an illegitimate purpose in this case.[6] ...

"On the other hand, this is not a case in which the City is planning to open the condemned land—at least not in its entirety—to use by the general public. Nor will the private lessees of the land in any sense be required to operate like common carriers, making their services available to all comers. But although such a projected use would be sufficient to satisfy the public use requirement, this 'Court long ago rejected any literal requirement that condemned property be put into use for the general public.' ... Not only was the 'use by the public' test difficult to administer (e.g., what proportion of the public need have access to the property? at what price?) but it proved to be impractical given the diverse and always evolving needs of society. Accordingly, when this Court began applying the Fifth Amendment to the States at the close of the 19th century, it embraced the broader and more natural interpretation of public use as 'public purpose.' ...

"The disposition of this case therefore turns on the question whether the City's development plan serves a 'public purpose.' Without exception, our cases have defined that concept broadly, reflecting our longstanding policy of deference to legislative judgments in this field.

"...

"Viewed as a whole, our jurisprudence has recognized that the needs of society have varied between different parts of the Nation, just as they have evolved over time in response to changed circumstances. Our earliest cases in particular embodied a strong theme of federalism, emphasizing the 'great respect' that we owe to state legislatures and state courts in discerning local public needs.... For more than a century, our public use jurisprudence has wisely eschewed rigid formulas and intrusive scrutiny in favor of affording legislatures broad latitude in determining what public needs justify the use of the takings power.

---

6. ... And while the City intends to transfer certain of the parcels to a private developer in a long-term lease—which developer, in turn, is expected to lease the office space and so forth to other private tenants— the identities of those private parties were not known when the plan was adopted. It is, of course, difficult to accuse the government of having taken A's property to benefit the private interests of B when the identity of B was unknown.

IV

"Those who govern the City were not confronted with the need to remove blight in the Fort Trumbull area, but their determination that the area was sufficiently distressed to justify a program of economic rejuvenation is entitled to our deference. The City has carefully formulated an economic development plan that it believes will provide appreciable benefits to the community, including—but by no means limited to—new jobs and increased tax revenue. As with other exercises in urban planning and development, the City is endeavoring to coordinate a variety of commercial, residential, and recreational uses of land, with the hope that they will form a whole greater than the sum of its parts. To effectuate this plan, the City has invoked a state statute that specifically authorizes the use of eminent domain to promote economic development. Given the comprehensive character of the plan, the thorough deliberation that preceded its adoption, and the limited scope of our review, it is appropriate for us, as it was in *Berman*, to resolve the challenges of the individual owners, not on a piecemeal basis, but rather in light of the entire plan. Because that plan unquestionably serves a public purpose, the takings challenged here satisfy the public use requirement of the Fifth Amendment.

"To avoid this result, petitioners urge us to adopt a new bright-line rule that economic development does not qualify as a public use. Putting aside the unpersuasive suggestion that the City's plan will provide only purely economic benefits, neither precedent nor logic supports petitioners' proposal. Promoting economic development is a traditional and long accepted function of government. There is, moreover, no principled way of distinguishing economic development from the other public purposes that we have recognized. In our cases upholding takings that facilitated agriculture and mining, for example, we emphasized the importance of those industries to the welfare of the States in question . . .; in *Berman*, we endorsed the purpose of transforming a blighted area into a 'well-balanced' community through redevelopment . . .; in *Midkiff*, we upheld the interest in breaking up a land oligopoly that 'created artificial deterrents to the normal functioning of the State's residential land market,' . . .; and in *Monsanto*, we accepted Congress' purpose of eliminating a 'significant barrier to entry in the pesticide market,' . . . . It would be incongruous to hold that the City's interest in the economic benefits to be derived from the development of the Fort Trumbull area has less of a public character than any of those other interests. Clearly, there is no basis for exempting economic development from our traditionally broad understanding of public purpose.

" . . . [T]he government's pursuit of a public purpose will often benefit individual private parties. . . . [16]

---

16. Nor do our cases support Justice O'Connor's novel theory that the government may only take property and transfer it to private parties when the initial taking eliminates some 'harmful property use.' There was nothing 'harmful' about the nonblighted department store at issue in *Berman* . . .; nothing 'harmful' about the lands at issue in the mining and agriculture cases . . .; and certainly nothing 'harmful' about the trade secrets owned by the pesticide manufacturers in *Monsanto*. . . . In each case, the public purpose we upheld depended on a private party's *future* use of the concededly nonharmful property that was taken. By focusing on a property's future use, as opposed to its past use, our cases are faithful to the text of the Takings Clause. . . . Justice O'Connor's intimation that a 'public purpose' may not be achieved by the action of private parties confuses the *purpose* of a taking with its *mechanics*, a mistake we warned of in *Midkiff*. . . .

"It is further argued that without a bright-line rule nothing would stop a city from transferring citizen A's property to citizen B for the sole reason that citizen B will put the property to a more productive use and thus pay more taxes. Such a one-to-one transfer of property, executed outside the confines of an integrated development plan, is not presented in this case. While such an unusual exercise of government power would certainly raise a suspicion that a private purpose was afoot, the hypothetical cases posited by petitioners can be confronted if and when they arise. They do not warrant the crafting of an artificial restriction on the concept of public use.

"Alternatively, petitioners maintain that for takings of this kind we should require a 'reasonable certainty' that the expected public benefits will actually accrue. Such a rule, however, would represent an even greater departure from our precedent. 'When the legislature's purpose is legitimate and its means are not irrational, our cases make clear that empirical debates over the wisdom of takings—no less than debates over the wisdom of other kinds of socioeconomic legislation—are not to be carried out in the federal courts.' *Midkiff*. . . . Indeed, earlier this Term we explained why similar practical concerns (among others) undermined the use of the 'substantially advances' formula in our regulatory takings doctrine. See *Lingle v. Chevron U.S.A. Inc.*, ... The disadvantages of a heightened form of review are especially pronounced in this type of case. Orderly implementation of a comprehensive redevelopment plan obviously requires that the legal rights of all interested parties be established before new construction can be commenced. A constitutional rule that required postponement of the judicial approval of every condemnation until the likelihood of success of the plan had been assured would unquestionably impose a significant impediment to the successful consummation of many such plans.

"Just as we decline to second-guess the City's considered judgments about the efficacy of its development plan, we also decline to second-guess the City's determinations as to what lands it needs to acquire in order to effectuate the project. . . .

". . . [N]othing in our opinion precludes any State from placing further restrictions on its exercise of the takings power. Indeed, many States already impose 'public use' requirements that are stricter than the federal baseline. . . . This Court's authority, however, extends only to determining whether the City's proposed condemnations are for a 'public use' within the meaning of the Fifth Amendment to the Federal Constitution. Because over a century of our case law interpreting that provision dictates an affirmative answer to that question, we may not grant petitioners the relief that they seek."

Justice Kennedy's concurring opinion emphasized the following:

"A court applying rational-basis review under the Public Use Clause should strike down a taking that, by a clear showing, is intended to favor a particular private party, with only incidental or pretextual public benefits, just as a court applying rational-basis review under the Equal Protection Clause must strike down a government classification that is clearly intended to injure a particular class of private parties, with only incidental or pretextual public justifications. See *Cleburne v. Cleburne Living Center, Inc.*, 473 U.S. 432, 446–447 (1985). . . .

"A court confronted with a plausible accusation of impermissible favoritism to private parties should treat the objection as a serious one and review the record to see if it has merit, though with the presumption that the government's actions were reasonable and intended to serve a public purpose. Here, the trial court conducted a careful and extensive inquiry. . . .

"The trial court concluded . . . that benefiting Pfizer was not 'the primary motivation or effect of this development plan'; instead, 'the primary motivation for [respondents] was to take advantage of Pfizer's presence.' . . . Likewise, the trial court concluded that '[t]here is nothing in the record to indicate that . . . [respondents] were motivated by a desire to aid [other] particular private entities.' . . . This case, then, survives the meaningful rational basis review that in my view is required under the Public Use Clause.

" . . .

"My agreement with the Court that a presumption of invalidity is not warranted for economic development takings in general, or for the particular takings at issue in this case, does not foreclose the possibility that a more stringent standard of review than that announced in *Berman* and *Midkiff* might be appropriate for a more narrowly drawn category of takings. There may be private transfers in which the risk of undetected impermissible favoritism of private parties is so acute that a presumption (rebuttable or otherwise) of invalidity is warranted under the Public Use Clause. . . . This demanding level of scrutiny, however, is not required simply because the purpose of the taking is economic development.

"This is not the occasion for conjecture as to what sort of cases might justify a more demanding standard, but . . . aspects of the instant case . . . convince me no departure from *Berman* and *Midkiff* is appropriate here. This taking occurred in the context of a comprehensive development plan meant to address a serious city-wide depression, and the projected economic benefits of the project cannot be characterized as *de minimus*. The identity of most of the private beneficiaries were unknown at the time the city formulated its plans. The city complied with elaborate procedural requirements that facilitate review of the record and inquiry into the city's purposes. In sum, while there may be categories of cases in which the transfers are so suspicious, or the procedures employed so prone to abuse, or the purported benefits are so trivial or implausible, that courts should presume an impermissible private purpose, no such circumstances are present in this case."

Justice O'Connor's dissent, joined by Chief Justice Rehnquist and Justices Scalia and Thomas, objected that the Court's reasoning "that the incidental public benefits resulting from the subsequent ordinary use of private property render economic development takings 'for public use' wash[es] out any distinction between private and public use of property—and thereby effectively delete[s] the words 'for public use' from the Takings Clause of the Fifth Amendment." Her opinion reasoned in part:

"Where is the line between 'public' and 'private' property use? . . . An external, judicial check on how the public use requirement is interpreted, however limited, is necessary if this constraint on government power is to retain any meaning. . . .

"Our cases have generally identified three categories of takings that comply with the public use requirement.... First, the sovereign may transfer private property to public ownership—such as for a road, a hospital, or a military base.... Second, the sovereign may transfer private property to private parties, often common carriers, who make the property available for the public's use—such as with a railroad, a public utility, or a stadium.... But 'public ownership' and 'use-by-the-public' are sometimes too constricting and impractical ways to define the scope of the Public Use Clause. Thus we have allowed that, in certain circumstances and to meet certain exigencies, takings that serve a public purpose also satisfy the Constitution even if the property is destined for subsequent private use. See, *e.g., Berman v. Parker* ...; *Hawaii Housing Authority v. Midkiff*....

"This case ... presents an issue of first impression: Are economic development takings constitutional? I would hold that they are not....

"...

"[F]or all the emphasis on deference, *Berman* and *Midkiff* hewed to a bedrock principle without which our public use jurisprudence would collapse: 'A purely private taking could not withstand the scrutiny of the public use requirement; it would serve no legitimate purpose of government and would thus be void.' ...

"The Court's holdings in *Berman* and *Midkiff* were true to the principle underlying the Public Use Clause. In both ... the extraordinary, precondemnation use of the targeted property inflicted affirmative harm on society—in *Berman* through blight resulting from extreme poverty and in *Midkiff* through oligopoly resulting from extreme wealth. And in both cases, the relevant legislative body had found that eliminating the existing property use was necessary to remedy the harm.... Thus a public purpose was realized when the harmful use was eliminated. Because each taking *directly* achieved a public benefit, it did not matter that the property was turned over to private use. Here, in contrast, New London does not claim that [petitioners'] well-maintained homes are the source of any social harm....

"In moving away from our decisions sanctioning the condemnation of harmful property use, the Court today significantly expands the meaning of public use. It holds that the sovereign may take private property currently put to ordinary private use, and give it over for new, ordinary private use, so long as the new use is predicted to generate some secondary benefit for the public— such as increased tax revenue, more jobs, maybe even aesthetic pleasure. But nearly any lawful use of real private property can be said to generate some incidental benefit to the public. Thus, if predicted (or even guaranteed) positive side-effects are enough to render transfer from one private party to another constitutional, then the words 'for public use' do not realistically exclude *any* takings, and thus do not exert any constraint on the eminent domain power.

"... The Court ... suggests two limitations on what can be taken after today's decision. First, it maintains a role for courts in ferreting out takings whose sole purpose is to bestow a benefit on the private transferee—without detailing how courts are to conduct that complicated inquiry. For his part, Justice Kennedy suggests that courts may divine illicit purpose by a careful review of the record and the process by which a legislature arrived at the decision to take—without specifying what courts should look for in a case with different facts, how they will know if they have found it, and what to do if they do not. . . . The trouble with economic development takings is that private benefit and incidental public benefit are, by definition, merged and mutually reinforcing. In this case, for example, any boon for Pfizer or the plan's developer is difficult to disaggregate from the promised public gains in taxes and jobs.

"Even if there were a practical way to isolate the motives behind a given taking, the gesture toward a purpose test is theoretically flawed. If it is true that incidental public benefits from new private use are enough to ensure the 'public purpose' in a taking, why should it matter, as far as the Fifth Amendment is concerned, what inspired the taking in the first place? How much the government does or does not desire to benefit a favored private party has no bearing on whether an economic development taking will or will not generate secondary benefit for the public. And whatever the reason for a given condemnation, the effect is the same from the constitutional perspective—private property is forcibly relinquished to new private ownership.

"A second proposed limitation is implicit in the Court's opinion[—]that eminent domain may only be used to upgrade—not downgrade—property. At best this makes the Public Use Clause redundant with the Due Process Clause, which already prohibits irrational government action. . . . The Court rightfully admits, however, that the judiciary cannot get bogged down in predictive judgments about whether the public will actually be better off after a property transfer. In any event, this constraint has no realistic import. For who among us can say she already makes the most productive or attractive possible use of her property? The specter of condemnation hangs over all property. Nothing is to prevent the State from replacing any Motel 6 with a Ritz-Carlton, any home with a shopping mall, or any farm with a factory. . . .

"The Court also puts special emphasis on facts peculiar to this case. . . . But none has legal significance to blunt the force of today's holding. If legislative prognostications about the secondary public benefits of a new use can legitimate a taking, there is nothing in the Court's rule or in Justice Kennedy's gloss on that rule to prohibit property transfers generated with less care, that are less comprehensive, that happen to result from less elaborate process, whose only projected advantage is the incidence of higher taxes, or that hope to transform an already prosperous city into an even more prosperous one.

" . . .

"Any property may now be taken for the benefit of another private party, but the fallout from this decision will not be random. The beneficiaries are likely to be those citizens with disproportionate influence and power in the political process, including large corporations and development firms. As for the victims, the government now has license to transfer property from those with fewer resources to those with more. The Founders cannot have intended this perverse result. . . ."

A separate dissent by Justice Thomas urged a return to what he perceived to be the "original meaning of the Public Use Clause: that the government may take property only if it actually uses or gives the public a legal right to use the property"—and not when "the purpose of the taking is legitimately public." In his view, the text of the Fifth Amendment, the early history of eminent domain practice, and the alleged mistake in conflating the public use requirement of the takings clause with the public purpose requirement of the due process clause, all point in the direction of reconsidering the error of *"Berman* and *Midkiff* [in] equating the eminent domain power with the police power of States." He contended that "[t]he 'public purpose' test applied by *Berman* and *Midkiff* ... cannot be applied in a principled manner" and that "[i]t is far easier to analyze whether the government owns or the public has a legal right to use the taken property than to ask whether the taking has a 'purely private purpose'—unless the Court means to eliminate public use scrutiny of takings entirely." Finally, he argued that "extending the concept of public purpose to encompass any economically beneficial goal guarantees that these losses will fall disproportionately on poor communities. Those communities are not only systematically less likely to put their lands to the highest and best social use, but are also the least politically powerful. If ever there were justification for intrusive judicial review of constitutional provisions that protect 'discrete and insular minorities,' *United States v. Carolene Products Co.* ..., surely that principle would apply with great force to the powerless groups and individuals the Public Use Clause protects."

1. RESTRICTIONS ON PROPERTY USE

Page 568. Add at end of subsection:

LINGLE v. CHEVRON U.S.A. INC., 544 U.S. 528, 125 S.Ct. 2074, 161 L.Ed.2d 876 (2005). Although the *Lucas* and *Tahoe–Sierra* cases both involve claims that government denial of economically viable use of property constitutes a taking, they each incidentally refer to the separate doctrinal formulation initially set forth in Agins v. City of Tiburon, 447 U.S. 255, 100 S.Ct. 2138, 65 L.Ed.2d 106 (1980), that government regulation of private property "effects a taking if [such regulation] does not substantially advance legitimate state interests...." Applying that independent rule, the lower federal courts in *Lingle* held that Act 257, a Hawaii statute designed to control retail gasoline prices by limiting the rent oil companies could charge dealers leasing service stations from them, effected "an unconstitutional regulatory taking." Because existing lessee-dealers could transfer occupancy rights to a new lessee and charge a premium reflecting the rent reduction, and because in any event the oil company lessors could unilaterally raise wholesale fuel prices in order to offset the reduction in their rental income, the lower courts ruled, there would be no savings to pass on to consumers of gasoline, and, hence, the statute failed to substantially advance a legitimate state interest.

A unanimous Supreme Court reversed, "correct[ing] course" by holding that the *Agins* " 'substantially advances' formula is not a valid takings test, and indeed ... has no proper place in our takings jurisprudence." Justice O'Connor's opinion for the Court noted that "in no case have we found a compensable taking based on such an inquiry" and reasoned in significant part as follows:

"Although our regulatory takings jurisprudence cannot be characterized as unified, the[] three inquiries reflected in ... *Loretto, Lucas*, and *Penn Central* ... share a common touchstone. Each aims to identify regulatory actions that are functionally equivalent to the classic taking in which government directly appropriates private property or ousts the owner from his domain. Accordingly, each ... focuses directly upon the severity of the burden that government imposes upon private property rights. [P]hysical takings require compensation because of the unique burden they impose: A permanent physical invasion, however minimal the economic cost it entails, eviscerates the owner's right to exclude others from entering and using her property—perhaps the most fundamental of all property interests.... In the *Lucas* context, ... the complete elimination of a property's value is the determinative factor.... And the *Penn Central* inquiry turns in large part, albeit not exclusively, upon the magnitude of a regulation's economic impact and the degree to which it interferes with legitimate property interests.

"... Although a number of our takings precedents have recited the 'substantially advances' formula minted in *Agins*, this is our first opportunity to consider its validity as a freestanding takings test. We conclude that this formula prescribes an inquiry in the nature of a due process, not a takings, test, and that it has no proper place in our takings jurisprudence.

"There is no question that the 'substantially advances' formula was derived from due process, not takings, precedents....

"... [W]hen *Agins* was decided, there had been some history of referring to deprivations of property without due process of law as 'takings,' ... and the Court had yet to clarify whether 'regulatory takings' claims were properly cognizable under the Takings Clause or the Due Process Clause....

"Although *Agins'* reliance on due process precedents is understandable, the language the Court selected was regrettably imprecise. The 'substantially advances' formula suggests a means-ends test: It asks, in essence, whether a regulation of private property is *effective* in achieving some legitimate public purpose. An inquiry of this nature has some logic in the context of a due process challenge, for a regulation that fails to serve any legitimate governmental objective may be so arbitrary or irrational that it runs afoul of the Due Process Clause.... But such a test is not a valid method of discerning whether private property has been 'taken' for purposes of the Fifth Amendment.

"In stark contrast to the three regulatory takings tests discussed above, the 'substantially advances' inquiry reveals nothing about the *magnitude or character of the burden* a particular regulation imposes upon private property rights. Nor does it provide any information about how any regulatory burden is *distributed* among property owners. In consequence, this test does not help to identify those regulations whose effects are functionally comparable to government appropriation or invasion of private property; it is tethered neither to the text of the Takings Clause nor to the basic justification for allowing regulatory actions to be challenged under the Clause.

"... A test that tells us nothing about the actual burden imposed on property rights, or how that burden is allocated[,] cannot tell us when justice might require that the burden be spread among taxpayers through the payment of compensation. The owner of a property subject to a regulation that *effectively* serves a legitimate state interest may be just as singled out and just as burdened as the owner of a property subject to an *ineffective* regulation. It would make little sense to say that the second owner has suffered a taking while the first has not. Likewise, an ineffective regulation may not significantly burden property rights at all, and it may distribute any burden broadly and evenly among property owners. The notion that such a regulation nevertheless 'takes' private property for public use merely by virtue of its ineffectiveness or foolishness is untenable.

"... [T]he 'substantially advances' inquiry probes the regulation's underlying validity. But such an inquiry is logically prior to and distinct from the question whether a regulation effects a taking, for the Takings Clause presupposes that the government has acted in pursuit of a valid public purpose....

"... Chevron has not clearly argued—let alone established—that it has been singled out to bear any particularly severe regulatory burden. Rather, the gravamen of Chevron's claim is simply that Hawaii's rent cap will not actually serve the State's legitimate interest in protecting consumers against high gasoline prices. Whatever the merits of that claim, it does not sound under the Takings Clause. Chevron plainly does not seek compensation for a taking of its property for a legitimate public use, but rather an injunction against the enforcement of a regulation that it alleges to be fundamentally arbitrary and irrational.

"... The *Agins* formula can be read to demand heightened means-ends review of virtually any regulation of private property. If so interpreted, it would require courts to scrutinize the efficacy of a vast array of state and federal regulations—a task for which courts are not well suited. Moreover, it would empower—and might often require—courts to substitute their predictive judgments for those of elected legislatures and expert agencies.

"... To resolve Chevron's takings claim, the District Court was required to choose between the views of two opposing economists as to whether Hawaii's rent control statute would help to prevent concentration and supracompetitive prices in the State's retail gasoline market. Finding one expert to be 'more persuasive' than the other, the court concluded that the Hawaii Legislature's chosen regulatory strategy would not actually achieve its objectives.... Along the way, the court determined that the State was not entitled to enact a prophylactic rent cap without actual evidence that oil companies had charged, or would charge, excessive rents.... We find the proceedings below remarkable, to say the least, given that we have long eschewed such heightened scrutiny when addressing substantive due process challenges to government regulation.... The reasons for deference to legislative judgments about the need for, and likely effectiveness of, regulatory actions are by now well established, and we think they are no less applicable here."

2. MANDATED ACCESS TO PROPERTY

Page 579. Add at end of subsection:

LINGLE v. CHEVRON U.S.A. INC., 544 U.S. 528, 125 S.Ct. 2074, 161 L.Ed.2d 876 (2005). As noted, supra, p. 33, the Court in *Lingle* unanimously repudiated the view it had expressed in Agins v. City of Tiburon, 447 U.S. 255, 100 S.Ct. 2138, 65 L.Ed.2d 106 (1980), and many subsequent cases, that government regulation of private property "effects a taking if [such regulation] does not substantially advance legitimate state interests...." Part III of Justice O'Connor's opinion "emphasize[d] that our holding today—that the 'substantially advances' formula is not a valid takings test—does not require us to disturb any of our prior holdings.'' It continued:

"It might be argued that this formula played a role in our decisions in *Nollan v. California Coastal Comm'n*, 483 U.S. 825 (1987), and *Dolan v. City of Tigard*, 512 U.S. 374 (1994). . . . But while the Court drew upon the language of *Agins* in these cases, it did not apply the 'substantially advances' test that is the subject of today's decision. Both *Nollan* and *Dolan* involved Fifth Amendment takings challenges to adjudicative land-use exactions—specifically, government demands that a landowner dedicate an easement allowing public access to her property as a condition of obtaining a development permit. . . .

"In each case, the Court began with the premise that, had the government simply appropriated the easement in question, this would have been a *per se* physical taking. . . . The question was whether the government could, without paying the compensation that would otherwise be required upon effecting such a taking, demand the easement as a condition for granting a development permit the government was entitled to deny. The Court in *Nollan* answered in the affirmative, provided that the exaction would substantially advance the same government interest that would furnish a valid ground for denial of the permit. . . . The Court further refined this requirement in *Dolan,* holding that an adjudicative exaction requiring dedication of private property must also be 'rough[ly] proportiona[l]' . . . both in nature and extent to the impact of the proposed development.''. . .

"Although *Nollan* and *Dolan* quoted *Agins'* language, . . . the rule those decisions established is entirely distinct from the 'substantially advances' test we address today. Whereas the 'substantially advances' inquiry before us now is unconcerned with the degree or type of burden a regulation places upon property, *Nollan* and *Dolan* both involved dedications of property so onerous that, outside the exactions context, they would be deemed *per se* physical takings. In neither case did the Court question whether the exaction would substantially advance *some* legitimate state interest. . . . Rather, the issue was whether the exactions substantially advanced the *same* interests that land-use authorities asserted would allow them to deny the permit altogether. As the Court explained in *Dolan*, these cases involve a special application of the 'doctrine of ''unconstitutional conditions,'' ' which provides that 'the government may not require a person to give up a constitutional right—here the right to receive just compensation when property is taken for a public use—in exchange for a discretionary benefit conferred by the government where the benefit has little or no relationship to the property.' . . . That is worlds apart from a rule that says a regulation affecting property constitutes a taking on its face solely because it does not substantially advance a legitimate government interest. In short, *Nollan* and *Dolan* cannot be characterized as applying the 'substantially advances' test we address today, and our decision should not be read to disturb these precedents.''

SECTION 2. PROTECTION OF PERSONAL LIBERTIES

C. PERSONAL AUTONOMY

Page 659. Replace Stenberg v. Carhart:

Gonzales v. Carhart

___ U.S. ___, 127 S.Ct. 1610, 167 L.Ed.2d 480 (2007).

Justice Kennedy delivered the opinion of the Court.

These cases require us to consider the validity of the Partial–Birth Abortion Ban Act of 2003(Act), 18 U.S.C. § 1531 (2000 ed., Supp. IV), a federal statute regulating abortion procedures. In recitations preceding its operative provisions the Act refers to the Court's opinion in *Stenberg v. Carhart,* 530 U.S. 914 (2000), which also addressed the subject of abortion procedures used in the later stages of pregnancy. Compared to the state statute at issue in *Stenberg,* the Act is more specific concerning the instances to which it applies and in this respect more precise in its coverage. We conclude the Act should be sustained against the objections lodged by the broad, facial attack brought against it.

... [D]octors who perform second-trimester abortions [successfully] challenged the constitutionality of the Act [in the District of Nebraska and Eight Circuit, as did some Planned Parenthood groups and the City and County of San Francisco in the Northern District of California and the Ninth Circuit.]

. . .

I

A

The Act proscribes a particular manner of ending fetal life, so it is necessary here, as it was in *Stenberg,* to discuss abortion procedures in some detail. . . .

... Between 85 and 90 percent of the approximately 1.3 million abortions performed each year in the United States take place in the first three months of pregnancy, ... most common[ly by] the physician vacuum[ing] out the embryonic tissue. [A]n alternative is to use medication, such as ... RU–486. . . . The Act does not regulate these procedures.

Of the remaining abortions ... most occur in the second trimester. The surgical procedure referred to as "dilation and evacuation" or "D & E" is the usual abortion method in this trimester. . . .

After sufficient dilation the ... doctor ... inserts grasping forceps through the woman's cervix and into the uterus to grab the fetus. The doctor grips a fetal part with the forceps and pulls it back through the cervix and vagina, continuing to pull even after meeting resistance from the cervix. The friction causes the fetus to tear apart. ... A doctor may make 10 to 15 passes with the forceps to evacuate the fetus in its entirety....

Some doctors, especially later in the second trimester, may kill the fetus a day or two before performing the surgical evacuation[, making] ... its removal ... easier....

The abortion procedure that was the impetus for the numerous bans on "partial-birth abortion," including the Act, is a variation of this standard D & E [sometimes called] ... intact D & E. The main difference between the two procedures is that in intact D & E a doctor extracts the fetus intact or largely intact with only a few passes. There are no comprehensive statistics indicating what percentage of all D & Es are performed in this manner.

. . .

In an intact D & E procedure the doctor extracts the fetus in a way conducive to pulling out its entire body, instead of ripping it apart....

Intact D & E gained public notoriety when, in 1992, Dr. Martin Haskell gave a presentation describing his method of performing the operation.... In the usual intact D & E the fetus' head lodges in the cervix, and dilation is insufficient to allow it to pass ... Haskell explained [how the surgeon should pierce the fetal skull,] enlarge the opening ... and evacuate[] the skull contents....

This is an abortion doctor's clinical description. Here is another description from a nurse who witnessed the same method performed on a 26½–week fetus and who testified before the Senate Judiciary Committee:

" 'Dr. Haskell went in with forceps and grabbed the baby's legs and pulled them down into the birth canal. Then he delivered the baby's body and the arms—everything but the head. The doctor kept the head right inside the uterus....

" 'The baby's little fingers were clasping and unclasping, and his little feet were kicking. Then the doctor stuck the scissors in the back of his head, and the baby's arms jerked out, like a startle reaction, like a flinch, like a baby does when he thinks he is going to fall.

" 'The doctor opened up the scissors, stuck a high-powered suction tube into the opening, and sucked the baby's brains out. Now the baby went completely limp....

" 'He cut the umbilical cord and delivered the placenta. He threw the baby in a pan, along with the placenta and the instruments he had just used.' " ...

Dr. Haskell's approach is not the only method of killing the fetus once its head lodges in the cervix, and "the process has evolved" since his presentation....

Some doctors performing an intact D & E attempt to remove the fetus without collapsing the skull.... Yet one doctor would not allow delivery of a live fetus younger than 24 weeks because "the objective of [his] procedure is to perform an abortion," not a birth.... Another doctor testified he crushes a fetus' skull not only to reduce its size but also to ensure the fetus is dead before it is removed. For the staff to have to deal with a fetus that has "some viability to it, some movement of limbs," according to this doctor, "[is] always a difficult situation." ...

D & E and intact D & E are not the only second-trimester abortion methods....

B

After Dr. Haskell's procedure received public attention, with ensuing and increasing public concern, bans on " 'partial birth abortion' " proliferated. By the time of the *Stenberg* decision, about 30 States had enacted bans designed to prohibit the procedure.... In 2003, after this Court's decision in *Stenberg,* Congress passed the Act at issue here [and] President Bush signed [it] into law....

The Act responded to *Stenberg* in two ways. First, Congress made factual findings. Congress determined that this Court in *Stenberg* "was required to accept the very questionable findings issued by the district court judge," ... but that Congress was "not bound to accept the same factual findings,".... Congress found, among other things, that "[a] moral, medical, and ethical consensus exists that the practice of performing a partial-birth abortion ... is a gruesome and inhumane procedure that is never medically necessary and should be prohibited." ...

Second, and more relevant here, the Act's language differs from that of the Nebraska statute struck down in *Stenberg*.... The operative provisions of the Act provide in relevant part:

> "(a) Any physician who, in or affecting interstate or foreign commerce, knowingly performs a partial-birth abortion and thereby kills a human fetus shall be fined under this title or imprisoned not more than 2 years, or both. This subsection does not apply to a partial-birth abortion that is necessary to save the life of a mother whose life is endangered by a physical disorder, physical illness, or physical injury, including a life-endangering physical condition caused by or arising from the pregnancy itself. This subsection takes effect 1 day after the enactment.

> "(b) As used in this section—

> > "(1) the term 'partial-birth abortion' means an abortion in which the person performing the abortion—

> > > "(A) deliberately and intentionally vaginally delivers a living fetus until, in the case of a head-first presentation, the entire fetal head is outside the body of the mother, or, in the case of breech presentation, any part of the fetal trunk past the navel is outside

the body of the mother, for the purpose of performing an overt act that the person knows will kill the partially delivered living fetus; and

"(B) performs the overt act, other than completion of delivery, that kills the partially delivered living fetus; and

"(2) the term 'physician' means a doctor of medicine or osteopathy legally authorized to practice medicine and surgery by the State in which the doctor performs such activity, or any other individual legally authorized by the State to perform abortions: *Provided, however,* That any individual who is not a physician or not otherwise legally authorized by the State to perform abortions, but who nevertheless directly performs a partial-birth abortion, shall be subject to the provisions of this section.

. . .

"(d)(1) A defendant accused of an offense under this section may seek a hearing before the State Medical Board on whether the physician's conduct was necessary to save the life of the mother whose life was endangered by a physical disorder, physical illness, or physical injury, including a life-endangering physical condition caused by or arising from the pregnancy itself.

"(2) The findings on that issue are admissible on that issue at the trial of the defendant. Upon a motion of the defendant, the court shall delay the beginning of the trial for not more than 30 days to permit such a hearing to take place.

"(e) A woman upon whom a partial-birth abortion is performed may not be prosecuted under this section, for a conspiracy to violate this section, or for an offense under section 2, 3, or 4 of this title based on a violation of this section." 18 U.S.C. § 1531 (2000 ed., Supp. IV).

. . .

II

The principles set forth in the joint opinion in Planned Parenthood of Southeastern Pa. v. Casey, 505 U.S. 833 (1992), did not find support from all those who join the instant opinion. See *id.,* at 979–1002 (Scalia, J., joined by Thomas, J., *inter alios,* concurring in judgment in part and dissenting in part). Whatever one's views concerning the *Casey* joint opinion, it is evident a premise central to its conclusion—that the government has a legitimate and substantial interest in preserving and promoting fetal life—would be repudiated were the Court now to affirm the judgments of the Courts of Appeals.

. . .

. . . [W]e must determine whether the Act furthers the legitimate interest of the Government in protecting the life of the fetus that may become a child.

To implement its holding, *Casey* rejected both *Roe's* rigid trimester framework and the interpretation of *Roe* that considered all previability regulations of abortion unwarranted. . . . On this point *Casey* overruled the holdings in two cases because they undervalued the State's interest in potential life. . . . (. . .

Thornburgh v. American College of Obstetricians and Gynecologists, 476 U.S. 747 (1986) and *Akron v. Akron Center for Reproductive Health, Inc.,* 462 U.S. 416 (1983)).

We assume the following principles for the purposes of this opinion. Before viability, a State "may not prohibit any woman from making the ultimate decision to terminate her pregnancy." . . . (plurality opinion). It also may not impose upon this right an undue burden, which exists if a regulation's "purpose or effect is to place a substantial obstacle in the path of a woman seeking an abortion before the fetus attains viability." *Id.,* . . . . On the other hand, "[r]egulations which do no more than create a structural mechanism by which the State, or the parent or guardian of a minor, may express profound respect for the life of the unborn are permitted, if they are not a substantial obstacle to the woman's exercise of the right to choose." *Id.* . . . *Casey* . . . struck a balance. The balance was central to its holding. We now apply its standard to the cases at bar.

III

. . .

. . . Respondents assert that . . . the Act is void for vagueness because its scope is indefinite. In the alternative, respondents argue the Act's text proscribes all D & Es. Because D & E is the most common second-trimester abortion method, respondents suggest the Act imposes an undue burden. In this litigation the Attorney General does not dispute that the Act would impose an undue burden if it covered standard D & E.

We conclude that the Act is not void for vagueness, does not impose an undue burden from any overbreadth, and is not invalid on its face.

[Interpreting the Act to punish only those who vaginally deliver a *living* fetus, past the point at which "either the fetal head or the fetal trunk past the navel is outside the body of the mother," and who thereafter perform an overt act causing the fetus' death that is separate from the act of delivery—all done "deliberately and intentionally"—the Court rejected the vagueness challenge.]

C

We next determine whether the Act imposes an undue burden, as a facial matter, because its restrictions on second-trimester abortions are too broad. . . . The Act prohibits intact D & E; and, notwithstanding respondents' arguments, it does not prohibit the D & E procedure in which the fetus is removed in parts.

1

. . .

The Act excludes most D & Es in which the fetus is removed in pieces, not intact. If the doctor intends to remove the fetus in parts from the outset, the doctor will not have the requisite intent to incur criminal liability. . . .

. . .

Congress, it is apparent, responded to [*Stenberg*'s] concerns because the Act departs in material ways from the statute in *Stenberg.* It adopts the phrase "delivers a living fetus," § 1531(b)(1)(A) (2000 ed., Supp. IV), instead of "'delivering ... a living unborn child, or a substantial portion thereof,'" 530 U.S., at 938 (quoting Neb.Rev.Stat. Ann. § 28–326(9) (Supp.1999)). The Act's language, unlike the statute in *Stenberg,* expresses the usual meaning of "deliver" when used in connection with "fetus," namely, extraction of an entire fetus rather than removal of fetal pieces.... The Act thus displaces the interpretation of "delivering" dictated by the Nebraska statute's reference to a "substantial portion" of the fetus. *Stenberg, supra,* at 944 (indicating that the Nebraska "statute itself specifies that it applies *both* to delivering 'an intact unborn child' *or* 'a substantial portion thereof' ").... D & E does not involve the delivery of a fetus because it requires the removal of fetal parts that are ripped from the fetus as they are pulled through the cervix.

The identification of specific anatomical landmarks to which the fetus must be partially delivered also differentiates the Act from the statute at issue in *Stenberg*.... The Act's anatomical landmarks ... clarify that the removal of a small portion of the fetus is not prohibited. The landmarks also require the fetus to be delivered so that it is partially "outside the body of the mother." ... To come within the ambit of the Nebraska statute, on the other hand, a substantial portion of the fetus only had to be delivered into the vagina; no part of the fetus had to be outside the body of the mother before a doctor could face criminal sanctions....

By adding an overt-act requirement Congress sought further to meet the Court's objections to the state statute considered in *Stenberg*.... The Act makes the distinction the Nebraska statute failed to draw ... by differentiating between the overall partial-birth abortion and the distinct overt act that kills the fetus.... The fatal overt act must occur after delivery to an anatomical landmark, and it must be something "other than [the] completion of delivery." ... This distinction matters because, unlike intact D & E, standard D & E does not involve a delivery followed by a fatal act.

The canon of constitutional avoidance, finally, extinguishes any lingering doubt as to whether the Act covers the prototypical D & E procedure.... It is true this longstanding maxim of statutory interpretation has, in the past, fallen by the wayside when the Court confronted a statute regulating abortion. The Court at times employed an antagonistic " 'canon of construction under which in cases involving abortion, a permissible reading of a statute [was] to be avoided at all costs.' " *Stenberg* ... (Kennedy, J., dissenting).... *Casey* put this novel statutory approach to rest. *Stenberg* ... (Kennedy, J., dissenting). *Stenberg* need not be interpreted to have revived it. We read that decision instead to stand for the uncontroversial proposition that the canon of constitutional avoidance does not apply if a statute is not "genuinely susceptible to two constructions." ... Here, ... interpreting the Act so that it does not prohibit standard D & E is the most reasonable reading and understanding of its terms.

2

... Respondents ... contend—relying on the testimony of numerous abortion doctors—that D & E may result in the delivery of a living fetus beyond the Act's anatomical landmarks in a significant fraction of cases....

Th[eir] reasoning, however, does not take account of the Act's intent requirements, which preclude liability from attaching to an accidental intact D

& E. If a doctor's intent at the outset is to perform a D & E in which the fetus would not be delivered to either of the Act's anatomical landmarks, but the fetus nonetheless is delivered past one of those points, the requisite and prohibited scienter is not present. . . .

The evidence also supports a legislative determination that an intact delivery is almost always a conscious choice rather than a happenstance. . . .

. . . Respondents have not shown that requiring doctors to intend dismemberment before delivery to an anatomical landmark will prohibit the vast majority of D & E abortions. The Act, then, cannot be held invalid on its face on these grounds.

IV

Under the principles accepted as controlling here, the Act, as we have interpreted it, would be unconstitutional "if its purpose or effect is to place a substantial obstacle in the path of a woman seeking an abortion before the fetus attains viability." *Casey,* . . . (plurality opinion). The abortions affected by the Act's regulations take place both previability and postviability; so the quoted language and the undue burden analysis it relies upon are applicable. The question is whether the Act, measured by its text in this facial attack, imposes a substantial obstacle to late-term, but previability, abortions. The Act does not on its face impose a substantial obstacle, and we reject this further facial challenge to its validity.

A

The Act's purposes are set forth in recitals preceding its operative provisions. A description of the prohibited abortion procedure demonstrates the rationale for the congressional enactment. The Act proscribes a method of abortion in which a fetus is killed just inches before completion of the birth process. Congress stated as follows: "Implicitly approving such a brutal and inhumane procedure by choosing not to prohibit it will further coarsen society to the humanity of not only newborns, but all vulnerable and innocent human life, making it increasingly difficult to protect such life." Congressional Findings (14)(N), in notes following 18 U.S.C. § 1531 (2000 ed., Supp. IV), p. 769. The Act expresses respect for the dignity of human life.

Congress was concerned, furthermore, with the effects on the medical community and on its reputation caused by the practice of partial-birth abortion. The findings in the Act explain:

> "Partial-birth abortion . . . confuses the medical, legal, and ethical duties of physicians to preserve and promote life, as the physician acts directly against the physical life of a child, whom he or she had just delivered, all but the head, out of the womb, in order to end that life." Congressional Findings (14)(J), *ibid.*

There can be no doubt the government "has an interest in protecting the integrity and ethics of the medical profession." *Washington v. Glucksberg,* 521 U.S. 702, 731 (1997). . . . .

Casey reaffirmed these governmental objectives. The government may use its voice and its regulatory authority to show its profound respect for the life within the woman. . . . The . . . premise . . . that the State, from the inception *going back to rational basis, not undue burden!*

of the pregnancy, maintains its own regulatory interest in protecting the life of the fetus that may become a child, cannot be set at naught by interpreting *Casey's* requirement of a health exception so it becomes tantamount to allowing a doctor to choose the abortion method he or she might prefer. Where it has a rational basis to act, and it does not impose an undue burden, the State may use its regulatory power to bar certain procedures and substitute others, all in furtherance of its legitimate interests in regulating the medical profession in order to promote respect for life, including life of the unborn.

The Act's ban on abortions that involve partial delivery of a living fetus furthers the Government's objectives. No one would dispute that, for many, D & E is a procedure itself laden with the power to devalue human life. Congress could nonetheless conclude that the type of abortion proscribed by the Act requires specific regulation because it implicates additional ethical and moral concerns that justify a special prohibition. Congress determined that the abortion methods it proscribed had a "disturbing similarity to the killing of a newborn infant," Congressional Findings (14)(L), ... and thus it was concerned with "draw[ing] a bright line that clearly distinguishes abortion and infanticide." Congressional Findings (14)(G), ... The Court has in the past confirmed the validity of drawing boundaries to prevent certain practices that extinguish life and are close to actions that are condemned. *Glucksberg* found reasonable the State's "fear that permitting assisted suicide will start it down the path to voluntary and perhaps even involuntary euthanasia." ...

Respect for human life finds an ultimate expression in the bond of love the mother has for her child. The Act recognizes this reality as well. Whether to have an abortion requires a difficult and painful moral decision.... While we find no reliable data to measure the phenomenon, it seems unexceptionable to conclude some women come to regret their choice to abort the infant life they once created and sustained.... Severe depression and loss of esteem can follow....

In a decision so fraught with emotional consequence some doctors may prefer not to disclose precise details of the means that will be used, confining themselves to the required statement of risks the procedure entails. From one standpoint this ought not to be surprising. Any number of patients facing imminent surgical procedures would prefer not to hear all details, lest the usual anxiety preceding invasive medical procedures become the more intense. This is likely the case with the abortion procedures here in issue....

It is, however, precisely this lack of information concerning the way in which the fetus will be killed that is of legitimate concern to the State. *Casey* ... The State has an interest in ensuring so grave a choice is well informed. It is self-evident that a mother who comes to regret her choice to abort must struggle with grief more anguished and sorrow more profound when she learns, only after the event, what she once did not know: that she allowed a doctor to pierce the skull and vacuum the fast-developing brain of her unborn child, a child assuming the human form.

It is a reasonable inference that a necessary effect of the regulation and the knowledge it conveys will be to encourage some women to carry the infant to full term, thus reducing the absolute number of late-term abortions. The medical profession, furthermore, may find different and less shocking methods to abort the fetus in the second trimester, thereby accommodating legislative demand. The State's interest in respect for life is advanced by the dialogue that better informs the political and legal systems, the medical profession, expectant mothers, and society as a whole of the consequences that follow from a decision to elect a late-term abortion.

It is objected that the standard D & E is in some respects as brutal, if not more, than the intact D & E, so that the legislation accomplishes little. What we have already said, however, shows ample justification for the regulation. Partial-birth abortion, as defined by the Act, differs from a standard D & E because the former occurs when the fetus is partially outside the mother to the point of one of the Act's anatomical landmarks. It was reasonable for Congress to think that partial-birth abortion, more than standard D & E, "undermines the public's perception of the appropriate role of a physician during the delivery process, and perverts a process during which life is brought into the world." Congressional Findings (14)(K).... There would be a flaw in this Court's logic, and an irony in its jurisprudence, were we first to conclude a ban on both D & E and intact D & E was overbroad and then to say it is irrational to ban only intact D & E because that does not proscribe both procedures. In sum, we reject the contention that the congressional purpose of the Act was "to place a substantial obstacle in the path of a woman seeking an abortion." ...

B

The Act's furtherance of legitimate government interests bears upon, but does not resolve, the next question: whether the Act has the effect of imposing an unconstitutional burden on the abortion right because it does not allow use of the barred procedure where " 'necessary, in appropriate medical judgment, for [the] preservation of the ... health of the mother.' " *Ayotte,* 546 U.S., at 327–328 (quoting *Casey....*) The prohibition in the Act would be unconstitutional, under precedents we here assume to be controlling, if it "subject[ed] [women] to significant health risks." ... In *Ayotte* the parties agreed a health exception to the challenged parental-involvement statute was necessary "to avert serious and often irreversible damage to [a pregnant minor's] health." ... Here, by contrast, whether the Act creates significant health risks for women has been a contested factual question. The evidence presented in the trial courts and before Congress demonstrates both sides have medical support for their position.

Respondents presented evidence that intact D & E may be the safest method of abortion, for reasons similar to those adduced in *Stenberg....*

These contentions were contradicted by other doctors who testified in the District Courts and before Congress. They concluded that the alleged health advantages were based on speculation without scientific studies to support them. They considered D & E always to be a safe alternative....

There is documented medical disagreement whether the Act's prohibition would ever impose significant health risks on women.... The three District Courts that considered the Act's constitutionality appeared to be in some disagreement on this central factual question....

The question becomes whether the Act can stand when this medical uncertainty persists. The Court's precedents instruct that the Act can survive this facial attack. The Court has given state and federal legislatures wide discretion to pass legislation in areas where there is medical and scientific uncertainty. . . .

This traditional rule is consistent with *Casey,* which confirms the State's interest in promoting respect for human life at all stages in the pregnancy. Physicians are not entitled to ignore regulations that direct them to use reasonable alternative procedures. The law need not give abortion doctors unfettered choice in the course of their medical practice, nor should it elevate their status above other physicians in the medical community. . . .

Medical uncertainty does not foreclose the exercise of legislative power in the abortion context any more than it does in other contexts. . . . The medical uncertainty over whether the Act's prohibition creates significant health risks provides a sufficient basis to conclude in this facial attack that the Act does not impose an undue burden.

The conclusion that the Act does not impose an undue burden is supported by other considerations. Alternatives are available to the prohibited procedure. As we have noted, the Act does not proscribe D & E. One District Court found D & E to have extremely low rates of medical complications. . . . If the intact D & E procedure is truly necessary in some circumstances, it appears likely an injection that kills the fetus is an alternative under the Act that allows the doctor to perform the procedure.

The instant cases, then, are different from *Planned Parenthood of Central Mo. v. Danforth,* 428 U.S. 52, 77–79 (1976), in which the Court invalidated a ban on saline amniocentesis, the then-dominant second-trimester abortion method. . . . Here the Act allows, among other means, a commonly used and generally accepted method, so it does not construct a substantial obstacle to the abortion right.

In reaching the conclusion the Act does not require a health exception we reject certain arguments made by the parties on both sides of these cases. On the one hand, the Attorney General urges us to uphold the Act on the basis of the congressional findings alone. . . . Although we review congressional factfinding under a deferential standard, we do not in the circumstances here place dispositive weight on Congress' findings. The Court retains an independent constitutional duty to review factual findings where constitutional rights are at stake. . . .

As respondents have noted, and the District Courts recognized, some recitations in the Act are factually incorrect. . . . Whether or not accurate at the time, some of the important findings have been superseded. . . . Congress determined no medical schools provide instruction on the prohibited procedure. . . . The testimony in the District Courts, however, demonstrated intact D & E is taught at medical schools. . . . Congress also found there existed a medical consensus that the prohibited procedure is never medically necessary. . . . The evidence presented in the District Courts contradicts that conclusion. . . . Uncritical deference to Congress' factual findings in these cases is inappropriate.

On the other hand, relying on . . . *Stenberg,* respondents contend that an abortion regulation must contain a health exception "if 'substantial medical authority supports the proposition that banning a particular procedure could endanger women's health.' " . . .

A zero tolerance policy would strike down legitimate abortion regulations, like the present one, if some part of the medical community were disinclined to follow the proscription. This is too exacting a standard to impose on the legislative power, exercised in this instance under the Commerce Clause, to regulate the medical profession. Considerations of marginal safety, including the balance of risks, are within the legislative competence when the regulation is rational and in pursuit of legitimate ends. When standard medical options are available, mere convenience does not suffice to displace them; and if some procedures have different risks than others, it does not follow that the State is altogether barred from imposing reasonable regulations. The Act is not invalid on its face where there is uncertainty over whether the barred procedure is ever necessary to preserve a woman's health, given the availability of other abortion procedures that are considered to be safe alternatives.

V

The considerations we have discussed support our further determination that these facial attacks should not have been entertained in the first instance. In these circumstances the proper means to consider exceptions is by as-applied challenge. The Government has acknowledged that preenforcement, as-applied challenges to the Act can be maintained.... This is the proper manner to protect the health of the woman if it can be shown that in discrete and well-defined instances a particular condition has or is likely to occur in which the procedure prohibited by the Act must be used. In an as-applied challenge the nature of the medical risk can be better quantified and balanced than in a facial attack.

.   .   .

... [R]espondents have not demonstrated that the Act would be unconstitutional in a large fraction of relevant cases. *Casey,* ... We note that the statute here applies to all instances in which the doctor proposes to use the prohibited procedure, not merely those in which the woman suffers from medical complications. It is neither our obligation nor within our traditional institutional role to resolve questions of constitutionality with respect to each potential situation that might develop....

The Act is open to a proper as-applied challenge in a discrete case....

.   .   .

Justice Thomas, with whom Justice Scalia joins, concurring.

I join the Court's opinion because it accurately applies current jurisprudence, including *Planned Parenthood of Southeastern Pa. v. Casey,* 505 U.S. 833 (1992). I write separately to reiterate my view that the Court's abortion jurisprudence, including *Casey* and *Roe v. Wade,* 410 U.S. 113 (1973), has no basis in the Constitution.... I also note that whether the Act constitutes a permissible exercise of Congress' power under the Commerce Clause is not before the Court....

Justice Ginsburg, with whom Justice Stevens, Justice Souter, and Justice Breyer join, dissenting.

.   .   .

Today's decision is alarming. It refuses to take *Casey* and *Stenberg* serious-ly. It tolerates, indeed applauds, federal intervention to ban nationwide a procedure found necessary and proper in certain cases by the American College of Obstetricians and Gynecologists (ACOG). It blurs the line, firmly drawn in *Casey,* between previability and postviability abortions. And, for the first time since *Roe,* the Court blesses a prohibition with no exception safeguarding a woman's health.

. . . Retreating from prior rulings that abortion restrictions cannot be imposed absent an exception safeguarding a woman's health, the Court upholds an Act that surely would not survive under the close scrutiny that previously attended state-decreed limitations on a woman's reproductive choices.

I

A

. . . [L]egal challenges to undue restrictions on abortion procedures do not seek to vindicate some generalized notion of privacy; rather, they center on a woman's autonomy to determine her life's course, and thus to enjoy equal citizenship stature. . . .

In keeping with this comprehension of the right to reproductive choice, the Court has consistently required that laws regulating abortion, at any stage of pregnancy and in all cases, safeguard a woman's health. . . .

We have thus ruled that a State must avoid subjecting women to health risks not only where the pregnancy itself creates danger, but also where state regulation forces women to resort to less safe methods of abortion. . . . Indeed, we have applied the rule that abortion regulation must safeguard a woman's health to the particular procedure at issue here—intact dilation and evacuation (D & E).[3]

In *Stenberg,* we expressly held that a statute banning intact D & E was unconstitutional in part because it lacked a health exception. . . . We noted that there existed a "division of medical opinion" about the relative safety of intact D & E, . . . but we made clear that as long as "substantial medical authority supports the proposition that banning a particular abortion procedure could endanger women's health," a health exception is required. . . . [D]ivision in medical opinion "at most means uncertainty, a factor that signals the presence of risk, not its absence." *Ibid.* "[A] statute that altogether forbids [intact D & E]. . . . consequently must contain a health exception." . . .

B

In 2003, a few years after our ruling in *Stenberg,* Congress passed the Partial–Birth Abortion Ban Act—without an exception for women's health. . . .[4] The congressional findings on which the Partial–Birth Abortion Ban Act rests

---

3. . . .

Adolescents and indigent women, re-search suggests, are more likely than other women to have difficulty obtaining an abor-tion during the first trimester of pregnan-cy. . . .

4. The Act's sponsors left no doubt that their intention was to nullify our ruling in *Stenberg.* . . .

do not withstand inspection, as the lower courts have determined and this Court is obliged to concede. . . .

Many of the Act's recitations are incorrect. . . .

More important, Congress claimed there was a medical consensus that the banned procedure is never necessary. . . . But the evidence "very clearly demonstrate[d] the opposite." . . .

Similarly, Congress found that "[t]here is no credible medical evidence that partial-birth abortions are safe or are safer than other abortion procedures." Congressional Findings (14)(B). . . . But the congressional record includes letters from numerous individual physicians stating that pregnant women's health would be jeopardized under the Act, as well as statements from nine professional associations, including ACOG, the American Public Health Association, and the California Medical Association, attesting that intact D & E carries meaningful safety advantages over other methods. . . .

C

In contrast to Congress, the District Courts made findings after full trials at which all parties had the opportunity to present their best evidence. . . .

During the District Court trials, "numerous" "extraordinarily accomplished" and "very experienced" medical experts explained that, in certain circumstances and for certain women, intact D & E is safer than alternative procedures and necessary to protect women's health. . . .

According to the expert testimony plaintiffs introduced, the safety advantages of intact D & E are marked for women with certain medical conditions, for example, uterine scarring, bleeding disorders, heart disease, or compromised immune systems. . . . Further, plaintiffs' experts testified that intact D & E is significantly safer for women with certain pregnancy-related conditions, . . . and for women carrying fetuses with certain abnormalities. . . .

Intact D & E, plaintiffs' experts explained, provides safety benefits over D & E by dismemberment for several reasons[, including] minimiz[ing] the number of times a physician must insert instruments through the cervix and into the uterus[;] . . . decreas[ing] the likelihood that fetal tissue will be retained in the uterus, a condition that can cause infection, hemorrhage, and infertility[;] diminish[ing] the chances of exposing the patient's tissues to sharp bony fragments sometimes resulting from dismemberment of the fetus[; and, because it] takes less operating time than D & E by dismemberment, [it] may reduce bleeding, the risk of infection, and complications relating to anesthesia. . . .

Based on thoroughgoing review of the trial evidence and the congressional record, each of the District Courts to consider the issue rejected Congress' findings as unreasonable and not supported by the evidence. . . .

The District Courts' findings merit this Court's respect. . . . Today's opinion supplies no reason to reject those findings. Nevertheless, despite the District Courts' appraisal of the weight of the evidence, and in undisguised conflict with *Stenberg,* the Court asserts that the Partial–Birth Abortion Ban Act can survive "when . . . medical uncertainty persists." This assertion is bewildering. Not only does it defy the Court's longstanding precedent affirming the necessity of a health exception, with no carve-out for circumstances of medical uncertainty; it gives short shrift to the records before us, carefully canvassed by the District Courts. Those records indicate that "the majority of highly-qualified experts on the subject believe intact D & E to be the safest, most appropriate procedure under certain circumstances."

The Court acknowledges some of this evidence, but insists that, because some witnesses disagreed with the ACOG and other experts' assessment of risk, the Act can stand. In this insistence, the Court brushes under the rug the District Courts' well-supported findings that the physicians who testified that intact D & E is never necessary to preserve the health of a woman had slim authority for their opinions. They had no training for, or personal experience with, the intact D & E procedure, and many performed abortions only on rare occasions.... Even indulging the assumption that the Government witnesses were equally qualified to evaluate the relative risks of abortion procedures, their testimony could not erase the "significant medical authority support[ing] the proposition that in some circumstances, [intact D & E] would be the safest procedure." *Stenberg*,.

II

A

The Court offers flimsy and transparent justifications for upholding a nationwide ban on intact D & E *sans* any exception to safeguard a women's health.... The law saves not a single fetus from destruction, for it targets only a *method* of performing abortion.... And surely the statute was not designed to protect the lives or health of pregnant women.... In short, the Court upholds a law that, while doing nothing to "preserv[e] ... fetal life," bars a woman from choosing intact D & E although her doctor "reasonably believes [that procedure] will best protect [her]." *Stenberg*, ... (Stevens, J., concurring).

As another reason for upholding the ban, the Court emphasizes that the Act does not proscribe the nonintact D & E procedure. But why not, one might ask. Nonintact D & E could equally be characterized as "brutal," involving as it does "tear[ing] [a fetus] apart" and "ripp[ing] off" its limbs. "[T]he notion that either of these two equally gruesome procedures ... is more akin to infanticide than the other, or that the State furthers any legitimate interest by banning one but not the other, is simply irrational." *Stenberg*, ... (Stevens, J., concurring).

Delivery of an intact, albeit nonviable, fetus warrants special condemnation, the Court maintains, because a fetus that is not dismembered resembles an infant. But so, too, does a fetus delivered intact after it is terminated by injection a day or two before the surgical evacuation, or a fetus delivered through medical induction or cesarean. Yet, the availability of those procedures—along with D & E by dismemberment—the Court says, saves the ban on intact D & E from a declaration of unconstitutionality. Never mind that the procedures deemed acceptable might put a woman's health at greater risk....

Ultimately, the Court admits that "moral concerns" are at work, concerns that could yield prohibitions on any abortion.... Notably, the concerns expressed are untethered to any ground genuinely serving the Government's interest in preserving life. By allowing such concerns to carry the day and case, overriding fundamental rights, the Court dishonors our precedent....

Revealing in this regard, the Court invokes an antiabortion shibboleth for which it concededly has no reliable evidence: Women who have abortions come to regret their choices, and consequently suffer from "[s]evere depression and loss of esteem."[7] Because of women's fragile emotional state and because of the "bond of love the mother has for her child," the Court worries, doctors may withhold information about the nature of the intact D & E procedure. The solution the Court approves, then, is *not* to require doctors to inform women, accurately and adequately, of the different procedures and their attendant risks.... Instead, the Court deprives women of the right to make an autonomous choice, even at the expense of their safety.[9]

This way of thinking reflects ancient notions about women's place in the family and under the Constitution—ideas that have long since been discredited....

.   .   .

B

In cases on a "woman's liberty to determine whether to [continue] her pregnancy," this Court has identified viability as a critical consideration. See *Casey* ... (plurality opinion)....

Today, the Court blurs that line.... Instead of drawing the line at viability, the Court refers to Congress' purpose to differentiate "abortion and infanticide" based not on whether a fetus can survive outside the womb, but on where a fetus is anatomically located when a particular medical procedure is performed....

One wonders how long a line that saves no fetus from destruction will hold in face of the Court's "moral concerns." ... The Court's hostility to the right *Roe* and *Casey* secured is not concealed. Throughout, the opinion refers to obstetrician-gynecologists and surgeons who perform abortions not by the titles of their medical specialties, but by the pejorative label "abortion doctor." A fetus is described as an "unborn child," and as a "baby"; second-trimester, previability abortions are referred to as "late-term"; and the reasoned medical judgments of highly trained doctors are dismissed as "preferences" motivated by "mere convenience." Instead of the heightened scrutiny we have previously applied, the Court determines that a "rational" ground is enough to uphold the Act. And, most troubling, *Casey's* principles, confirming the continuing vitality of "the essential holding of *Roe,*" are merely "assume[d]" for the moment, rather than "retained" or "reaffirmed," *Casey....*

---

7. The Court is surely correct that, for most women, abortion is a painfully difficult decision. But "neither the weight of the scientific evidence to date nor the observable reality of 33 years of legal abortion in the United States comports with the idea that having an abortion is any more dangerous to a woman's long-term mental health than de-livering and parenting a child that she did not intend to have...." [Citing studies.]

9. Eliminating or reducing women's reproductive choices is manifestly *not* a means of protecting them. When safe abortion procedures cease to be an option, many women seek other means to end unwanted or coerced pregnancies....

III

A

The Court further confuses our jurisprudence when it declares that "facial attacks" are not permissible ... where *medical uncertainty exists*.... This holding is perplexing given that, in materially identical circumstances we held that a statute lacking a health exception was unconstitutional on its face. *Stenberg*....

... *Casey* makes clear that, in determining whether any restriction poses an undue burden on a "large fraction" of women, the relevant class is *not* "all women," nor "all pregnant women," nor even all women "seeking abortions." ... Rather, a provision restricting access to abortion, "must be judged by reference to those [women] for whom it is an actual rather than an irrelevant restriction," *ibid.* Thus the absence of a health exception burdens *all* women for whom it is relevant—women who, in the judgment of their doctors, require an intact D & E because other procedures would place their health at risk.... It makes no sense to conclude that this facial challenge fails because respondents have not shown that a health exception is necessary for a large fraction of second-trimester abortions, including those for which a health exception is unnecessary: The very purpose of a health *exception* is to protect women in *exceptional* cases.

B

If there is anything at all redemptive to be said of today's opinion, it is that the Court is not willing to foreclose entirely a constitutional challenge to the Act.... But the Court offers no clue on what a "proper" lawsuit might look like. Nor does the Court explain why the injunctions ordered by the District Courts should not remain in place, trimmed only to exclude instances in which another procedure would safeguard a woman's health at least equally well. Surely the Court cannot mean that no suit may be brought until a woman's health is immediately jeopardized by the ban on intact D & E. A woman "suffer[ing] from medical complications" needs access to the medical procedure at once and cannot wait for the judicial process to unfold....

. . .

The Court envisions that in an as-applied challenge, "the nature of the medical risk can be better quantified and balanced." But it should not escape notice that the record already includes hundreds and hundreds of pages of testimony identifying "discrete and well-defined instances" in which recourse to an intact D & E would better protect the health of women with particular conditions. Record evidence also documents that medical exigencies, unpredictable in advance, may indicate to a well-trained doctor that intact D & E is the safest procedure. In light of this evidence, our unanimous decision just one year ago in *Ayotte* counsels against reversal. See 546 U.S., at 331 (remanding for reconsideration of the remedy for the absence of a health exception, suggesting that an injunction prohibiting unconstitutional applications might suffice).

The Court's allowance only of an "as-applied challenge in a discrete case" jeopardizes women's health and places doctors in an untenable position. Even if courts were able to carve-out exceptions through piecemeal litigation for "discrete and well-defined instances," women whose circumstances have not been anticipated by prior litigation could well be left unprotected. In treating those women, physicians would risk criminal prosecution, conviction, and imprisonment if they exercise their best judgment as to the safest medical procedure for their patients. The Court is thus gravely mistaken to conclude that narrow as-applied challenges are "the proper manner to protect the health of the woman."

IV

. . .

Though today's opinion does not go so far as to discard *Roe* or *Casey,* the Court, differently composed than it was when we last considered a restrictive abortion regulation, is hardly faithful to our earlier invocations of "the rule of law" and the "principles of *stare decisis.*" Congress imposed a ban despite our clear prior holdings that the State cannot proscribe an abortion procedure when its use is necessary to protect a woman's health. Although Congress' findings could not withstand the crucible of trial, the Court defers to the legislative override of our Constitution-based rulings. A decision so at odds with our jurisprudence should not have staying power.

In sum, the notion that the Partial–Birth Abortion Ban Act furthers any legitimate governmental interest is, quite simply, irrational. The Court's defense of the statute provides no saving explanation. In candor, the Act, and the Court's defense of it, cannot be understood as anything other than an effort to chip away at a right declared again and again by this Court—and with increasing comprehension of its centrality to women's lives. When "a statute burdens constitutional rights and all that can be said on its behalf is that it is the vehicle that legislators have chosen for expressing their hostility to those rights, the burden is undue." *Stenberg,* . . . (Ginsburg, J., concurring). . . .

. . .

CHAPTER 10

THE EQUAL PROTECTION CLAUSE AND THE REVIEW OF THE REASONABLENESS OF LEGISLATION

SECTION 3. SUSPECT CLASSIFICATIONS

B. RACIAL SEGREGATION IN SCHOOLS AND OTHER PUBLIC FACILITIES

Page 731. Add at end of Note, "Segregation in Public Facilities Other than Schools":

More than four decades later, in Johnson v. California, 543 U.S. 499, 125 S.Ct. 1141, 160 L.Ed.2d 949 (2005), a divided Court insisted that strict scrutiny be applied to an unwritten California policy segregating prisoners in double cells (but not the prison generally) for up to 60 days after they arrive at a new prison, despite the claims of corrections officials that the temporary segregation was necessary during a period of inmate evaluation to prevent violence associated with racial gangs. With Chief Justice Rehnquist not participating, Justice O'Connor's majority opinion reasoned in part that "by insisting that inmates be housed only with other inmates of the same race, it is possible that prison officials will breed further hostility among prisoners and reinforce racial and ethnic divisions. By perpetuating the notion that race matters most, racial segregation of inmates 'may exacerbate the very patterns of [violence that it is] said to counteract.'" She "decline[d] the invitation" to make an exception for the prison context, where for certain fundamental constitutional rights the Court in Turner v. Safley, 482 U.S. 78, 89, 107 S.Ct. 2254, 96 L.Ed.2d 64 (1987), has required only that a burdensome regulation be "reasonably related" to "legitimate penological interests." Unlike the constitutional rights to which the deferential standard of *Turner* properly applied, "[t]he right not to be discriminated against based on one's race is ... not a right that need necessarily be compromised for the sake of proper prison administration. On the contrary, compliance with the Fourteenth Amendment's ban on racial discrimination ... bolsters the legitimacy of the entire criminal justice system." The majority was convinced that "[i]n the prison context, when the government's power is at its apex, ... searching judicial review of racial classifications is necessary to guard against invidious discrimination"; that "[t]he 'necessities of prison security and discipline' ... are a compelling government interest justifying only those uses of race that are narrowly tailored to address those necessities"; and that on remand, although "[s]trict scrutiny does not preclude the ability of prison officials to address the compelling interest in prison safety[, p]rison administrators . . . will have to demonstrate that any race-based policies are narrowly tailored to that end."

A dissent by Justice Stevens concluded that the record as it stood showed the policy was unconstitutional, for it was "based on a conclusive presumption that housing inmates of different races together creates an unacceptable risk of racial violence"; "scant empirical evidence" supported that presumption; and a "very real risk that prejudice (whether conscious or not) partly underlies the . . . policy" undermined it. A polar opposite dissent by Justice Thomas, joined by Justice Scalia, emphasized "how limited the policy . . . is" of racial segregation of "a portion of [California's] inmates, in a part of its prisons, for brief periods . . . until the State can arrange permanent housing" and argued that the Court should apply *Turner* and defer to the expert judgment of prison officials. Those officials had asserted that "housing inmates in double cells without regard to race threatens not only prison discipline, but also the physical safety of inmates and staff . . . because double cells are especially dangerous. The risk of racial violence in public areas of prisons is high, and the tightly confined, private conditions of cells hazard even more violence." Furthermore, "Johnson has never argued that California's policy is motivated by anything other than a desire to protect inmates and staff." In any event, "the Constitution's usual demands . . . have always been lessened inside . . . prison walls" and the majority's "second-guessing" fell "far short of the compelling showing needed to overcome the deference we owe to prison administrators."

Page 734. Add footnote a. after first full sentence:

    a. More than 35 years later, in Parents Involved in Community Schools v. Seattle School District No. 1, reported in full, *infra*, the Court divided deeply over the meaning and significance of these two sentences for assessing the constitutionality of the voluntary use of race in student assignments in school districts that were not currently subject to desegregation orders.

Page 749. Add after Note, "When Is Desegregation Achieved and Judicial Authority at an End":

Parents Involved in Community Schools v. Seattle School District No. 1

___ U.S. ___, 127 S.Ct. 2738, ___ L.Ed.2d ___ (2007).

[The report in this case appears *infra* at p. 56]

E. "BENIGN" DISCRIMINATION: AFFIRMATIVE ACTION, QUOTAS, PREFERENCES BASED ON GENDER OR RACE

2. CLASSIFICATIONS ADVANTAGING RACIAL MINORITIES

Page 835. Add footnote a. after first full paragraph of Note, "Race–Conscious Affirmative Action, 1974–1989":

    a. A deeply divided Court revisited the meaning and significance of this statement more than 35 years later in Parents Involved in Community Schools v. Seattle School District No. 1, reported in full, *infra*, p. 56.

Page 901. Add at end of subsection:

Parents Involved in Community Schools v. Seattle School District No. 1

___ U.S. ___, 127 S.Ct. 2738, ___ L.Ed.2d ___ (2007).

Chief Justice Roberts announced the judgment of the Court, and delivered the opinion of the Court with respect to Parts I, II, III–A, and III–C, and an opinion with respect to Parts III–B and IV, in which Justices Scalia, Thomas, and Alito join.

The school districts in these cases voluntarily adopted student assignment plans that rely upon race to determine which public schools certain children may attend. The Seattle school district classifies children as white or nonwhite; the Jefferson County school district as black or "other." In Seattle, this racial classification is used to allocate slots in oversubscribed high schools. In Jefferson County, it is used to make certain elementary school assignments and to rule on transfer requests. In each case, the school district relies upon an individual student's race in assigning that student to a particular school, so that the racial balance at the school falls within a predetermined range based on the racial composition of the school district as a whole. Parents of students denied assignment to particular schools under these plans solely because of their race brought suit, contending that allocating children to different public schools on the basis of race violated the Fourteenth Amendment guarantee of equal protection. The Courts of Appeals below upheld the plans. We ... reverse.

I

Both cases present the same underlying legal question—whether a public school that had not operated legally segregated schools or has been found to be unitary may choose to classify students by race and rely upon that classification in making school assignments. . . .

A

Seattle School District No. 1 operates 10 regular public high schools. In 1998, it adopted the plan at issue[, which] allows incoming ninth graders to choose from among any of the district's high schools. . . .

. . . If too many students list the same school as their first choice, the district employs a series of "tiebreakers" [for] the oversubscribed school. The first [is] a sibling currently enrolled. . . . The next tiebreaker depends upon the racial composition of the particular school and the race of the individual student. In the district's public schools approximately 41 percent of enrolled students are white; the remaining 59 percent, comprising all other racial groups, are classified by Seattle for assignment purposes as nonwhite. . . .[2] If an oversubscribed school is not within 10 percentage points of the district's overall

2. The racial breakdown of this nonwhite group is approximately 23.8 percent Asian–American, 23.1 percent African–American, 10.3 percent Latino, and 2.8 percent Native–American. . . .

white/nonwhite racial balance, it is what the district calls "integration positive," and the district employs a tiebreaker that selects for assignment students whose race "will serve to bring the school into balance." ... If ... necessary ..., the next tiebreaker is the geographic proximity of the school to the student's residence....

Seattle has never operated segregated schools—legally separate schools for students of different races—nor has it ever been subject to court-ordered desegregation. It nonetheless employs the racial tiebreaker in an attempt to address the effects of racially identifiable housing patterns on school assignments....

For the 2000–2001 school year, five ... schools were oversubscribed—... so much so that 82 percent of incoming ninth graders ranked one of these schools as their first choice.... Three of the[m] were "integration positive" because the school's white enrollment the previous school year was greater than 51 percent.... Thus, more nonwhite students (107, 27, and 82, respectively) who selected one of these three schools as a top choice received placement at the school than would have been the case had race not been considered, and proximity been the next tiebreaker.... [Another] was "integration positive" because its nonwhite enrollment the previous school year was greater than 69 percent; 89 more white students were assigned ... by operation of the racial tiebreaker in the 2000–2001 school year than otherwise would have been.... Garfield was the only oversubscribed school whose composition during the 1999–2000 school year was within the racial guidelines, although in previous years Garfield's enrollment had been predominantly nonwhite, and the racial tiebreaker had been used to give preference to white students....

... [P]arents of children who have been or may be denied assignment to their chosen high school in the district because of their race[—such as ninth-grader Andy Meeks, who was accepted into a selective program but, because of the racial tiebreaker, was denied assignment to the relevant high school—challenged the policy as a denial of equal protection. They lost in the District Court and eventually in an en banc decision of the Ninth Circuit, which affirmed] the District Court's determination that Seattle's plan was narrowly tailored to serve a compelling government interest....

B

Jefferson County Public Schools operates the public school system in metropolitan Louisville, Kentucky. In 1973 a federal court found that Jefferson County had maintained a segregated school system, ... and in 1975 the District Court entered a desegregation decree.... Jefferson County operated under this decree until 2000, when the District Court dissolved the decree after finding that the district had achieved unitary status by eliminating "[t]o the greatest extent practicable" the vestiges of its prior policy of segregation....

In 2001, after the decree had been dissolved, Jefferson County adopted the voluntary student assignment plan at issue in this case.... Approximately 34 percent of the district's 97,000 students are black; most of the remaining 66 percent are white.... The plan requires all nonmagnet schools to maintain a minimum black enrollment of 15 percent, and a maximum black enrollment of 50 percent....

At the elementary school level, based on his or her address, each student is designated a "resides" school to which students within a specific geographic area are assigned; elementary resides schools are "grouped into clusters in order to facilitate integration." . . . "Decisions to assign students to schools within each cluster are based on available space within the schools and the racial guidelines in the District's current student assignment plan." . . . If a school has reached the "extremes of the racial guidelines," a student whose race would contribute to the school's racial imbalance will not be assigned there. . . . After assignment, students . . . are permitted to apply to transfer . . . for any number of reasons, [but they] may be denied because of lack of available space or on the basis of the racial guidelines.

When petitioner Crystal Meredith moved into the school district . . . she sought to enroll her son, Joshua McDonald, in kindergarten for the 2002–2003 school year. His resides school was only a mile from his new home, but it had no available space [and he was] assigned . . . to another elementary school in his cluster, Young Elementary. This school was 10 miles from home, and Meredith sought to transfer Joshua to a school in a different cluster . . . only a mile from home[,] but Joshua's transfer was . . . denied because, in the words of Jefferson County, "[t]he transfer would have an adverse effect on desegregation compliance" of Young. . . .

Meredith['s] suit . . . alleging violations of the Equal Protection Clause [was unsuccessful in the District Court and the Sixth Circuit.]

. . .

III

A

It is well established that when the government distributes burdens or benefits on the basis of individual racial classifications, that action is reviewed under strict scrutiny. *Johnson* v. *California*, 543 U.S. 499, 505–506 (2005); *Grutter* v. *Bollinger*, 539 U.S. 306, 326 (2003). . . . In order to satisfy this searching standard of review, the school districts must demonstrate that the use of individual racial classifications in the assignment plans here under review is "narrowly tailored" to achieve a "compelling" government interest. . . .

[O]ur prior cases, in evaluating the use of racial classifications in the school context, have recognized two interests that qualify as compelling. The first is . . . remedying the effects of past intentional discrimination. . . . Yet the Seattle public schools have not shown that they were ever segregated by law, and were not subject to court-ordered desegregation decrees. The Jefferson County public schools were previously segregated by law and were subject to a desegregation decree entered in 1975. In 2000, the District Court that entered that decree dissolved it, finding that Jefferson County had "eliminated the vestiges associated with the former policy of segregation and its pernicious effects," and thus had achieved "unitary" status. . . . Jefferson County accordingly does not rely upon an interest in remedying the effects of past intentional discrimination in defending its present use of race in assigning students. . . .

Nor could it. We have emphasized that the harm being remedied by mandatory desegregation plans is the harm that is traceable to segregation, and that "the Constitution is not violated by racial imbalance in the schools, without more." ... Once Jefferson County achieved unitary status, it had remedied the constitutional wrong that allowed race-based assignments. Any continued use of race must be justified on some other basis.[10]

The second government interest we have recognized as compelling ... is the interest in diversity in higher education upheld in *Grutter*.... The diversity interest was not focused on race alone but encompassed "all factors that may contribute to student body diversity." ...

. . .

The entire gist of the analysis in *Grutter* was that the admissions program at issue there focused on each applicant as an individual, and not simply as a member of a particular racial group. The classification of applicants by race upheld in *Grutter* was only as part of a "highly individualized, holistic review,".... The point of the narrow tailoring analysis in which the *Grutter* Court engaged was to ensure that the use of racial classifications was indeed part of a broader assessment of diversity, and not simply an effort to achieve racial balance, which the Court explained would be "patently unconstitutional." ...

In the present cases, by contrast, race is not considered as part of a broader effort to achieve "exposure to widely diverse people, cultures, ideas, and viewpoints," ...; race, for some students, is determinative standing alone. The districts argue that other factors, such as student preferences, affect assignment decisions under their plans, but under each plan when race comes into play, it is decisive by itself. It is not simply one factor weighed with others in reaching a decision, as in *Grutter*; it is *the* factor. Like the ... undergraduate plan struck down in *Gratz*, ... the plans here "do not provide for a meaningful individualized review of applicants" but instead rely on racial classifications in a "nonindividualized, mechanical" way ... (O'Connor, J., concurring).

Even when it comes to race, the plans here employ only a limited notion of diversity, viewing race exclusively in white/nonwhite terms in Seattle and black/"other" terms in Jefferson County.... The Seattle "Board Statement Reaffirming Diversity Rationale" speaks of the "inherent educational value" in "[p]roviding students the opportunity to attend schools with diverse student enrollment,".... But under the Seattle plan, a school with 50 percent Asian–American students and 50 percent white students but no African–American, Native–American, or Latino students would qualify as balanced, while a school with 30 percent Asian–American, 25 percent African–American, 25 percent Latino, and 20 percent white students would not. It is hard to understand how a plan that could allow these results can be viewed as being concerned with achieving enrollment that is " 'broadly diverse,' " *Grutter*....

---

10. The districts point to dicta in a prior opinion in which the Court suggested that, while not constitutionally mandated, it would be constitutionally permissible for a school district to seek racially balanced schools as a matter of "educational policy." See *Swann* v. *Charlotte-Mecklenburg Bd. of Ed.*, 402 U.S. 1, 16 (1971).... *Swann*, evaluating a school district engaged in court-or-dered desegregation, had no occasion to consider whether a district's voluntary adoption of race-based assignments in the absence of a finding of prior *de jure* segregation was constitutionally permissible, an issue that was again expressly reserved in *Washington* v. *Seattle School Dist. No. 1*, 458 U.S. 457, 472, n. 15 (1982)....

Prior to *Grutter*, the courts of appeals rejected as unconstitutional attempts to implement race-based assignment plans—such as the plans at issue here—in primary and secondary schools.... After *Grutter*, however, the two Courts of Appeals in these cases, and one other, found that race-based assignments were permissible at the elementary and secondary level, largely in reliance on that case....

In upholding the admissions plan in *Grutter*, though, this Court relied upon considerations unique to institutions of higher education, noting that in light of "the expansive freedoms of speech and thought associated with the university environment, universities occupy a special niche in our constitutional tradition." ... The Court explained that "[c]ontext matters" in applying strict scrutiny, and repeatedly noted that it was addressing the use of race "in the context of higher education." ... The Court in *Grutter* expressly articulated key limitations on its holding—defining a specific type of broad-based diversity and noting the unique context of higher education—but these limitations were largely disregarded by the lower courts in extending *Grutter* to uphold race-based assignments in elementary and secondary schools. The present cases are not governed by *Grutter*.

B

Perhaps recognizing that reliance on *Grutter* cannot sustain their plans, both school districts assert additional interests, distinct from the interest upheld in *Grutter*, to justify their race-based assignments.... Seattle contends that its use of race helps to reduce racial concentration in schools and to ensure that racially concentrated housing patterns do not prevent nonwhite students from having access to the most desirable schools.... Jefferson County has articulated a similar goal, phrasing its interest in terms of educating its students "in a racially integrated environment." ...[12] Each school district argues that educational and broader socialization benefits flow from a racially diverse learning environment, and each contends that because the diversity they seek is racial diversity—not the broader diversity at issue in *Grutter*—it makes sense to promote that interest directly by relying on race alone.

The parties and their *amici* dispute whether racial diversity in schools in fact has a marked impact on test scores and other objective yardsticks or achieves intangible socialization benefits. The debate is not one we need to resolve, however, because it is clear that the racial classifications employed by the districts are not narrowly tailored to the goal of achieving the educational and social benefits asserted to flow from racial diversity. In design and operation, the plans are directed only to racial balance, pure and simple, an objective this Court has repeatedly condemned as illegitimate.

---

12. Jefferson County also argues that it would be incongruous to hold that what was constitutionally required of it one day—race-based assignments pursuant to the desegregation decree—can be constitutionally prohibited the next. But what was constitutionally required of the district prior to 2000 was the elimination of the vestiges of prior segregation—not racial proportionality in its own right. See *Freeman* v. *Pitts*, 503 U.S. 467, 494–496 (1992). Once those vestiges were eliminated, Jefferson County was on the same footing as any other school district, and its use of race must be justified on other grounds.

The plans are tied to each district's specific racial demographics, rather than to any pedagogic concept of the level of diversity needed to obtain the asserted educational benefits. In Seattle, ... the benefits of racial diversity require enrollment of at least 31 percent white students; in Jefferson County, at least 50 percent. There must be at least 15 percent nonwhite students under Jefferson County's plan; in Seattle, more than three times that figure. This comparison makes clear that the racial demographics in each district—whatever they happen to be—drive the required "diversity" numbers. The plans here are not tailored to achieving a degree of diversity necessary to realize the asserted educational benefits; instead the plans are tailored, in the words of Seattle's Manager of Enrollment Planning, Technical Support, and Demographics, to "the goal established by the school board of attaining a level of diversity within the schools that approximates the district's overall demographics." ...

The districts offer no evidence that the level of racial diversity necessary to achieve the asserted educational benefits happens to coincide with the racial demographics of the respective school districts—or rather the white/nonwhite or black/"other" balance of the districts, since that is the only diversity addressed by the plans. ... The [Seattle] district did not ... demonstrate in any way how the educational and social benefits of racial diversity or avoidance of racial isolation are more likely to be achieved at a school that is 50 percent white and 50 percent Asian–American, which would qualify as diverse under Seattle's plan, than at a school that is 30 percent Asian–American, 25 percent African–American, 25 percent Latino, and 20 percent white, which under Seattle's definition would be racially concentrated.

Similarly, Jefferson County's expert referred to the importance of having "at least 20 percent" minority group representation for the group "to be visible enough to make a difference," and noted that "small isolated minority groups in a school are not likely to have a strong effect on the overall school." ... The Jefferson County plan, however, is based on a goal of replicating at each school "an African–American enrollment equivalent to the average district-wide African–American enrollment." ... Joshua McDonald's requested transfer was denied because his race was listed as "other" rather than black, and allowing the transfer would have had an adverse effect on the racial guideline compliance of Young Elementary, the school he sought to leave.... At the time, however, Young Elementary was 46.8 percent black.... The transfer might have had an adverse effect on the effort to approach district-wide racial proportionality at Young, but it had nothing to do with preventing either the black or "other" group from becoming "small" or "isolated" at Young.

In fact, in each case the extreme measure of relying on race in assignments is unnecessary to achieve the stated goals, even as defined by the districts. For example, at Franklin High School in Seattle, the racial tiebreaker was applied because nonwhite enrollment exceeded 69 percent, and resulted in an incoming ninth-grade class in 2000–2001 that was 30.3 percent Asian–American, 21.9 percent African–American, 6.8 percent Latino, 0.5 percent Native–American, and 40.5 percent Caucasian. Without the racial tiebreaker, the class would have been 39.6 percent Asian–American, 30.2 percent African–American, 8.3 percent Latino, 1.1 percent Native–American, and 20.8 percent Caucasian.... When the actual racial breakdown is considered, enrolling students without regard to their race yields a substantially diverse student body under any definition of diversity.

In *Grutter*, the number of minority students the school sought to admit was an undefined "meaningful number" necessary to achieve a genuinely diverse student body.... Although the matter was the subject of disagreement on the Court, ... the majority concluded that the law school did not count back from its applicant pool to arrive at the "meaningful number" it regarded as necessary to diversify its student body.... Here the racial balance the districts seek is a defined range set solely by reference to the demographics of the respective school districts.

This working backward to achieve a particular type of racial balance, rather than working forward from some demonstration of the level of diversity that provides the purported benefits, is a fatal flaw under our existing precedent. We have many times over reaffirmed that "[r]acial balance is not to be achieved for its own sake." ... *Grutter* itself reiterated that "outright racial balancing" is "patently unconstitutional." ...

Accepting racial balancing as a compelling state interest would justify the imposition of racial proportionality throughout American society, contrary to our repeated recognition that "[a]t the heart of the Constitution's guarantee of equal protection lies the simple command that the Government must treat citizens as individuals, not as simply components of a racial, religious, sexual or national class." ...[14] Allowing racial balancing as a compelling end in itself would "effectively assur[e] that race will always be relevant in American life, and that the 'ultimate goal' of 'eliminating entirely from governmental decisionmaking such irrelevant factors as a human being's race' will never be achieved." ...

The validity of our concern that racial balancing has "no logical stopping point," ... is demonstrated here by the degree to which the districts tie their racial guidelines to their demographics. As the districts' demographics shift, so too will their definition of racial diversity....

... [I]n Seattle the plans are defended as necessary to address the consequences of racially identifiable housing patterns. The sweep of the mandate claimed by the district is contrary to our rulings that remedying past societal discrimination does not justify race-conscious government action....

The principle that racial balancing is not permitted is one of substance, not semantics. Racial balancing is not transformed from "patently unconstitutional" to a compelling state interest simply by relabeling it "racial diversity." While the school districts use various verbal formulations to describe the interest they seek to promote—racial diversity, avoidance of racial isolation, racial integration—they offer no definition of the interest that suggests it differs from racial balance....

---

14. In contrast, Seattle's website formerly described "emphasizing individualism as opposed to a more collective ideology" as a form of "cultural racism," and currently states that the district has no intention "to hold onto unsuccessful concepts such as [a] ... colorblind mentality." ...

Jefferson County phrases its interest as "racial integration," but integration certainly does not require the sort of racial proportionality reflected in its plan. Even in the context of mandatory desegregation, we have stressed that racial proportionality is not required, ... and here Jefferson County has already been found to have eliminated the vestiges of its prior segregated school system.

... To the extent the objective is sufficient diversity so that students see fellow students as individuals rather than solely as members of a racial group, using means that treat students solely as members of a racial group is fundamentally at cross-purposes with that end.

C

The districts assert ... that the way in which they have employed individual racial classifications is necessary to achieve their stated ends. The minimal effect these classifications have on student assignments, however, suggests that other means would be effective. Seattle's racial tiebreaker results, in the end, only in shifting a small number of students between schools.... In over one-third of the assignments affected by the racial tiebreaker ... the use of race in the end made no difference, and the district could identify only 52 students who were ultimately affected adversely by the racial tiebreaker in that it resulted in assignment to a school they had not listed as a preference and to which they would not otherwise have been assigned.

. . .

Similarly, Jefferson County's use of racial classifications has only a minimal effect on the assignment of students. Elementary school students are assigned to their first-or second-choice school 95 percent of the time, and transfers, which account for roughly 5 percent of assignments, are only denied 35 percent of the time—and presumably an even smaller percentage are denied on the basis of the racial guidelines, given that other factors may lead to a denial.... Jefferson County estimates that the racial guidelines account for only 3 percent of assignments....

While we do not suggest that *greater* use of race would be preferable, the minimal impact of the districts' racial classifications on school enrollment casts doubt on the necessity of using racial classifications. In *Grutter*, the consideration of race was viewed as indispensable in more than tripling minority representation at the law school—from 4 to 14.5 percent.... Here the most Jefferson County itself claims is that "because the guidelines provide a firm definition of the Board's goal of racially integrated schools, they 'provide administrators with the authority to facilitate, negotiate and collaborate with principals and staff to maintain schools within the 15–50% range.'" ... Classifying and assigning schoolchildren according to a binary conception of race is an extreme approach in light of our precedents and our Nation's history of using race in public schools, and requires more than such an amorphous end to justify it.

The districts have also failed to show that they considered methods other than explicit racial classifications to achieve their stated goals.... [I]n Seattle several alternative assignment plans—many of which would not have used express racial classifications—were rejected with little or no consideration....

Jefferson County has failed to present any evidence that it considered alternatives, even though the district already claims that its goals are achieved primarily through means other than the racial classifications. . . .

IV

Justice Breyer's dissent takes a different approach to these cases, one that fails to ground the result it would reach in law. Instead, it selectively relies on inapplicable precedent and even dicta while dismissing contrary holdings, alters and misapplies our well-established legal framework for assessing equal protection challenges to express racial classifications, and greatly exaggerates the consequences of today's decision.

To begin with, Justice Breyer seeks to justify the plans at issue under our precedents recognizing the compelling interest in remedying past intentional discrimination. . . . Not even the school districts go this far, and for good reason. The distinction between segregation by state action and racial imbalance caused by other factors has been central to our jurisprudence in this area for generations. . . . The dissent elides this distinction between *de jure* and *de facto* segregation, casually intimates that Seattle's school attendance patterns reflect illegal segregation, and fails to credit the judicial determination—under the most rigorous standard—that Jefferson County had eliminated the vestiges of prior segregation. The dissent thus alters in fundamental ways not only the facts presented here but the established law.

. . . The present cases are before us . . . because the Seattle school district was never segregated by law, and the Jefferson County district has been found to be unitary, having eliminated the vestiges of its prior dual status. The justification for race-conscious remedies . . . is therefore not applicable here. The dissent's persistent refusal to accept this distinction . . . explains its inability to understand why the remedial justification for racial classifications cannot decide these cases.

Justice Breyer's dissent next relies heavily on dicta from *Swann* v. *Charlotte-Mecklenburg Bd. of Ed.*, . . . [W]hen *Swann* was decided, this Court had not yet confirmed that strict scrutiny applies to racial classifications like those before us. . . .

Justice Breyer would not only put such extraordinary weight on admitted dicta, but relies on the statement for something it does not remotely say. *Swann* addresses only a possible state objective; it says nothing of the permissible *means*—race conscious or otherwise—that a school district might employ to achieve that objective. . . .

Further, for all the lower court cases Justice Breyer cites as evidence of the "prevailing legal assumption" embodied by *Swann*, very few are pertinent. . . .[16]

. . .

---

16. [A]ll the cases Justice Breyer's dissent cites as evidence of the "prevailing legal assumption" were decided before this Court definitively determined that "all racial classifications . . . must be analyzed by a reviewing court under strict scrutiny." *Adarand Constructors, Inc.* v. *Pena*, 515 U.S. 200, 227 (1995). Many proceeded under the now-rejected view that classifications seeking to benefit a disadvantaged racial group should

Justice Breyer's dissent also asserts that these cases are controlled by *Grutter,* claiming that the existence of a compelling interest in these cases "follows *a fortiori*" from *Grutter,* and accusing us of tacitly overruling that case. The dissent overreads *Grutter,* however, in suggesting that it renders pure racial balancing a constitutionally compelling interest; *Grutter* itself recognized that using race simply to achieve racial balance would be "patently unconstitutional," . . . The Court was exceedingly careful in describing the interest furthered in *Grutter* as "not an interest in simple ethnic diversity" but rather a "far broader array of qualifications and characteristics" in which race was but a single element. . . . We take the *Grutter* Court at its word. We simply do not understand how Justice Breyer can maintain that classifying every schoolchild as black or white, and using that classification as a determinative factor in assigning children to achieve pure racial balance, can be regarded as "less burdensome, and hence more narrowly tailored" than the consideration of race in *Grutter,* when the Court in *Grutter* stated that "[t]he importance of . . . individualized consideration" in the program was "paramount," and consideration of race was one factor in a "highly individualized, holistic review." . . . Certainly if the constitutionality of the stark use of race in these cases were as established as the dissent would have it, there would have been no need for the extensive analysis undertaken in *Grutter.* In light of the foregoing, Justice Breyer's appeal to *stare decisis* rings particularly hollow.

At the same time it relies on inapplicable desegregation cases, misstatements of admitted dicta, and other noncontrolling pronouncements, Justice Breyer's dissent candidly dismisses the significance of this Court's repeated *holdings* that all racial classifications must be reviewed under strict scrutiny, arguing that a different standard of review should be applied because the districts use race for beneficent rather than malicious purposes.

. . . Our cases clearly reject the argument that motives affect the strict scrutiny analysis. . . .

This argument that different rules should govern racial classifications designed to include rather than exclude is not new; it has been repeatedly pressed in the past, . . . and has been repeatedly rejected. . . .

The reasons . . . are clear enough. "The Court's emphasis on 'benign racial classifications' suggests confidence in its ability to distinguish good from harmful governmental uses of racial criteria. History should teach greater humility. . . . '[B]enign' carries with it no independent meaning, but reflects only acceptance of the current generation's conclusion that a politically acceptable burden, imposed on particular citizens on the basis of race, is reasonable." *Metro Broadcasting,* 497 U.S., at 609–610 (O'Connor, J., dissenting). . . .

Justice Breyer speaks of bringing "the races" together (putting aside the purely black-and-white nature of the plans), as the justification for excluding individuals on the basis of their race. Again, this approach to racial classifica-

---

be held to a lesser standard of review. . . . Even if this purported distinction, which Justice Stevens would adopt, had not been already rejected by this Court, the distinction has no relevance to these cases, in which students of all races are excluded from the schools they wish to attend based solely on the racial classifications. See, *e.g.,* App. . . . (noting that 89 nonwhite students were denied assignment to a particular school by operation of Seattle's racial tiebreaker).

. . .

tions is fundamentally at odds with our precedent, which makes clear that the Equal Protection Clause "protect[s] *persons*, not *groups*," *Adarand*, 515 U.S., at 227 (emphasis in original).... This fundamental principle goes back, in this context, to *Brown* itself. See *Brown* v. *Board of Education*, 349 U.S. 294, 300 (1955) (*Brown II*) ("At stake is the *personal* interest of the plaintiffs in admission to public schools ... on a nondiscriminatory basis" (emphasis added)). For the dissent, in contrast, " 'individualized scrutiny' is simply beside the point."

Justice Breyer's position comes down to a familiar claim: The end justifies the means.... Our established strict scrutiny test for racial classifications, however, insists on "detailed examination, both as to ends *and* as to means." *Adarand*, ... (emphasis added). Simply because the school districts may seek a worthy goal does not mean they are free to discriminate on the basis of race to achieve it, or that their racial classifications should be subject to less exacting scrutiny.

Despite his argument that these cases should be evaluated under a "standard of review that is not 'strict' in the traditional sense of that word," Justice Breyer still purports to apply strict scrutiny to these cases. It is evident, however, that Justice Breyer's brand of narrow tailoring is quite unlike anything found in our precedents. Without any detailed discussion of the operation of the plans, the students who are affected, or the districts' failure to consider race-neutral alternatives, the dissent concludes that the districts have shown that these racial classifications are necessary to achieve the districts' stated goals. This conclusion is divorced from any evaluation of the actual impact of the plans at issue in these cases—other than to note that the plans "often have no effect." Instead, the dissent suggests that some combination of the development of these plans over time, the difficulty of the endeavor, and the good faith of the districts suffices to demonstrate that these stark and controlling racial classifications are constitutional. The Constitution and our precedents require more.

... Justice Breyer repeatedly urges deference to local school boards on these issues. Such deference "is fundamentally at odds with our equal protection jurisprudence. We put the burden on state actors to demonstrate that their race-based policies are justified." *Johnson*, ...

Justice Breyer's dissent ends on an unjustified note of alarm. It predicts that today's decision "threaten[s]" the validity of "[h]undreds of state and federal statutes and regulations." But the examples the dissent mentions—for example, a provision of the No Child Left Behind Act that requires States to set measurable objectives to track the achievement of students from major racial and ethnic groups, 20 U.S.C. § 6311(b)(2)(C)(v)—have nothing to do with the pertinent issues in these cases.

Justice Breyer also suggests that other means for achieving greater racial diversity in schools are necessarily unconstitutional if the racial classifications at issue in these cases cannot survive strict scrutiny. These other means—*e.g.*, where to construct new schools, how to allocate resources among schools, and which academic offerings to provide to attract students to certain schools— implicate different considerations than the explicit racial classifications at issue in these cases, and we express no opinion on their validity—not even in dicta. Rather, we employ the familiar and well-established analytic approach of strict scrutiny to evaluate the plans at issue today, an approach that in no way warrants the dissent's cataclysmic concerns. Under that approach, the school districts have not carried their burden of showing that the ends they seek justify the particular extreme means they have chosen—classifying individual students on the basis of their race and discriminating among them on that basis.

* * *

If the need for the racial classifications ... is unclear, even on the districts' own terms, the costs are undeniable. "[D]istinctions between citizens solely because of their ancestry are by their very nature odious to a free people whose institutions are founded upon the doctrine of equality." ... Government action dividing us by race is inherently suspect because such classifications promote "notions of racial inferiority and lead to a politics of racial hostility," *Croson*, ... "reinforce the belief, held by too many for too much of our history, that individuals should be judged by the color of their skin," *Shaw* v. *Reno*, ... and "endorse race-based reasoning and the conception of a Nation divided into racial blocs, thus contributing to an escalation of racial hostility and conflict." *Metro Broadcasting*, ... (O'Connor, J., dissenting). As the Court explained in *Rice* v. *Cayetano*, 528 U.S. 495, 517 (2000), "[o]ne of the principal reasons race is treated as a forbidden classification is that it demeans the dignity and worth of a person to be judged by ancestry instead of by his or her own merit and essential qualities."

All this is true enough in the contexts in which these statements were made—government contracting, voting districts, allocation of broadcast licenses, and electing state officers—but when it comes to using race to assign children to schools, history will be heard. In *Brown* v. *Board of Education*, ... we held that segregation deprived black children of equal educational opportunities regardless of whether school facilities and other tangible factors were equal, because government classification and separation on grounds of race themselves denoted inferiority.... The next Term, we accordingly stated that "full compliance" with *Brown I* required school districts "to achieve a system of determining admission to the public schools *on a nonracial basis.*" *Brown II,* ....

The parties and their *amici* debate which side is more faithful to the heritage of *Brown*, but the position of the plaintiffs in *Brown* was spelled out in their brief and could not have been clearer: "[T]he Fourteenth Amendment prevents states from according differential treatment to American children on the basis of their color or race." ... What do the racial classifications at issue here do, if not accord differential treatment on the basis of race? ... [T]his Court ... emphasized in its remedial opinion that what was "[a]t stake is the personal interest of the plaintiffs in admission to public schools as soon as practicable *on a nondiscriminatory basis,*" and what was required was "determining admission to the public schools *on a nonracial basis.*" *Brown II,* .... What do the racial classifications do in these cases, if not determine admission to a public school on a racial basis? Before *Brown*, schoolchildren were told where they could and could not go to school based on the color of their skin. The school districts in these cases have not carried the heavy burden of demonstrating that we should allow this once again—even for very different reasons. For schools that never segregated on the basis of race, such as Seattle, or that have removed the vestiges of past segregation, such as Jefferson County, the way "to achieve a system of determining admission to the public schools on a nonracial basis," *Brown II,* . . . is to stop assigning students on a racial basis. The way to stop discrimination on the basis of race is to stop discriminating on the basis of race.

. . . [R]eversed, and . . . remanded for further proceedings.

Justice Thomas, concurring.

. . . Disfavoring a color-blind interpretation of the Constitution, the dissent would give school boards a free hand to make decisions on the basis of race—an approach reminiscent of that advocated by the segregationists in *Brown* v. *Board of Education,* 347 U. S 483 (1954). This approach is just as wrong today as it was a half-century ago. . . .

. . .

. . . Racial imbalance is not segregation.[2] . . .

. . . To raise the specter of resegregation to defend these programs is to ignore the meaning of the word and the nature of the cases before us.[3]

. . . [T]he school districts . . . also have no present interest in remedying past segregation. . . .

. . . .[A]s a general rule, all race-based government decisionmaking—regardless of context—is unconstitutional.

This Court has carved out a narrow exception to that general rule for cases . . . of state-enforced racial separation, [which require] race-based remedial measures to eliminate segregation and its vestiges.

Neither of the programs before us today is compelled as a remedial measure, and no one makes such a claim. . . .

. . .

. . .[8]

. . .

---

2. [O]utside of the context of remediation for past *de jure* segregation, "integration" is simply racial balancing. Therefore, the school districts' attempts to further "integrate" are properly thought of as little more than attempts to achieve a particular racial balance.

3. . . . To equate the achievement of a certain statistical mix in several schools with the elimination of the system of systematic *de jure* segregation trivializes the latter accomplishment. Nothing but an interest in classroom aesthetics and a hypersensitivity to elite sensibilities justifies the school districts' racial balancing programs. . . .

8. Contrary to the dissent's argument, the Louisville school district's interest in remedying its past *de jure* segregation did vanish the day the District Court found that Louisville had eliminated the vestiges of its historic *de jure* segregation. . . . Because Louisville could use race-based measures only as a remedy for past *de jure* segregation, it is not "incoherent" to say that race-based decisionmaking was allowed to Louisville one day—while it was still remedying—and forbidden to it the next—when remediation was finished. That seemingly odd turnaround is merely a result of the fact that the remediation of *de jure* segregation is a jealously guarded exception to the Equal Protection Clause's general rule against government race-based decisionmaking.

. . . [I]t is wrong to place the remediation of segregation on the same plane as the remediation of racial imbalance. First, . . . the further we get from the era of state-sponsored racial separation, the less likely it is that racial imbalance has a traceable connection to any prior segregation. . . .

Second, a school cannot "remedy" racial imbalance in the same way that it can remedy segregation. Remediation of past *de jure* segregation is a one-time process involving the redress of a discrete legal injury inflicted by an identified entity. At some point, the discrete injury will be remedied, and the school district will be declared unitary. . . . Unlike *de jure* segregation, there is no ultimate remedy for racial imbalance. Individual schools will fall in and out of balance in the natural course, and the appropriate balance itself will shift with a school district's changing demographics. Thus, racial balancing will have to take place on an indefinite basis—a continuous process with no identifiable culpable party and no discernable end point. In part for those reasons, the Court has never permitted outright racial balancing solely for the purpose of achieving a particular racial balance.

II

Lacking a cognizable interest in remediation, neither of these plans can survive strict scrutiny because neither plan serves a genuinely compelling state interest. . . .

. . .

. . . The constitutional problems with government race-based decisionmaking are not diminished in the slightest by the presence or absence of an intent to oppress any race or by the real or asserted well-meaning motives for the race-based decisionmaking. . . .

Even supposing it mattered . . ., the race-based student assignment programs before us are not as benign as the dissent believes. . . . [E]very time the government uses racial criteria to "bring the races together," someone gets excluded, and the person excluded suffers an injury solely because of his or her race. . . . This . . . is precisely the sort of government action that pits the races against one another, exacerbates racial tension, and "provoke[s] resentment among those who believe that they have been wronged by the government's use of race." . . .

. . .

[T]he dissent . . . asserts that racially balanced schools improve educational outcomes for black children. . . . In reality, it is far from apparent that coerced racial mixing has any educational benefits, much less that integration is necessary to black achievement.

. . .

Add to the inconclusive social science the fact of black achievement in "racially isolated" environments. . . . Even after *Brown*, some schools with predominantly black enrollments have achieved outstanding educational results. . . .

The Seattle school board itself must believe that racial mixing is not necessary to black achievement. Seattle operates a K–8 "African–American

Academy," which has a "nonwhite" enrollment of 99%.... Contrary to what the dissent would have predicted, the children in Seattle's African American Academy have shown gains when placed in a "highly segregated" environment.

Given this tenuous relationship between forced racial mixing and improved educational results for black children, the dissent cannot plausibly maintain that an educational element supports the integration interest, let alone makes it compelling....

. . .

Finally, the dissent asserts a "democratic element" to the integration interest[—] define[d] as "an interest in producing an educational environment that reflects the 'pluralistic society' in which our children will live." Environmental reflection, though, is just another way to say racial balancing....

. . .

Moreover, ... it will always be important for students to learn cooperation among the races. If this interest justifies race-conscious measures today, then logically it will justify race-conscious measures forever. Thus, the democratic interest, limitless in scope and "timeless in [its] ability to affect the future," ... cannot justify government race-based decisionmaking.

. . .

... [E]ven supposing interracial contact leads directly to improvements in racial attitudes and race relations, a program that assigns students of different races to the same schools might not capture those benefits. Simply putting students together under the same roof does not necessarily mean that the students will learn together or even interact.

Furthermore, it is unclear whether increased interracial contact improves racial attitudes and relations....

Given our case law and the paucity of evidence supporting the dissent's belief that these plans improve race relations, no democratic element can support the integration interest.

The dissent attempts to buttress the integration interest by claiming that it follows *a fortiori* from the interest this Court recognized as compelling in *Grutter*.... *Grutter* recognized a compelling interest in a law school's attainment of a diverse student body [that] was critically dependent upon features unique to higher education: "the expansive freedoms of speech and thought associated with the university environment," the "special niche in our constitutional tradition" occupied by universities, and "[t]he freedom of a university to make its own judgments as to education[,] includ[ing] the selection of its student body." ... None of these features is present in elementary and secondary schools. Those schools do not select their own students, and education in the elementary and secondary environment generally does not involve the free interchange of ideas thought to be an integral part of higher education.... [O]nly by ignoring *Grutter*'s reasoning can the dissent claim that recognizing a compelling interest in these cases is an *a fortiori* application of *Grutter*.

. . .

III

Most of the dissent's criticisms of today's result can be traced to its rejection of the color-blind Constitution. . . .

The dissent appears to pin its interpretation of the Equal Protection Clause to current societal practice and expectations, deference to local officials, likely practical consequences, and reliance on previous statements from this and other courts. Such a view was ascendant in this Court's jurisprudence for several decades. It first appeared in *Plessy*. . . .

The segregationists in *Brown* embraced the arguments the Court endorsed in *Plessy*. Though *Brown* decisively rejected those arguments, today's dissent replicates them to a distressing extent. . . .

. . .

What was wrong in 1954 cannot be right today.[27] . . . [N]o . . . contextual details . . . can "provide refuge from the principle that under our Constitution, the government may not make distinctions on the basis of race." . . .

In place of the color-blind Constitution, the dissent would permit measures to keep the races together and proscribe measures to keep the races apart. . . . The Constitution is not that malleable. . . . [O]ur history has taught us . . . to beware of elites bearing racial theories. . . . Can we really be sure that the racial theories that motivated *Dred Scott* and *Plessy* are a relic of the past or that future theories will be nothing but beneficent and progressive? That is a gamble I am unwilling to take, and it is one the Constitution does not allow.

. . .

Justice Kennedy, concurring in part and concurring in the judgment.

. . .

I . . . join Parts I and II of the Court's opinion [and] also . . . Parts III–A and III–C. . . . My views do not allow me to join the balance of the opinion by The Chief Justice, which seems to me to be inconsistent in both its approach and its implications with the history, meaning, and reach of the Equal Protection Clause. Justice Breyer's dissenting opinion, on the other hand, rests on what in my respectful submission is a misuse and mistaken interpretation of our precedents. This leads it to advance propositions . . . both erroneous and in fundamental conflict with basic equal protection principles. As a consequence, this separate opinion is necessary. . . .

I

. . . The dissent finds that the school districts have identified a compelling interest in increasing diversity, including for the purpose of avoiding racial

---

27. It is no answer to say that these cases can be distinguished from *Brown* because *Brown* involved invidious racial classifications whereas the racial classifications here are benign. How does one tell when a racial classification is invidious? The segregation- ists in *Brown* argued that their racial classifications were benign . . . . It is the height of arrogance for Members of this Court to assert blindly that their motives are better than others.

isolation. The plurality, by contrast, does not acknowledge that the school districts have identified a compelling interest here. For this reason, among others, I do not join Parts III–B and IV. Diversity, depending on its meaning and definition, is a compelling educational goal a school district may pursue.

. . . [T]he inquiry into less restrictive alternatives demanded by the narrow tailoring analysis requires in many cases a thorough understanding of how a plan works. The government bears the burden of justifying its use of individual racial classifications. As part of that burden it must establish, in detail, how decisions based on an individual student's race are made in a challenged governmental program. The Jefferson County Board of Education fails to meet this threshold mandate.

. . .

. . . While it acknowledges that racial classifications are used to make certain assignment decisions, it fails to make clear, for example, who makes the decisions; what if any oversight is employed; the precise circumstances in which an assignment decision will or will not be made on the basis of race; or how it is determined which of two similarly situated children will be subjected to a given race-based decision. . . .

. . .

. . . When a court subjects governmental action to strict scrutiny, it cannot construe ambiguities in favor of the State.

As for the Seattle case, the school district . . . has failed to explain why, in a district composed of a diversity of races, with fewer than half of the students classified as "white," it has employed the crude racial categories of "white" and "non-white" as the basis for its assignment decisions. . . .

The district has identified its purposes as follows: "(1) to promote the educational benefits of diverse school enrollments; (2) to reduce the potentially harmful effects of racial isolation by allowing students the opportunity to opt out of racially isolated schools; and (3) to make sure that racially segregated housing patterns did not prevent non-white students from having equitable access to the most popular over-subscribed schools." . . . Yet the school district does not explain how, in the context of its diverse student population, a blunt distinction between "white" and "non-white" furthers these goals. As the Court explains, "a school with 50 percent Asian–American students and 50 percent white students but no African–American, Native–American, or Latino students would qualify as balanced, while a school with 30 percent Asian–American, 25 percent African–American, 25 percent Latino, and 20 percent white students would not." . . . Far from being narrowly tailored to its purposes, this system threatens to defeat its own ends, and the school district has provided no convincing explanation for its design. Other problems are evident in Seattle's system, but there is no need to address them now. As the district fails to account for the classification system it has chosen, despite what appears to be its ill fit, Seattle has not shown its plan to be narrowly tailored to achieve its own ends; and thus it fails to pass strict scrutiny.

II

. . .

. . . [P]arts of the opinion by The Chief Justice imply an all-too-unyielding insistence that race cannot be a factor in instances when, in my view, it may be taken into account. The plurality opinion is too dismissive of the legitimate interest government has in ensuring all people have equal opportunity regardless of their race. . . . The plurality opinion is at least open to the interpretation that the Constitution requires school districts to ignore the problem of *de facto* resegregation in schooling. I cannot endorse that conclusion. To the extent the plurality opinion suggests the Constitution mandates that state and local school authorities must accept the status quo of racial isolation in schools, it is, in my view, profoundly mistaken.

. . .

In the administration of public schools by the state and local authorities it is permissible to consider the racial makeup of schools and to adopt general policies to encourage a diverse student body, one aspect of which is its racial composition. Cf. *Grutter* v. *Bollinger*, ... If school authorities are concerned that the student-body compositions of certain schools interfere with the objective of offering an equal educational opportunity to all of their students, they are free to devise race-conscious measures to address the problem in a general way and without treating each student in different fashion solely on the basis of a systematic, individual typing by race.

School boards may pursue the goal of bringing together students of diverse backgrounds and races through other means, including strategic site selection of new schools; drawing attendance zones with general recognition of the demographics of neighborhoods; allocating resources for special programs; recruiting students and faculty in a targeted fashion; and tracking enrollments, performance, and other statistics by race. These mechanisms are race conscious but do not lead to different treatment based on a classification that tells each student he or she is to be defined by race, so it is unlikely any of them would demand strict scrutiny to be found permissible. . . . Executive and legislative branches, which for generations now have considered these types of policies and procedures, should be permitted to employ them with candor and with confidence that a constitutional violation does not occur whenever a decisionmaker considers the impact a given approach might have on students of different races. Assigning to each student a personal designation according to a crude system of individual racial classifications is quite a different matter; and the legal analysis changes accordingly.

Each respondent has asserted that its assignment of individual students by race is permissible because there is no other way to avoid racial isolation in the school districts. Yet, as explained, each has failed to provide the support necessary for that proposition. . . . And individual racial classifications employed in this manner may be considered legitimate only if they are a last resort to achieve a compelling interest. . . .

In the cases before us it is noteworthy that the number of students whose assignment depends on express racial classifications is limited. I join Part III–C of the Court's opinion because I agree that in the context of these plans, the small number of assignments affected suggests that the schools could have achieved their stated ends through different means. These include the facially race-neutral means set forth above or, if necessary, a more nuanced, individual evaluation of school needs and student characteristics that might include race as a component. The latter approach would be informed by *Grutter*, though of course the criteria relevant to student placement would differ based on the age of the students, the needs of the parents, and the role of the schools.

III

The dissent rests on the assumptions that these sweeping race-based classifications of persons are permitted by existing precedents; that its confident endorsement of race categories for each child in a large segment of the community presents no danger to individual freedom in other, prospective realms of governmental regulation; and that the racial classifications used here cause no hurt or anger of the type the Constitution prevents. Each of these premises is, in my respectful view, incorrect.

A

... I am in many respects in agreement with ... [t]he conclusions [The Chief Justice] has set forth in Part III–A of the Court's opinion ..., because the compelling interests implicated in the cases before us are distinct from the interests the Court has recognized in remedying the effects of past intentional discrimination and in increasing diversity in higher education.... At the same time, ... to the extent the plurality opinion can be interpreted to foreclose consideration of these interests, I disagree with that reasoning.

As to the dissent, the general conclusions upon which it relies have no principled limit and would result in the broad acceptance of governmental racial classifications in areas far afield from schooling. The dissent's permissive strict scrutiny (which bears more than a passing resemblance to rational-basis review) could invite widespread governmental deployment of racial classifications....

This brings us to the dissent's reliance on the Court's opinions in *Gratz* v. *Bollinger*, 539 U.S. 244 (2003), and *Grutter*, ... To say ... that we must ratify the racial classifications here at issue based on the majority opinions in *Gratz* and *Grutter* is, with all respect, simply baffling.

Gratz involved a system where race was not the entire classification. The procedures in *Gratz* placed much less reliance on race than do the plans at issue here. The issue in *Gratz* arose, moreover, in the context of college admissions where students had other choices and precedent supported the proposition that First Amendment interests give universities particular latitude in defining diversity.... Even so the race factor was found to be invalid.... If *Gratz* is to be the measure, the racial classification systems here are *a fortiori* invalid. If the dissent were to say that college cases are simply not applicable to public school systems in kindergarten through high school, this would seem to me wrong, but at least an arguable distinction. Under no fair reading, though, can the majority opinion in *Gratz* be cited as authority to sustain the racial classifications under consideration here.

The same must be said for the controlling opinion in *Grutter*. There the Court sustained a system that, it found, was flexible enough to take into account "all pertinent elements of diversity," ... and considered race as only one factor among many.... Seattle's plan, by contrast, relies upon a mechanical formula that has denied hundreds of students their preferred schools on the basis of three rigid criteria: placement of siblings, distance from schools, and race. If those students were considered for a whole range of their talents and school needs with race as just one consideration, *Grutter* would have some application. That, though, is not the case. The only support today's dissent can draw from *Grutter* must be found in its various separate opinions, not in the opinion filed for the Court.

B

To uphold these programs the Court is asked to brush aside two concepts of central importance for determining the validity of laws and decrees designed to alleviate the hurt and adverse consequences resulting from race discrimination. The first is the difference between *de jure* and *de facto* segregation; the second, the presumptive invalidity of a State's use of racial classifications to differentiate its treatment of individuals.

. . .

[L]ike so many other legal categories that can overlap in some instances, the constitutional distinction between *de jure* and *de facto* segregation has been thought to be an important one. It must be conceded its primary function in school cases was to delimit the powers of the Judiciary in the fashioning of remedies. . . . The distinction ought not to be altogether disregarded, however, when we come to that most sensitive of all racial issues, an attempt by the government to treat whole classes of persons differently based on the government's systematic classification of each individual by race. There, too, the distinction serves as a limit on the exercise of a power that reaches to the very verge of constitutional authority. Reduction of an individual to an assigned racial identity for differential treatment is among the most pernicious actions our government can undertake. The allocation of governmental burdens and benefits, contentious under any circumstances, is even more divisive when allocations are made on the basis of individual racial classifications. . . . .

Notwithstanding these concerns, allocation of benefits and burdens through individual racial classifications was found sometimes permissible in the context of remedies for *de jure* wrong. . . . The remedy, though, was limited in time and limited to the wrong. . . . The limitation of this power to instances where there has been *de jure* segregation serves to confine the nature, extent, and duration of governmental reliance on individual racial classifications.

The cases here were argued upon the assumption, and come to us on the premise, that the discrimination in question did not result from *de jure* actions. And when *de facto* discrimination is at issue our tradition has been that the remedial rules are different. The State must seek alternatives to the classification and differential treatment of individuals by race, at least absent some extraordinary showing not present here.

C

The dissent refers to [lower court opinions], one of [whose] main concerns . . . was this: If it is legitimate for school authorities to work to avoid racial isolation in their schools, must they do so only by indirection and general policies? Does the Constitution mandate this inefficient result? Why may the authorities not recognize the problem in candid fashion and solve it altogether through resort to direct assignments based on student racial classifications? So, the argument proceeds, if race is the problem, then perhaps race is the solution.

The argument ignores the dangers presented by individual classifications, dangers that are not as pressing when the same ends are achieved by more indirect means. When the government classifies an individual by race, it must first define what it means to be of a race. Who exactly is white and who is nonwhite? To be forced to live under a state-mandated racial label is inconsistent with the dignity of individuals in our society. And it is a label that an individual is powerless to change. Governmental classifications that command people to march in different directions based on racial typologies can cause a new divisiveness. The practice can lead to corrosive discourse, where race serves not as an element of our diverse heritage but instead as a bargaining chip in the political process. On the other hand race-conscious measures that do not rely on differential treatment based on individual classifications present these problems to a lesser degree.

The idea that if race is the problem, race is the instrument with which to solve it cannot be accepted as an analytical leap forward. And if this is a frustrating duality of the Equal Protection Clause it simply reflects the duality of our history and our attempts to promote freedom in a world that sometimes seems set against it. Under our Constitution the individual, child or adult, can find his own identity, can define her own persona, without state intervention that classifies on the basis of his race or the color of her skin.

* * *

This Nation has a moral and ethical obligation to fulfill its historic commitment to creating an integrated society that ensures equal opportunity for all of its children. A compelling interest exists in avoiding racial isolation, an interest that a school district, in its discretion and expertise, may choose to pursue. Likewise, a district may consider it a compelling interest to achieve a diverse student population. Race may be one component of that diversity, but other demographic factors, plus special talents and needs, should also be considered. What the government is not permitted to do, absent a showing of necessity not made here, is to classify every student on the basis of race and to assign each of them to schools based on that classification. Crude measures of this sort threaten to reduce children to racial chits valued and traded according to one school's supply and another's demand.

That statement, to be sure, invites this response: A sense of stigma may already become the fate of those separated out by circumstances beyond their immediate control. But to this the replication must be: Even so, measures other than differential treatment based on racial typing of individuals first must be exhausted.

The decision today should not prevent school districts from continuing the important work of bringing together students of different racial, ethnic, and economic backgrounds. Due to a variety of factors—some influenced by government, some not—neighborhoods in our communities do not reflect the diversity of our Nation as a whole. Those entrusted with directing our public schools can bring to bear the creativity of experts, parents, administrators, and other concerned citizens to find a way to achieve the compelling interests they face without resorting to widespread governmental allocation of benefits and burdens on the basis of racial classifications.

With this explanation I concur in the judgment of the Court.

Justice Stevens, dissenting.

. . .

There is a cruel irony in The Chief Justice's reliance on our decision in *Brown* v. *Board of Education,* 349 U.S. 294 (1955). . . . [T]he history books do not tell stories of white children struggling to attend black schools. In this and other ways, The Chief Justice rewrites the history of one of this Court's most important decisions. . . .

The Chief Justice rejects the conclusion that the racial classifications at issue here should be viewed differently than others, because they do not impose burdens on one race alone and do not stigmatize or exclude. The only justification for refusing to acknowledge the obvious importance of that difference is the citation of a few recent opinions—none of which even approached unanimity—grandly proclaiming that all racial classifications must be analyzed under "strict scrutiny." . . .

. . . It is my firm conviction that no Member of the Court that I joined in 1975 would have agreed with today's decision.

Justice Breyer, with whom Justice Stevens, Justice Souter, and Justice Ginsburg join, dissenting.

These cases consider the longstanding efforts of two local school boards to integrate their public schools. The school board plans before us resemble many others adopted in the last 50 years by primary and secondary schools throughout the Nation. All of those plans represent local efforts to bring about the kind of racially integrated education that *Brown* v. *Board of Education*, 347 U.S. 483 (1954), long ago promised—efforts that this Court has repeatedly required, permitted, and encouraged local authorities to undertake. This Court has recognized that the public interests at stake in such cases are "compelling." We have approved of "narrowly tailored" plans that are no less race-conscious than the plans before us. And we have understood that the Constitution *permits* local communities to adopt desegregation plans even where it does not *require* them to do so.

The plurality . . . distorts precedent, . . . misapplies the relevant constitutional principles, . . . announces legal rules that will obstruct efforts by state and local governments to deal effectively with the growing resegregation of public schools, . . . threatens to substitute for present calm a disruptive round of race-related litigation, and . . . undermines *Brown*'s promise of integrated primary and secondary education that local communities have sought to make a reality. This cannot be justified in the name of the Equal Protection Clause.

I

Facts

. . . *Brown* . . . set the Nation on a path toward public school integration.

. . .

... [I]n respect to race-conscious desegregation measures that the Constitution *permitted,* but did not *require* ..., this Court unanimously stated:

> "School authorities are traditionally charged with broad power to formulate and implement educational policy and might well conclude, for example, that in order to prepare students to live in a pluralistic society each school should have a prescribed ratio of Negro to white students reflecting the proportion for the district as a whole. *To do this as an educational policy is within the broad discretionary powers of school authorities."* Swann v. Charlotte–Mecklenburg Bd. of Ed., 402 U.S. 1, 16 (1971) (emphasis added).

As a result, different districts—some acting under court decree, some acting in order to avoid threatened lawsuits, some seeking to comply with federal administrative orders, some acting purely voluntarily, some acting after federal courts had dissolved earlier orders—adopted, modified, and experimented with hosts of different kinds of plans, including race-conscious plans, all with a similar objective: greater racial integration of public schools....

Overall these efforts brought about considerable racial integration. More recently, however, progress has stalled.... In light of the evident risk of a return to school systems that are in fact (though not in law) resegregated, many school districts have felt a need to maintain or to extend their integration efforts.

The upshot is that myriad school districts operating in myriad circumstances have devised myriad plans, often with race-conscious elements, all for the sake of eradicating earlier school segregation, bringing about integration, or preventing retrogression. Seattle and Louisville are two such districts, and the histories of their present plans set forth typical school integration stories.

I describe those histories at length ... to highlight three important features of these cases. First, the school districts' plans serve "compelling interests" and are "narrowly tailored" on any reasonable definition of those terms. Second, the distinction between *de jure* segregation (caused by school systems) and *de facto* segregation (caused, *e.g.*, by housing patterns or generalized societal discrimination) is meaningless in the present context, thereby dooming the plurality's endeavor to find support for its views in that distinction. Third, real-world efforts to substitute racially diverse for racially segregated schools (however caused) are complex, to the point where the Constitution cannot plausibly be interpreted to rule out categorically all local efforts to use means that are "conscious" of the race of individuals.

In both Seattle and Louisville, ... plaintiffs filed lawsuits claiming unconstitutional segregation.... In Louisville, a federal court entered a remedial decree. In Seattle, the parties settled after the school district pledged to undertake a desegregation plan. In both cities, the school boards adopted plans designed to achieve integration by bringing about more racially diverse schools. In each city the school board modified its plan several times in light of, for example, hostility to busing, the threat of resegregation, and the desirability of introducing greater student choice. And in each city, the school boards' plans have evolved over time in ways that progressively *diminish* the plans' use of explicit race-conscious criteria.

[Justice Breyer's detailed recitation is omitted.]

... When formulating the plans under review, both districts drew upon their considerable experience with earlier plans, having revised their policies periodically in light of that experience. Both districts rethought their methods over time and explored a wide range of other means, including non-race-conscious policies. Both districts also considered elaborate studies and consulted widely within their communities.

Both districts sought greater racial integration for educational and democratic, as well as for remedial, reasons. Both sought to achieve these objectives while preserving their commitment to other educational goals, *e.g.*, districtwide commitment to high quality public schools, increased pupil assignment to neighborhood schools, diminished use of busing, greater student choice, reduced risk of white flight, and so forth. Consequently, the present plans expand student choice; they limit the burdens (including busing) that earlier plans had imposed upon students and their families; and they use race-conscious criteria in limited and gradually diminishing ways. In particular, they use race-conscious criteria only to mark the outer bounds of broad population-related ranges.

The histories also make clear the futility of looking simply to whether earlier school segregation was *de jure* or *de facto* in order to draw firm lines separating the constitutionally permissible from the constitutionally forbidden use of "race-conscious" criteria. . . .

No one here disputes that Louisville's segregation was *de jure*. But what about Seattle's? Was it *de facto? De jure?* A mixture? Opinions differed. Or is it that a prior federal court had not adjudicated the matter? Does that make a difference? Is Seattle free on remand to say that its schools were *de jure* segregated, just as in 1956 a memo for the School Board admitted? The plurality does not seem confident as to the answer. . . .

A court finding of *de jure* segregation cannot be the crucial variable. After all, a number of school districts in the South that the Government or private plaintiffs challenged as segregated *by law* voluntarily desegregated their schools *without a court order*—just as Seattle did. . . .

Moreover, Louisville's history makes clear that a community under a court order to desegregate might submit a race-conscious remedial plan *before* the court dissolved the order, but with every intention of following that plan even *after* dissolution. How could such a plan be lawful the day before dissolution but then become unlawful the very next day? On what legal ground can the majority rest its contrary view? . . .

Are courts really to treat as merely *de facto* segregated those school districts that avoided a federal order by voluntarily complying with *Brown*'s requirements? . . . . This Court has previously done just the opposite, permitting a race-conscious remedy without any kind of court decree. . . . Because the Constitution emphatically does not forbid the use of race-conscious measures by districts in the South that voluntarily desegregated their schools, on what basis does the plurality claim that the law forbids Seattle to do the same? . . .

The histories also indicate the complexity of the tasks and the practical difficulties that local school boards face when they seek to achieve greater racial integration. The boards work in communities where demographic patterns change, where they must meet traditional learning goals, where they must attract and retain effective teachers, where they should (and will) take account of parents' views and maintain *their* commitment to public school education, where they must adapt to court intervention, where they must encourage voluntary student and parent action—where they will find that their own good faith, their knowledge, and their understanding of local circumstances are always necessary but often insufficient to solve the problems at hand.

These facts and circumstances help explain why in this context, as to means, the law often leaves legislatures, city councils, school boards, and voters with a broad range of choice, thereby giving "different communities" the opportunity to "try different solutions to common problems and gravitate toward those that prove most successful or seem to them best to suit their individual needs." ...

. . .

II

The Legal Standard

A longstanding and unbroken line of legal authority tells us that the Equal Protection Clause permits local school boards to use race-conscious criteria to achieve positive race-related goals, even when the Constitution does not compel it. Because of its importance, I shall repeat what this Court said about the matter in *Swann* . . . .

[Justice Breyer quotes other opinions with similar statements.]

These statements nowhere suggest that this freedom is limited to school districts where court-ordered desegregation measures are also in effect. . . .

. . .

This Court has also held that school districts may be required by federal statute to undertake race-conscious desegregation efforts even when there is no likelihood that *de jure* segregation can be shown. . . .

Lower state and federal courts had considered the matter settled and uncontroversial even before this Court decided *Swann*. Indeed, in 1968, the Illinois Supreme Court rejected an equal protection challenge to a race-conscious state law seeking to undo *de facto* segregation. . . .

. . .

I quote the Illinois Supreme Court at length to illustrate the prevailing legal assumption at the time *Swann* was decided. In this respect, *Swann* was not a sharp or unexpected departure from prior rulings; it reflected a consensus that had already emerged among state and lower federal courts.

If there were doubts before *Swann* was decided, they did not survive this Court's decision. Numerous state and federal courts explicitly relied upon *Swann*'s guidance for decades to follow. . . .

. . .

Courts are not alone in accepting as constitutionally valid the legal principle that *Swann* enunciated-*i.e.*, that the government may voluntarily adopt race-conscious measures to improve conditions of race even when it is not under a constitutional obligation to do so. That principle has been accepted by every branch of government and is rooted in the history of the Equal Protection Clause itself. Thus, Congress has enacted numerous race-conscious statutes that illustrate that principle or rely upon its validity. See, *e.g.*, 20 U.S.C. § 6311(b)(2)(C)(v) (No Child Left Behind Act); § 1067 *et seq.* (authorizing aid to minority institutions). In fact, without being exhaustive, I have counted 51 federal statutes that use racial classifications. I have counted well over 100 state statutes that similarly employ racial classifications. Presidential administrations for the past half-century have used and supported various race-conscious measures.... And during the same time, hundreds of local school districts have adopted student assignment plans that use race-conscious criteria....

That *Swann*'s legal statement should find such broad acceptance is not surprising.... [A] well-established legal view of the Fourteenth Amendment ... understands the basic objective of those who wrote the Equal Protection Clause as forbidding practices that lead to racial exclusion. The Amendment sought to bring into American society as full members those whom the Nation had previously held in slavery....

There is reason to believe that those who drafted an Amendment with this basic purpose in mind would have understood the legal and practical difference between the use of race-conscious criteria in defiance of that purpose, namely to keep the races apart, and the use of race-conscious criteria to further that purpose, namely to bring the races together....

Sometimes Members of this Court have disagreed about the degree of leniency that the Clause affords to programs designed to include.... But I can find no case in which this Court has followed Justice Thomas' "colorblind" approach. And I have found no case that otherwise repudiated this constitutional asymmetry between that which seeks to *exclude* and that which seeks to *include* members of minority races.

What does the plurality say in response? First, it seeks to distinguish *Swann* and other similar cases on the ground that those cases involved remedial plans in response to *judicial findings* of *de jure* segregation. [T]hat is historically untrue. Many school districts in the South adopted segregation remedies (to which *Swann* clearly applies) without any such federal order. Seattle's circumstances are not meaningfully different .... Louisville's plan was created and initially adopted when a compulsory district court order was in place. And, in any event, the histories of Seattle and Louisville make clear that this distinction—between court-ordered and voluntary desegregation—seeks a line that sensibly cannot be drawn.

Second, the plurality downplays the importance of *Swann* and related cases by frequently describing their relevant statements as "dicta." ... *Swann* ... set forth its view prominently in an important opinion joined by all nine Justices, knowing that it would be read and followed throughout the Nation.... The constitutional principle enunciated in *Swann,* reiterated in subsequent cases, and relied upon over many years, provides, and has widely been thought to provide, authoritative legal guidance. And if the plurality now chooses to reject that principle, it cannot adequately justify its retreat simply by affixing the label "dicta" to reasoning with which it disagrees. Rather, it must explain to the courts and to the Nation *why* it would abandon guidance set forth many years before, guidance that countless others have built upon over time, and which the law has continuously embodied.

Third, a more important response is the plurality's claim that later cases— in particular *Johnson, Adarand,* and *Grutter*—supplanted *Swann*. . . .

Several of these cases were significantly more restrictive than *Swann* in respect to the degree of leniency the Fourteenth Amendment grants to programs designed to *include* people of all races. . . . But that legal circumstance cannot make a critical difference here for two separate reasons.

First, . . . the cases to which the plurality refers, though all applying strict scrutiny, do not treat exclusive and inclusive uses the same. Rather, they apply the strict scrutiny test in a manner that is "fatal in fact" only to racial classifications that harmfully *exclude;* they apply the test in a manner that is *not* fatal in fact to racial classifications that seek to *include*.

. . . Today's opinion reveals that the plurality would rewrite this Court's prior jurisprudence, at least in practical application, transforming the "strict scrutiny" test into a rule that is fatal in fact across the board. In doing so, the plurality parts company from this Court's prior cases, and it takes from local government the longstanding legal right to use race-conscious criteria for inclusive purposes in limited ways.

Second, as *Grutter* specified, "[c]ontext matters when reviewing race-based governmental action under the Equal Protection Clause." . . .

. . .

This context is *not* a context that involves the use of race to decide who will receive goods or services that are normally distributed on the basis of merit and which are in short supply. It is not one in which race-conscious limits stigmatize or exclude; the limits at issue do not pit the races against each other or otherwise significantly exacerbate racial tensions. They do not impose burdens unfairly upon members of one race alone but instead seek benefits for members of all races alike. The context here is one of racial limits that seek, not to keep the races apart, but to bring them together.

. . .

If one examines the context more specifically, one finds that the districts' plans reflect efforts to overcome a history of segregation, embody the results of broad experience and community consultation, seek to expand student choice while reducing the need for mandatory busing, and use race-conscious criteria in highly limited ways that diminish the use of race compared to preceding integration efforts. . . . They do not seek to award a scarce commodity on the basis of merit, for they are not magnet schools; rather, by design and in practice, they offer substantially equivalent academic programs and electives. . . . In a word, [they] do not involve the kind of race-based harm that has led this Court, in other contexts, to find the use of race-conscious criteria unconstitutional.

. . .

The view that a more lenient standard than "strict scrutiny" should apply in the present context would not imply abandonment of judicial efforts carefully to determine the need for race-conscious criteria and the criteria's tailoring in light of the need. And the present context requires a court to examine carefully the race-conscious program at issue. In doing so, a reviewing judge must be fully aware of the potential dangers and pitfalls that Justice Thomas and Justice Kennedy mention. . . .

But unlike the plurality, such a judge would also be aware that a legislature or school administrators, ultimately accountable to the electorate, could *nonetheless* properly conclude that a racial classification sometimes serves a purpose important enough to overcome the risks they mention, for example, helping to end racial isolation or to achieve a diverse student body in public schools. . . . Where that is so, the judge would carefully examine the program's details to determine whether the use of race-conscious criteria is proportionate to the important ends it serves.

. . . I believe that the law requires application here of a standard of review that is not "strict" in the traditional sense of that word, although it does require the careful review I have just described. . . . Apparently Justice Kennedy also agrees that strict scrutiny would not apply in respect to certain "race-conscious" school board policies. . . .

Nonetheless, in light of *Grutter* and other precedents, . . . I shall apply the version of strict scrutiny that those cases embody. . . . If the plans survive this strict review, they would survive less exacting review *a fortiori*. . . .

III

Applying the Legal Standard

A

Compelling Interest

The principal interest advanced . . . [is] promoting or preserving greater racial "integration" of public schools. By this term, I mean the school districts' interest in eliminating school-by-school racial isolation and increasing the degree to which racial mixture characterizes each of the district's schools and each individual student's public school experience.

. . . [T]he interest at stake possesses three essential elements. First, there is a historical and remedial element: an interest in setting right the consequences of prior conditions of segregation. This refers back to a time when public schools were highly segregated, often as a result of legal or administrative policies that facilitated racial segregation in public schools. It is an interest in continuing to combat the remnants of segregation caused in whole or in part by these school-related policies, which have often affected not only schools, but also housing patterns, employment practices, economic conditions, and social attitudes. It is an interest in maintaining hard-won gains. And it has its roots in preventing what gradually may become the *de facto* resegregation of America's public schools. . . .

Second, there is an educational element: an interest in overcoming the adverse educational effects produced by and associated with highly segregated schools. . . .

... [T]he evidence supporting an educational interest in racially integrated schools is well established and strong enough to permit a democratically elected school board reasonably to determine that this interest is a compelling one.

. . . .

Third, there is a democratic element: an interest in producing an educational environment that reflects the "pluralistic society" in which our children will live....

. . .

... Again, ... the evidence supporting a democratic interest in racially integrated schools is firmly established and sufficiently strong to permit a school board to determine, as this Court has itself often found, that this interest is compelling.

For example, one study documented that "black and white students in desegregated schools are less racially prejudiced than those in segregated schools," and that "interracial contact in desegregated schools leads to an increase in interracial sociability and friendship." ... Other studies have found that both black and white students who attend integrated schools are more likely to work in desegregated companies after graduation than students who attended racially isolated schools.... Further research has shown that the desegregation of schools can help bring adult communities together by reducing segregated housing. Cities that have implemented successful school desegregation plans have witnessed increased interracial contact and neighborhoods that tend to become less racially segregated.... These effects not only reinforce the prior gains of integrated primary and secondary education; they also foresee a time when there is less need to use race-conscious criteria.

Moreover, this Court from *Swann* to *Grutter* has treated these civic effects as an important virtue of racially diverse education....

In light of this Court's conclusions in *Grutter,* the "compelling" nature of these interests in the context of primary and secondary public education follows here *a fortiori*. Primary and secondary schools are where the education of this Nation's children begins, where each of us begins to absorb those values we carry with us to the end of our days....

. . .

The compelling interest at issue here, then, includes an effort to eradicate the remnants, not of general "societal discrimination," but of primary and secondary school segregation; it includes an effort to create school environments that provide better educational opportunities for all children; it includes an effort to help create citizens better prepared to know, to understand, and to work with people of all races and backgrounds, thereby furthering the kind of democratic government our Constitution foresees. If an educational interest that combines these three elements is not "compelling," what is?

. . .

The plurality tries to draw a distinction by reference to the well-established conceptual difference between *de jure* ... and *de facto* segregation .... But that distinction concerns what the Constitution *requires* school boards to do, not what it *permits* them to do....

... No case of this Court has ever relied upon the *de jure/de facto* distinction in order to limit what a school district is voluntarily allowed to do.... And *Swann* [and subsequent cases] made one thing clear: significant as the difference between *de jure* and *de facto* segregation may be to the question of what a school district *must* do, that distinction is not germane to the question of what a school district *may* do.

Nor does any precedent indicate ... that remedial interests vanish the day after a federal court declares that a district is "unitary." ... Louisville adopted those portions of the plan at issue here *before* a court declared Louisville "unitary." ... I do not understand why this Court's cases, which rest the significance of a "unitary" finding in part upon the wisdom and desirability of returning schools to local control, should deprive those local officials of legal *permission* to use means they once found necessary to combat persisting injustices.

For his part, Justice Thomas faults my citation of various studies supporting the view that school districts can find compelling educational and civic interests in integrating their public schools. He is entitled of course to his own opinion as to which studies he finds convincing—although it bears mention that even the author of some of Justice Thomas' preferred studies has found *some* evidence linking integrated learning environments to increased academic achievement.... If we are to insist upon unanimity in the social science literature before finding a compelling interest, we might never find one. I believe only that the Constitution allows democratically elected school boards to make up their own minds as to how best to include people of all races in one America.

B

Narrow Tailoring

... Several factors, taken together, lead me to conclude that the boards' use of race-conscious criteria in these plans passes even the strictest "tailoring" test.

First, the race-conscious criteria at issue only help set the outer bounds of *broad* ranges....

In fact, the defining feature of both plans is greater emphasis upon student choice. In Seattle, for example, in more than 80% of all cases, that choice alone determines which high schools Seattle's ninth graders will attend. After ninth grade, students can decide voluntarily to transfer to a preferred district high school (without any consideration of race-conscious criteria). *Choice*, therefore, is the "predominant factor" in these plans. *Race* is not....

Indeed, the race-conscious ranges at issue in these cases often have no effect, either because the particular school is not oversubscribed in the year in question, or because the racial makeup of the school falls within the broad range, or because the student is a transfer applicant or has a sibling at the school. In these respects, the broad ranges are less like a quota and more like the kinds of "useful starting points" that this Court has consistently found permissible, even when they set boundaries upon voluntary transfers, and even when they are based upon a community's general population....

Second, broad-range limits on voluntary school choice plans are less burdensome, and hence more narrowly tailored, ... than other race-conscious restrictions this Court has previously approved.... Indeed, the plans before us are *more narrowly tailored* than the race-conscious admission plans that this Court approved in *Grutter*. Here, race becomes a factor only in a fraction of students' non-merit-based assignments—not in large numbers of students' merit-based applications. Moreover, the effect of applying race-conscious criteria here affects potentially disadvantaged students *less severely,* not more severely, than the criteria at issue in *Grutter*. Disappointed students are not rejected from a State's flagship graduate program; they simply attend a different one of the district's many public schools, which in aspiration and in fact are substantially equal.... And, in Seattle, the disadvantaged student loses at most one year at the high school of his choice. One will search *Grutter* in vain for similarly persuasive evidence of narrow tailoring as the school districts have presented here.

Third, the manner in which the school boards developed these plans itself reflects "narrow tailoring." Each plan was devised to overcome a history of segregated public schools. Each plan embodies the results of local experience and community consultation. Each plan is the product of a process that has sought to enhance student choice, while diminishing the need for mandatory busing. And each plan's use of race-conscious elements is *diminished* compared to the use of race in preceding integration plans.

The school boards' widespread consultation, their experimentation with numerous other plans, indeed, the 40–year history that Part I sets forth, make clear that plans that are less explicitly race-based are unlikely to achieve the board's "compelling" objectives. The history of each school system reveals highly segregated schools, followed by remedial plans that involved forced busing, followed by efforts to attract or retain students through the use of plans that abandoned busing and replaced it with greater student choice. Both cities once tried to achieve more integrated schools by relying solely upon measures such as redrawn district boundaries, new school building construction, and unrestricted voluntary transfers. In neither city did these prior attempts prove sufficient to achieve the city's integration goals....

Moreover, giving some degree of weight to a local school board's knowledge, expertise, and concerns in these particular matters is not inconsistent with rigorous judicial scrutiny. It simply recognizes that judges are not well suited to act as school administrators. Indeed, in the context of school desegregation, this Court has repeatedly stressed the importance of acknowledging that local school boards better understand their own communities and have a better knowledge of what in practice will best meet the educational needs of their pupils....

. . .

Having looked at dozens of *amicus* briefs, public reports, news stories, and the records in many of this Court's prior cases, which together span 50 years of desegregation history in school districts across the Nation, I have discovered many examples of districts that sought integration through explicitly race-conscious methods, including mandatory busing. Yet, I have found *no* example or model that would permit this Court to say to Seattle and to Louisville: "Here is an instance of a desegregation plan that is likely to achieve your objectives and also makes less use of race-conscious criteria than your plans." And, if the plurality cannot suggest such a model—and it cannot—then it seeks to impose a "narrow tailoring" requirement that in practice would never be met.

Indeed, if there is no such plan, or if such plans are purely imagined, it is understandable why, as the plurality notes, Seattle school officials concentrated on diminishing the racial component of their districts' plan, but did not pursue eliminating that element entirely. For the plurality now to insist as it does that these school districts ought to have said so officially is either to ask for the superfluous (if they need only make explicit what is implicit) or to demand the impossible (if they must somehow provide more proof that there is no hypothetical *other* plan that could work as well as theirs). I am not aware of any case in which this Court has read the "narrow tailoring" test to impose such a requirement. . . .

The plurality also points to the school districts' use of numerical goals based upon the racial breakdown of the general school population, and it faults the districts for failing to prove that *no other set of numbers will work*. The plurality refers to no case in support of its demand. Nor is it likely to find such a case. After all, this Court has in many cases explicitly permitted districts to use target ratios based upon the district's underlying population. . . . The reason is obvious: In Seattle, where the overall student population is 41% white, permitting 85% white enrollment at a single school would make it much more likely that other schools would have very few white students, whereas in Jefferson County, with a 60% white enrollment, one school with 85% white students would be less likely to skew enrollments elsewhere.

Moreover, there is research-based evidence supporting, for example, that a ratio no greater than 50% minority—which is Louisville's starting point, and as close as feasible to Seattle's starting point—is helpful in limiting the risk of "white flight." . . . Federal law also assumes that a similar target percentage will help avoid detrimental "minority group isolation." See No Child Left Behind Act of 2001, Title V, Part C, 115 Stat. 1806, 20 U.S.C. § 7231 *et seq.* (2000 ed., Supp. IV); 34 CFR §§ 280.2, 280.4 (2006) (implementing regulations). What other numbers are the boards to use as a "starting point"? Are they to spend days, weeks, or months seeking independently to validate the use of ratios that this Court has repeatedly authorized in prior cases? Are they to draw numbers out of thin air? These districts have followed this Court's holdings and advice in "tailoring" their plans. That, too, strongly supports the lawfulness of their methods.

Nor could the school districts have accomplished their desired aims (*e.g.*, avoiding forced busing, countering white flight, maintaining racial diversity) by other means. Nothing in the extensive history of desegregation efforts over the past 50 years gives the districts, or this Court, any reason to believe that another method is possible to accomplish these goals. Nevertheless, Justice Kennedy suggests that school boards:

> "may pursue the goal of bringing together students of diverse backgrounds and races through other means, including strategic site selection of new schools; drawing attendance zones with general recognition of the

demographics of neighborhoods; allocating resources for special programs; recruiting students and faculty in a targeted fashion; and tracking enrollments, performance, and other statistics by race.''

But, as to "strategic site selection," Seattle has built one new high school in the last 44 years (and that specialized school serves only 300 students).... As to "drawing" neighborhood "attendance zones" on a racial basis, Louisville tried it, and it worked only when forced busing was also part of the plan. As to "allocating resources for special programs," Seattle and Louisville have both experimented with this; indeed, these programs are often referred to as "magnet schools," but the limited desegregation effect of these efforts extends at most to those few schools to which additional resources are granted. In addition, there is no evidence from the experience of these school districts that it will make any meaningful impact.... As to "recruiting faculty" on the basis of race, both cities have tried, but only as one part of a broader program. As to "tracking enrollments, performance and other statistics by race," tracking *reveals* the problem; it does not cure it.

Justice Kennedy sets forth two additional concerns related to "narrow tailoring." . . .

....I am not certain just how ... Justice Kennedy's concerns affect the lawfulness of the Louisville program, for they seem to be failures of explanation, not of administration. But Louisville should be able to answer the relevant questions on remand.

Justice Kennedy's second concern is directly related to the merits of Seattle's plan: Why does Seattle's plan group Asian–Americans, Hispanic–Americans, Native–Americans, and African–Americans together, treating all as similar minorities? The majority suggests that Seattle's classification system could permit a school to be labeled "diverse" with a 50% Asian–American and 50% white student body, and no African–American students, Hispanic students, or students of other ethnicity....

The 50/50 hypothetical has no support in the record here; it is conjured from the imagination. In fact, Seattle apparently began to treat these different minority groups alike in response to the federal Emergency School Aid Act's requirement that it do so.... Moreover, maintaining this federally mandated system of classification makes sense insofar as Seattle's experience indicates that the relevant circumstances in respect to each of these different minority groups are roughly similar, *e.g.*, in terms of residential patterns, and call for roughly similar responses. This is confirmed by the fact that Seattle has been able to achieve a desirable degree of diversity without the *greater* emphasis on race that drawing fine lines among minority groups would require. Does the plurality's view of the Equal Protection Clause mean that courts must give no weight to such a board determination? Does it insist upon especially strong evidence supporting inclusion of multiple minority groups in an otherwise lawful government minority-assistance program? If so, its interpretation threatens to produce divisiveness among minority groups that is incompatible with the basic objectives of the Fourteenth Amendment. Regardless, the plurality cannot object that the constitutional defect is the individualized use of race and simultaneously object that not enough account of individuals' race has been taken.

Finally, I recognize that the Court seeks to distinguish *Grutter* from these cases by claiming that *Grutter* arose in " 'the context of higher education.' " But that is not a meaningful legal distinction. I have explained why I do not believe the Constitution could possibly find "compelling" the provision of a racially diverse education for a 23–year–old law student but not for a 13–year–old high school pupil. And I have explained how the plans before us are more narrowly tailored than those in *Grutter*. I add that one cannot find a relevant distinction in the fact that these school districts did not examine the merits of applications "individual[ly]." The context here does not involve admission by merit; a child's academic, artistic, and athletic "merits" are not at all relevant to the child's placement. These are not affirmative action plans, and hence "individualized scrutiny" is simply beside the point.

The upshot is that these plans' specific features—(1) their limited and historically-diminishing use of race, (2) their strong reliance upon other non-race-conscious elements, (3) their history and the manner in which the districts developed and modified their approach, (4) the comparison with prior plans, and (5) the lack of reasonably evident alternatives—together show that the districts' plans are "narrowly tailored" to achieve their "compelling" goals. In sum, the districts' race-conscious plans satisfy "strict scrutiny" and are therefore lawful.

IV

. . .

. . . [I]f the [Louisville] plan was lawful when . . . first adopted and . . . the day before the District Court dissolved its order, how can the plurality now suggest that it became *unlawful* the following day? Is it conceivable that the Constitution, implemented through a court desegregation order, could permit (perhaps *require*) the district to make use of a race-conscious plan the day before the order was dissolved and then *forbid* the district to use the identical plan the day after? . . . The Equal Protection Clause is not incoherent. And federal courts would rightly hesitate to find unitary status if the consequences of the ruling were so dramatically disruptive.

Second, *Seattle School Dist. No. 1*, 458 U.S. 457, is directly on point. That case involves the original Seattle Plan, a *more heavily race-conscious predecessor* of the very plan now before us. [T]his Court struck down a state referendum that effectively barred implementation of Seattle's desegregation plan and "burden[ed] all future attempts to integrate Washington schools in districts throughout the State." . . . Because the referendum would have prohibited the adoption of a school-integration plan that involved mandatory busing, and because it would have imposed a special burden on school integration plans (plans that sought to integrate previously segregated schools), the Court found it unconstitutional. . . .

. . .

It is difficult to believe that the Court that held unconstitutional a referendum that would have interfered with the implementation of this plan thought that the integration plan it sought to preserve was itself an *unconstitutional* plan. And if *Seattle School Dist. No. 1* is premised upon the constitutionality of the original Seattle Plan, it is equally premised upon the constitutionality of the present plan, for the present plan *is* the Seattle Plan, modified only insofar as it places even *less* emphasis on race-conscious elements than its predecessors.

It is even more difficult to accept the plurality's contrary view, namely that the underlying plan was unconstitutional. If that is so, then *all* of Seattle's earlier (even more race-conscious) plans must also have been unconstitutional.... How could the plurality adopt a constitutional standard that would hold unconstitutional large numbers of race-conscious integration plans adopted by numerous school boards over the past 50 years while remaining true to this Court's desegregation precedent?

V

Consequences

. . .

At a minimum, the plurality's views would threaten a surge of race-based litigation. Hundreds of state and federal statutes and regulations use racial classifications for educational or other purposes. In many such instances, the contentious force of legal challenges to these classifications, meritorious or not, would displace earlier calm.

... [T]hat the controlling opinion would make a school district's use of [racial] criteria often unlawful (and the plurality's "colorblind" view would make such use always unlawful) suggests that today's opinion will require setting aside the laws of several States and many local communities.

[D]e *facto* resegregation is on the rise.... It is reasonable to conclude that such resegregation can create serious educational, social, and civic problems.... [S]chool boards ... may need all of the means presently at their disposal to combat those problems. Yet the plurality would deprive them of at least one tool that some districts now consider vital—the limited use of broad race-conscious student population ranges.

... The Court should leave [the people] ... to decide, to quote the plurality's slogan, whether the best "way to stop discrimination on the basis of race is to stop discriminating on the basis of race." ... That is why the Equal Protection Clause outlaws invidious discrimination, but does not similarly forbid all use of race-conscious criteria.

Until today, this Court understood the Constitution as affording the people, acting through their elected representatives, freedom to select the use of "race-conscious" criteria from among their available options.... Today, however, the Court restricts (and some Members would eliminate) that leeway. I fear the consequences of doing so for the law, for the schools, for the democratic process, and for America's efforts to create, out of its diversity, one Nation.

VI

Conclusions

. . .

. . . [I]t is the plurality's opinion, not this dissent that "fails to ground the result it would reach in law."

Four basic considerations have led me to this view. *First,* the histories of Louisville and Seattle reveal complex circumstances and a long tradition of conscientious efforts by local school boards to resist racial segregation in public schools. . . .

Second, since . . . *Brown,* the law has consistently and unequivocally approved of both voluntary and compulsory race-conscious measures to combat segregated schools. The Equal Protection Clause . . . has always distinguished in practice between state action that excludes and thereby subordinates racial minorities and state action that seeks to bring together people of all races. . . .

Third, the plans before us, subjected to rigorous judicial review, are supported by compelling state interests and are narrowly tailored to accomplish those goals. Just as diversity in higher education was deemed compelling in *Grutter,* diversity in public primary and secondary schools—where there is even more to gain—must be, *a fortiori,* a compelling state interest. Even apart from *Grutter,* five Members of this Court agree that "avoiding racial isolation" and "achiev[ing] a diverse student population" remain today compelling interests. *Ante,* . . . (opinion of Kennedy, J.). These interests combine remedial, educational, and democratic objectives. For the reasons discussed above, however, I disagree with Justice Kennedy that Seattle and Louisville have not done enough to demonstrate that their present plans are necessary to continue upon the path set by *Brown.* These plans are *more* "narrowly tailored" than the race-conscious law school admissions criteria at issue in *Grutter.* . . .

Fourth, the plurality's approach risks serious harm to the law and for the Nation. . . . [T]he Court's decision today slows down and sets back the work of local school boards to bring about racially diverse schools. . . .

. . .

The Court's decision undermines . . . *stare decisis.* . . .

And . . . respect for democratic local decisionmaking by States and school boards. . . .

And . . . today's holding upsets settled expectations, creates legal uncertainty, and threatens to produce considerable further litigation, aggravating race-related conflict.

And what of the long history and moral vision that the Fourteenth Amendment itself embodies? The plurality cites in support those who argued in *Brown* against segregation, and Justice Thomas likens the approach that I have taken to that of segregation's defenders. . . . But segregation policies did not simply tell schoolchildren "where they could and could not go to school based on the color of their skin"; they perpetuated a caste system rooted in the institutions of slavery and 80 years of legalized subordination. The lesson of history is not that efforts to continue racial segregation are constitutionally indistinguishable from efforts to achieve racial integration. Indeed, it is a cruel distortion of history to compare Topeka, Kansas, in the 1950's to Louisville and Seattle in the modern day—to equate the plight of Linda Brown (who was ordered to attend a Jim Crow school) to the circumstances of Joshua McDonald (whose request to transfer to a school closer to home was initially declined).

This is not to deny that there is a cost in applying "a state-mandated racial label." But that cost does not approach, in degree or in kind, the terrible harms of slavery, the resulting caste system, and 80 years of legal racial segregation.

* * *

Finally, what of the hope and promise of *Brown?* ... *Brown* held out a promise ... of true racial equality—not as a matter of fine words on paper, but as a matter of everyday life in the Nation's cities and schools. It was about the nature of a democracy that must work for all Americans. It sought one law, one Nation, one people, not simply as a matter of legal principle but in terms of how we actually live.

... Today, ... attitudes toward race in this Nation have changed dramatically. Many parents, white and black alike, want their children to attend schools with children of different races. Indeed, the very school districts that once spurned integration now strive for it. The long history of their efforts reveals the complexities and difficulties they have faced. And in light of those challenges, they have asked us not to take from their hands the instruments they have used to rid their schools of racial segregation, instruments that they believe are needed to overcome the problems of cities divided by race and poverty. The plurality would decline their modest request.

... This is a decision that the Court and the Nation will come to regret.

I must dissent.

SECTION 4.   PROTECTION OF PERSONAL LIBERTIES

D.   COURT ACCESS, WELFARE, AND THE POOR

Page 1057.   Add at end of Note, "The Rights of the Poor Defendant in the Criminal Justice System":

The Due Process and Equal Protection Clauses were held to require the appointment of counsel, however, in connection with preparing an application for discretionary leave to seek a first-tier appeal from a challenged conviction based on a guilty plea or a plea of nolo contendere. Halbert v. Michigan, 545 U.S. 605, 125 S.Ct. 2582, 162 L.Ed.2d 552 (2005). Justice Ginsburg's majority opinion reasoned that a discretionary first appeal should be treated the same as a first appeal as of right under Douglas v. California, rather than as a discretionary subsequent appeal under Ross v. Moffitt, largely because of two features of Michigan's appellate process following plea-based convictions: "First, in determining how to dispose of an application for leave to appeal, Michigan's intermediate appellate court looks to the merits of the claims made in the application. Second, indigent defendants pursuing first-tier review in the Court of Appeals are generally ill equipped to represent themselves." Unlike discretionary review following a first appeal as of right, as in *Ross,* when the first appeal is discretionary a "first-tier review applicant, forced to act *pro se,* will face a record unreviewed by appellate counsel, and will be equipped with no attorney's brief prepared for, or reasoned opinion by, a court of review[,]" rendering "a *pro se* applicant's entitlement to seek leave to appeal ... more formal than real." Justice Ginsburg also noted the low rates of inmate literacy and reasoned that "[n]avigating the appellate process without a lawyer's assistance is a perilous endeavor for a layperson, and well beyond the competence of individuals, like Halbert, who have little education, learning disabilities, and mental impairments."

Justice Thomas, joined by Justice Scalia and Chief Justice Rehnquist, dissented, finding the Court's decision "an unwarranted extension of" *Douglas*.

CHAPTER 11

DEFINING THE SCOPE OF "LIBERTY" AND "PROPERTY" PROTECTED BY THE DUE PROCESS CLAUSE—THE PROCEDURAL DUE PROCESS CASES

SECTION 1. WHEN DOES DUE PROCESS MANDATE CONSTITUTIONAL PROCEDURES?

A. WHAT "PROPERTY" AND "LIBERTY" IS PROTECTED?

Page 1103. Add after American Manufacturers Mutual Insurance Co. v. Sullivan:

TOWN OF CASTLE ROCK v. GONZALES, 545 U.S. 748, 125 S.Ct. 2796, 162 L.Ed.2d 658 (2005). In violation of a restraining order issued in conjunction with divorce proceedings, and without notice, an estranged father took his three daughters from the front of the family home. Tragically, several hours later he murdered them and thereafter was killed in a shoot-out with police. The mother sued the Town, alleging that her repeated, unsuccessful efforts throughout the night to have the police enforce the restraining order were thwarted by a police department policy or custom of failing to respond properly and tolerating non-enforcement of restraining orders, thereby depriving her, without due process, of a statutorily-based property interest in police enforcement of the restraining order.

The Court held that she "did not, for purposes of the Due Process Clause, have a property interest in police enforcement of the restraining order against her husband." Noting that "a benefit is not a protected entitlement if government officials may grant or deny it in their discretion[,]" Justice Scalia's opinion wrote that "the central state-law question is whether Colorado law gave respondent a right to police enforcement of the restraining order"—a question as to which the Court found deference to the Tenth Circuit Court of Appeals "inappropriate," primarily because its opinion "did not draw upon a deep well of state-specific expertise, but consisted primarily of quoting language from the restraining order, the statutory text, and a state-legislative-hearing transcript." The Court's own examination led it to conclude that Colorado statutory provisions apparently obligating police to use "every reasonable means to enforce a restraining order," and to "arrest, or if an arrest would be impractical under the circumstances, seek a warrant for the arrest of a restrained person" when there is probable cause that the person has violated the order, did not "truly ma[k]e enforcement of restraining orders *mandatory*. A well established tradition of police discretion has long coexisted with apparently mandatory arrest statutes." Accordingly, "a true mandate of police action would require some stronger indication from the Colorado Legislature...."

Justice Scalia also wrote:

"Respondent does not specify the precise means of enforcement that the Colorado restraining-order statute assertedly mandated—whether her interest lay in having police arrest her husband, having them seek a warrant for his arrest, or having them 'use every reasonable means, up to and including arrest, to enforce the order's terms ...' Such indeterminacy is not the hallmark of a duty that is mandatory. Nor can someone be safely deemed 'entitled' to something when the identity of the alleged entitlement is vague. ... The dissent ultimately contends that the obligations under the statute were quite precise: either make an arrest or (if that is impractical) seek an arrest warrant. The problem with this is that the seeking of an arrest warrant would be an entitlement to nothing but procedure—which ... can[not] be the basis for a property interest.... After the warrant is sought, it remains within the discretion of a judge whether to grant it, and after it is granted, it remains within the discretion of the police whether and when to execute it. Respondent would have been assured nothing but the seeking of a warrant. This is not the sort of 'entitlement' out of which a property interest is created.

"Even if the statute could be said to have made enforcement of restraining orders 'mandatory' because of the domestic-violence context of the underlying statute, that would not necessarily mean that state law gave *respondent* an entitlement to *enforcement* of the mandate. Making the actions of government employees obligatory can serve various legitimate ends other than the conferral of a benefit on a specific class of people. ...

"Respondent's alleged interest stems only from a State's *statutory* scheme—from a restraining order that was authorized by and tracked precisely the statute on which the Court of Appeals relied. She does not assert that she has any common-law or contractual entitlement to enforcement. If she was given a statutory entitlement, we would expect to see some indication of that in the statute itself. Although Colorado's statute spoke of 'protected person[s]' such as respondent, it did so in connection with matters other than a right to enforcement.... Perhaps most importantly, the statute spoke directly to the protected person's power to 'initiate contempt proceedings against the restrained person if the order [was] issued in a civil action or request the prosecuting attorney to initiate contempt proceedings if the order [was] issued in a criminal action.' ... The protected person's express power to 'initiate' civil contempt proceedings contrasts tellingly with the mere ability to 'request' initiation of criminal contempt proceedings—and even more dramatically with the complete silence about any power to 'request' (much less demand) that an arrest be made.

" ...

"Even if we were to think otherwise concerning the creation of an entitlement by Colorado, it is by no means clear that an individual entitlement to enforcement of a restraining order could constitute a 'property' interest for purposes of the Due Process Clause. Such a right would not, of course, resemble any traditional conception of property. Although that alone does not disqualify it from due process protection, as *Roth* and its progeny show, the right to have a restraining order enforced does not 'have some ascertainable monetary value,' as even our '*Roth*-type property-as-entitlement' cases have implicitly required. . . . Perhaps most radically, the alleged property interest here arises *incidentally*, not out of some new species of government benefit or service, but out of a function that government actors have always performed—to wit, arresting people who they have probable cause to believe have committed a criminal offense.

". . . In this case . . . '[t]he simple distinction between government action that directly affects a citizen's legal rights . . . and action that is directed against a third party and affects the citizen only indirectly or incidentally, provides a sufficient answer to' respondent's reliance on cases that found government-provided services to be entitlements.'"

Justice Souter's concurring opinion, joined by Justice Breyer, said in part:

"[Gonzales'] argument is unconventional because the state-law benefit for which it claims federal procedural protection is itself a variety of procedural regulation, a set of rules to be followed by officers exercising the State's executive power: use all reasonable means to enforce, arrest upon demonstrable probable cause, get a warrant, and so on.

"When her argument is [so] understood . . . , a further reason appears for rejecting its call to apply *Roth,* a reason that would apply even if the statutory mandates to the police were absolute, leaving the police with no discretion when the beneficiary of a protective order insists upon its enforcement. . . . [The] argument is at odds with the rule that '[p]rocess is not an end in itself. Its constitutional purpose is to protect a substantive interest to which the individual has a legitimate claim of entitlement.' . . . Just as a State cannot diminish a property right, once conferred, by attaching less than generous procedure to its deprivation, . . . neither does a State create a property right merely by ordaining beneficial procedure unconnected to some articulable substantive guarantee. . . . [W]e have not identified property with procedure as such. State rules of executive procedure, however important, may be nothing more than rules of executive procedure.

 "Thus, in every instance of property recognized by this Court as calling for federal procedural protection, the property has been distinguishable from the procedural obligations imposed on state officials to protect it. Whether welfare benefits, *Goldberg v. Kelly,* 397 U.S. 254 (1970), attendance at public schools, *Goss v. Lopez,* 419 U.S. 565 (1975), utility services, *Memphis Light, Gas & Water Div. v. Craft,* 436 U.S. 1 (1978), public employment, *Perry v. Sindermann,* 408 U.S. 593 (1972), professional licenses, *Barry v. Barchi,* 443 U.S. 55 (1979), and so on, the property interest recognized in our cases has always existed apart from state procedural protection before the Court has recognized a constitutional claim to protection by federal process. . . . There is no articulable distinction between the object of Gonzales's asserted entitlement and the process she desires in order to protect her entitlement; both amount to certain steps to be taken by the police to protect her family and herself. Gonzales's claim would thus take us beyond *Roth* or any other recognized theory of Fourteenth Amendment due process, by collapsing the distinction between property protected and the process that protects it, and would federalize every mandatory state-law direction to executive officers whose performance on the job can be vitally significant to individuals affected.

"The procedural directions involved here ... presuppose no enforceable substantive entitlement, and *Roth* does not raise them to federally enforceable status in the name of due process."

Justice Stevens dissented, joined by Justice Ginsburg. Among the points he emphasized were that the States had passed a wave of "mandatory arrest" statutes in the domestic violence context in the 1980s and 1990s "with the unmistakable goal of eliminating police discretion in this area"; that "the Colorado statute at issue in this case was enacted for the benefit of the narrow class of persons who are beneficiaries of domestic restraining orders, and ... the order at issue in this case was specifically intended to provide protection to respondent and her children"; and "that a citizen's interest in the government's commitment to provide police enforcement in certain defined circumstances ... is just as concrete and worthy of protection as her interest in any other important service the government or a private firm has undertaken to provide." In his view, "under the statute, the police were *required* to provide enforcement; *they lacked the discretion to do nothing*.... Under the statute, if the police have probable cause that a violation has occurred, enforcement consists of either making an immediate arrest or seeking a warrant and then executing an arrest—traditional, well-defined tasks that law enforcement officers perform every day." Moreover, "[b]ecause the statute's guarantee of police enforcement is triggered by, and operates only in reference to, a judge's granting of a restraining order in favor of an identified ' "protected person," ' there is simply no room to suggest that such a person has received merely an ' "incidental" ' or ' "indirect" ' benefit." In the concluding section of his dissent, Justice Stevens wrote in part:

"Given that Colorado law has quite clearly eliminated the police's discretion to deny enforcement, respondent is correct that she had much more than a 'unilateral expectation' that the restraining order would be enforced; rather, she had a 'legitimate claim of entitlement' to enforcement. *Roth* ....

"Police enforcement of a restraining order is a government service that is no less concrete and no less valuable than other government services, such as education. The relative novelty of recognizing this type of property interest is explained by the relative novelty of the domestic violence statutes creating a mandatory arrest duty; before this innovation, the unfettered discretion that characterized police enforcement defeated any citizen's 'legitimate claim of entitlement' to this service.... Colorado law *guaranteed* the provision of a certain service, in certain defined circumstances, to a certain class of beneficiaries, and respondent reasonably relied on that guarantee. As we observed in *Roth*, '[i]t is a purpose of the ancient institution of property to protect those claims upon which people rely in their daily lives, reliance that must not be arbitrarily undermined.' ... Surely, if respondent had contracted with a private security firm to provide her and her daughters with protection from her husband, it would be apparent that she possessed a property interest in such a contract. Here, Colorado undertook a comparable obligation, and respondent— with restraining order in hand—justifiably relied on that undertaking. Respondent's claim of entitlement to this promised service is no less legitimate than the other claims our cases have upheld, and no less concrete than a hypothetical agreement with a private firm. The fact that it is based on a statutory enactment and a judicial order entered for her special protection, rather than on a formal contract, does not provide a principled basis for refusing to consider it 'property' worthy of constitutional protection.[20]"

Page 1114. Add after Sandin v. Conner:

WILKINSON v. AUSTIN, 545 U.S. 209, 125 S.Ct. 2384, 162 L.Ed.2d 174 (2005). Prisoners challenged the procedures Ohio adopted for assignment to the Ohio State Penitentiary (OSP)—its most restrictive, highest security prison, designed to segregate the most dangerous prisoners from the general prison population. The Court unanimously held that under *Sandin* the inmates possessed a liberty interest in avoiding assignment to OSP but that Ohio's informal, nonadversary procedures were adequate to satisfy due process under *Mathews v. Eldridge*, 424 U.S. 319, 96 S.Ct. 893, 47 L.Ed.2d 18 (1976), discussed infra, p. 1120. With respect to the existence of a cognizable liberty interest, the Court noted but did not resolve a divergence among the Courts of Appeals about the application of *Sandin*'s criterion of whether a freedom from restraint "imposes atypical and significant hardship on the inmate in relation to the ordinary incidents of prison life" stemming from the difficulty of "identifying the baseline from which to measure what is atypical and significant in any prison system." Instead, the Court said:

" . . . [W]e are satisfied that assignment to OSP imposes an atypical and significant hardship under any plausible baseline.

"For an inmate placed in OSP, almost all human contact is prohibited, even to the point that conversation is not permitted cell to cell; the light, though it may be dimmed, is on for 24 hours; exercise is for 1 hour per day, but only in a small indoor room. Save perhaps for the especially severe limitations on all human contact, these conditions likely would apply to most solitary confinement facilities, but here there are two added components. First is the duration. Unlike the 30–day placement in *Sandin*, placement at OSP is indefinite and, after an initial 30–day review, is reviewed just annually. Second is that placement disqualifies an otherwise eligible inmate for parole consideration. . . . While any of these conditions standing alone might not be sufficient to create a liberty interest, taken together they impose an atypical and significant hardship within the correctional context. It follows that respondents have a liberty interest in avoiding assignment to OSP. . . .

"OSP's harsh conditions may well be necessary and appropriate in light of the danger that high-risk inmates pose both to prison officials and to other prisoners. That necessity, however, does not diminish our conclusion that the conditions give rise to a liberty interest in their avoidance."

---

20. . . . Justice Souter . . . misunderstands respondent's claim. . . . [R]espondent is in fact asserting a substantive interest in the "enforcement of the restraining order."[—]a tangible, substantive act. If an estranged husband violates a restraining order by abducting children, and the police succeed in enforcing the order, the person holding the restraining order has undeniably just received a substantive benefit. As in other procedural due process cases, respondent is ar-guing that the police officers failed to follow fair procedures in ascertaining whether the statutory criteria that trigger their obligation to provide enforcement—*i.e.*, an outstanding order plus probable cause that it is being violated—were satisfied in her case. . . . It is Justice Souter, not respondent, who makes the mistake of "collapsing the distinction between property protected and the process that protects it."

. . .

PART IV

Constitutional Protection of Expression and Conscience

CHAPTER 13

Governmental Control of the Content of Expression

SECTION 3. Speech Conflicting With Other Community values: Government Control of the Content of Speech

D. Regulation of Commercial Speech

Page 1423. Add footnote a. to end of Note, "Attorney Advertising":

a. In Tennessee Secondary School Athletic Association v. Brentwood Academy, ___ U.S. ___, 127 S.Ct. 2489, ___ L.Ed.2d ___ (2007), the Court unanimously rejected a first amendment challenge to an interscholastic athletic association rule prohibiting high school coaches from recruiting middle school athletes. The principal opinion by Justice Stevens spoke only for a plurality of four Justices, however, insofar as it relied on *Oh-* *ralik* in reasoning that "the dangers of undue influence and overreaching that exist when a lawyer chases an ambulance are also present when a high school coach contacts an eighth grader." Five Justices subscribed to Justice Kennedy's separate position disagreeing "with the principal opinion's reliance on *Oh-* *ralik*[,]" which "the Court has declined to extend ... beyond the attorney-client relationship." He objected that "[t]o allow freestanding state regulation of speech by coaches and other representatives of nonmember schools would be a dramatic expansion of *Ohralik* to a whole new field of endeavor."

Accordingly, he declined to join any portion of the principal opinion "that suggests *Ohralik* is applicable here."

CHAPTER 14

RESTRICTIONS ON TIME, PLACE, OR MANNER OF EXPRESSION

SECTION 4. SPEECH IN THE PUBLIC SCHOOLS

Page 1535. Add at end of section:

Morse v. Frederick

___ U.S. ___, 127 S.Ct. 2618, ___ L.Ed.2d ___ (2007).

Chief Justice Roberts delivered the opinion of the Court.

At a school-sanctioned and school-supervised event, a high school principal saw some of her students unfurl a large banner conveying a message she reasonably regarded as promoting illegal drug use. Consistent with established school policy prohibiting such messages at school events, the principal directed the students to take down the banner. One student—among those who had brought the banner to the event—refused to do so. The principal confiscated the banner and later suspended the student....

Our cases make clear that students do not "shed their constitutional rights to freedom of speech or expression at the schoolhouse gate." *Tinker v. Des Moines Independent Community School Dist.*, 393 U.S. 503 (1969). At the same time, we have held that "the constitutional rights of students in public school are not automatically coextensive with the rights of adults in other settings," *Bethel School Dist. No. 403 v. Fraser*, 478 U.S. 675, 682 (1986), and that the rights of students "must be 'applied in light of the special characteristics of the school environment.'" *Hazelwood School Dist. v. Kuhlmeier*, 484 U.S. 260, 266 (1988) (quoting *Tinker*, ...). Consistent with these principles, we hold that schools may take steps to safeguard those entrusted to their care from speech that can reasonably be regarded as encouraging illegal drug use. We conclude that the school officials in this case did not violate the First Amendment by confiscating the pro-drug banner and suspending the student responsible for it.

I

On January 24, 2002, the Olympic Torch Relay passed through Juneau, Alaska, ... along a street in front of Juneau–Douglas High School (JDHS) while school was in session. Petitioner ... school principal ... decided to permit staff and students to participate ... as an approved social event or class trip.... Students were allowed to leave class to observe the relay from either side of the street. Teachers and administrative officials monitored the students' actions.

Respondent Joseph Frederick, a JDHS senior, was late to school that day. When he arrived, he joined his friends (all but one ... JDHS students) across the street from the school to watch the event.... As the torchbearers and camera crews passed by, Frederick and his friends unfurled a 14–foot banner bearing the phrase: "BONG HiTS 4 JESUS." ... The large banner was easily readable by the students on the other side of the street.

Principal Morse immediately crossed the street and demanded that the banner be taken down. Everyone but Frederick complied. Morse confiscated the banner and told Frederick to report to her office, where she suspended him for 10 days. Morse later explained that she told Frederick to take the banner down because she thought it encouraged illegal drug use, in violation of established school policy....

[On appeal,] the superintendent ... explained that Frederick "was not disciplined because the principal of the school 'disagreed' with his message, but because his speech appeared to advocate the use of illegal drugs." ...

The superintendent continued:

"The common-sense understanding of the phrase 'bong hits' is that it is a reference to a means of smoking marijuana. Given [Frederick's] inability or unwillingness to express any other credible meaning for the phrase, I can only agree with the principal and countless others who saw the banner as advocating the use of illegal drugs. [Frederick's] speech was not political. He was not advocating the legalization of marijuana or promoting a religious belief. He was displaying a fairly silly message promoting illegal drug usage in the midst of a school activity, for the benefit of television cameras covering the Torch Relay. [Frederick's] speech was potentially disruptive to the event and clearly disruptive of and inconsistent with the school's educational mission to educate students about the dangers of illegal drugs and to discourage their use." ...

Relying on our decision in *Fraser, supra,* the superintendent concluded that the principal's actions were permissible because Frederick's banner was "speech or action that intrudes upon the work of the schools." ... The Juneau School District Board of Education upheld the suspension.

[Frederick sued, alleging that the school board and Morse had violated his First Amendment rights.... The District Court granted summary judgment for the school board and Morse, but the Ninth Circuit reversed.]

II

... [T]his is ... a school speech case..... The event occurred during normal school hours[,] was sanctioned by Principal Morse "as an approved social event or class trip," ... and the school district's rules expressly provide that pupils in "approved social events and class trips are subject to district rules for student conduct." ... Teachers and administrators were interspersed among the students and charged with supervising them. The high school band and cheerleaders performed. Frederick, standing among other JDHS students across the street from the school, directed his banner toward the school, making it plainly visible to most students. Under these circumstances, we agree with the superintendent that Frederick cannot "stand in the midst of his fellow students, during school hours, at a school-sanctioned activity and claim he is not at school." ... There is some uncertainty at the outer boundaries as to when courts should apply school-speech precedents, ... but not on these facts.

III

The message on Frederick's banner is cryptic. It is no doubt offensive to some, perhaps amusing to others. To still others, it probably means nothing at all. Frederick himself claimed "that the words were just nonsense meant to attract television cameras." ... But Principal Morse thought the banner would be interpreted by those viewing it as promoting illegal drug use, and that interpretation is plainly a reasonable one.

. . .

... At least two interpretations of the words on the banner demonstrate that the sign advocated the use of illegal drugs. First, the phrase could be interpreted as an imperative: "[Take] bong hits ... "—a message equivalent, as Morse explained in her declaration, to "smoke marijuana" or "use an illegal drug." Alternatively, the phrase could be viewed as celebrating drug use—"bong hits [are a good thing]," or "[we take] bong hits"—and we discern no meaningful distinction between celebrating illegal drug use in the midst of fellow students and outright advocacy or promotion. . . .

The pro-drug interpretation of the banner gains further plausibility given the paucity of alternative meanings the banner might bear. The best Frederick can come up with is that the banner is "meaningless and funny." ... The dissent similarly refers to the sign's message as "curious," "ambiguous," "nonsense," "ridiculous," "obscure," "silly," "quixotic," and "stupid." Gibberish is surely a possible interpretation of the words on the banner, but it is not the only one, and dismissing the banner as meaningless ignores its undeniable reference to illegal drugs.

The dissent mentions Frederick's "credible and uncontradicted explanation for the message—he just wanted to get on television." But that is a description of Frederick's *motive* for displaying the banner; it is not an interpretation of what the banner says. The *way* Frederick was going to fulfill his ambition of appearing on television was by unfurling a pro-drug banner at a school event, in the presence of teachers and fellow students.

Elsewhere in its opinion, the dissent emphasizes the importance of political speech and the need to foster "national debate about a serious issue," as if to suggest that the banner is political speech. But not even Frederick argues that the banner conveys any sort of political or religious message. Contrary to the dissent's suggestion, this is plainly not a case about political debate over the criminalization of drug use or possession.

IV

The question thus becomes whether a principal may, consistent with the First Amendment, restrict student speech at a school event, when that speech is reasonably viewed as promoting illegal drug use. We hold that she may.

. . .

Tinker held that student expression may not be suppressed unless school officials reasonably conclude that it will "materially and substantially disrupt the work and discipline of the school." ... The essential facts of *Tinker* are quite stark, implicating concerns at the heart of the First Amendment. The students sought to engage in political speech, using the armbands to express their "disapproval of the Vietnam hostilities and their advocacy of a truce, to make their views known, and, by their example, to influence others to adopt them." ... The only interest the Court discerned underlying the school's actions was the "mere desire to avoid the discomfort and unpleasantness that always accompany an unpopular viewpoint," or "an urgent wish to avoid the controversy which might result from the expression." ... That interest was not enough to justify banning "a silent, passive expression of opinion, unaccompanied by any disorder or disturbance." ...

[In *Fraser,* this Court held] that the "School District acted entirely within its permissible authority in imposing sanctions upon Fraser in response to his offensively lewd and indecent speech." ...

The mode of analysis employed in *Fraser* is not entirely clear. The Court was plainly attuned to the content of Fraser's speech, citing the "marked distinction between the political 'message' of the armbands in *Tinker* and the sexual content of [Fraser's] speech." ... But the Court also reasoned that school boards have the authority to determine "what manner of speech in the classroom or in school assembly is inappropriate." ...

We need not resolve this debate to decide this case. For present purposes, it is enough to distill from *Fraser* two basic principles. First, *Fraser's* holding demonstrates that "the constitutional rights of students in public school are not automatically coextensive with the rights of adults in other settings." ... Had Fraser delivered the same speech in a public forum outside the school context, it would have been protected.... Second, *Fraser* established that the mode of analysis set forth in *Tinker* is not absolute. Whatever approach *Fraser* employed, it certainly did not conduct the "substantial disruption" analysis prescribed by *Tinker....*

. . .

Kuhlmeier [also] is ... instructive because it confirms both principles cited above....

Drawing on ... our student speech cases, we have held in the Fourth Amendment context that "while children assuredly do not 'shed their constitutional rights ... at the schoolhouse gate,' ... the nature of those rights is what is appropriate for children in school." ... In particular, "the school setting requires some easing of the restrictions to which searches by public authorities are ordinarily subject."

Even more to the point, these cases also recognize that deterring drug use by schoolchildren is an "important—indeed, perhaps compelling" interest.... Drug abuse can cause severe and permanent damage to the health and well-being of young people....

. . .

Congress has declared that part of a school's job is educating students about the dangers of illegal drug use....

Thousands of school boards throughout the country—including JDHS—have adopted policies aimed at effectuating this message.... Those school boards know that peer pressure is perhaps "the single most important factor leading schoolchildren to take drugs," and that students are more likely to use drugs when the norms in school appear to tolerate such behavior.... Student speech celebrating illegal drug use at a school event, in the presence of school administrators and teachers, thus poses a particular challenge for school officials working to protect those entrusted to their care from the dangers of drug abuse.

The "special characteristics of the school environment," ... and the governmental interest in stopping student drug abuse ... allow schools to restrict student expression that they reasonably regard as promoting illegal drug use. *Tinker* warned that schools may not prohibit student speech because of "undifferentiated fear or apprehension of disturbance" or "a mere desire to avoid the discomfort and unpleasantness that always accompany an unpopular viewpoint." ... The danger here is far more serious and palpable. The particular concern to prevent student drug abuse at issue here, embodied in established school policy, ... extends well beyond an abstract desire to avoid controversy.

Petitioners urge us to adopt the broader rule that Frederick's speech is proscribable because it is plainly "offensive" as that term is used in *Fraser*.... We think this stretches *Fraser* too far; that case should not be read to encompass any speech that could fit under some definition of "offensive." After all, much political and religious speech might be perceived as offensive to some. The concern here is not that Frederick's speech was offensive, but that it was reasonably viewed as promoting illegal drug use.

Although accusing this decision of doing "serious violence to the First Amendment" by authorizing "viewpoint discrimination," the dissent concludes that "it might well be appropriate to tolerate some targeted viewpoint discrimination in this unique setting." Nor do we understand the dissent to take the position that schools are required to tolerate student advocacy of illegal drug use at school events, even if that advocacy falls short of inviting "imminent" lawless action.... Stripped of rhetorical flourishes, then, the debate between the dissent and this opinion is less about constitutional first principles than about whether Frederick's banner constitutes promotion of illegal drug use. We have explained our view that it does. The dissent's contrary view on that relatively narrow question hardly justifies sounding the First Amendment bugle.

* * *

School principals have a difficult job, and a vitally important one. When Frederick suddenly and unexpectedly unfurled his banner, Morse had to decide to act—or not act—on the spot. It was reasonable for her to conclude that the banner promoted illegal drug use—in violation of established school policy—and that failing to act would send a powerful message to the students in her charge, including Frederick, about how serious the school was about the dangers of illegal drug use. The First Amendment does not require schools to tolerate at school events student expression that contributes to those dangers.

[R]eversed, and . . . remanded for further proceedings consistent with this opinion.

Justice Thomas, concurring.

. . .

Tinker effected a sea change in students' speech rights, extending them well beyond traditional bounds. . . .

. . .

Of course, *Tinker's* reasoning conflicted with the traditional understanding of the judiciary's role in relation to public schooling, a role limited by *in loco parentis*. Perhaps for that reason, the Court has since scaled back *Tinker's* standard, or rather set the standard aside on an ad hoc basis[—in *Fraser* and *Kuhlmeier*.]

Today, the Court creates another exception. In doing so, we continue to distance ourselves from *Tinker,* but we neither overrule it nor offer an explanation of when it operates and when it does not. . . . In my view, petitioners could prevail for a much simpler reason: As originally understood, the Constitution does not afford students a right to free speech in public schools.

III

In light of the history of American public education, it cannot seriously be suggested that the First Amendment "freedom of speech" encompasses a student's right to speak in public schools. Early public schools gave total control to teachers, who expected obedience and respect from students. And courts routinely deferred to schools' authority to make rules and to discipline students for violating those rules. . . .

. . .

. . . If parents do not like the rules imposed by those schools, they can seek redress in school boards or legislatures; they can send their children to private schools or home school them; or they can simply move. Whatever rules apply to student speech in public schools, those rules can be challenged by parents in the political process.

In place of that democratic regime, *Tinker* substituted judicial oversight of the day-to-day affairs of public schools. The *Tinker* Court made little attempt to ground its holding in the history of education or in the original understanding of the First Amendment. . . .

And because *Tinker* utterly ignored the history of public education, courts (including this one) routinely find it necessary to create ad hoc exceptions to its central premise. This doctrine of exceptions creates confusion without fixing the underlying problem by returning to first principles. Just as I cannot accept *Tinker's* standard, I cannot subscribe to *Kuhlmeier's* alternative. Local school boards, not the courts, should determine what pedagogical interests are "legitimate" and what rules "reasonably relat[e]" to those interests. . . .

. . .

I join the Court's opinion because it erodes *Tinker's* hold in the realm of student speech, even though it does so by adding to the patchwork of exceptions to the *Tinker* standard. I think the better approach is to dispense with *Tinker* altogether, and given the opportunity, I would do so.

Justice Alito, with whom Justice Kennedy joins, concurring.

I join the opinion of the Court on the understanding that (a) it goes no further than to hold that a public school may restrict speech that a reasonable observer would interpret as advocating illegal drug use and (b) it provides no support for any restriction of speech that can plausibly be interpreted as commenting on any political or social issue, including speech on issues such as "the wisdom of the war on drugs or of legalizing marijuana for medicinal use." (Stevens, J., dissenting).

The opinion of the Court correctly reaffirms the recognition in *Tinker* . . . of the fundamental principle that students do not "shed their constitutional rights to freedom of speech or expression at the schoolhouse gate." The Court is also correct in noting that *Tinker,* which permits the regulation of student speech that threatens a concrete and "substantial disruption," . . . does not set out the only ground on which in-school student speech may be regulated by state actors in a way that would not be constitutional in other settings.

But I do not read the opinion to mean that there are necessarily any grounds for such regulation that are not already recognized in the holdings of this Court [in *Tinker,* the present case, *Fraser,* and *Kuhlmeier.*] . . . I join the opinion of the Court on the understanding that the opinion does not hold that the special characteristics of the public schools necessarily justify any other speech restrictions.

The opinion of the Court does not endorse the broad argument advanced by petitioners and the United States that the First Amendment permits public school officials to censor any student speech that interferes with a school's "educational mission." . . . This argument can easily be manipulated in dangerous ways, and I would reject it before such abuse occurs. The "educational mission" of the public schools is defined by the elected and appointed public officials with authority over the schools and by the school administrators and faculty. As a result, some public schools have defined their educational missions as including the inculcation of whatever political and social views are held by the members of these groups.

During the *Tinker* era, a public school could have defined its educational mission to include solidarity with our soldiers and their families and thus could have attempted to outlaw the wearing of black armbands on the ground that they undermined this mission. Alternatively, a school could have defined its educational mission to include the promotion of world peace and could have sought to ban the wearing of buttons expressing support for the troops on the ground that the buttons signified approval of war. The "educational mission" argument would give public school authorities a license to suppress speech on political and social issues based on disagreement with the viewpoint expressed. The argument, therefore, strikes at the very heart of the First Amendment.

. . . It is . . . wrong to treat public school officials, for purposes relevant to the First Amendment, as if they were private, nongovernmental actors standing *in loco parentis.*

[A]ny argument for altering the usual free speech rules in the public schools cannot rest on a theory of delegation but must ... be based on some special characteristic of the school setting. The special characteristic ... relevant in this case is the threat to the physical safety of students.... [S]tudents, when not in school, may be able to avoid threatening individuals and situations. During school hours, however, parents are not present to provide protection and guidance, and students' movements and their ability to choose the persons with whom they spend time are severely restricted. Students may be compelled on a daily basis to spend time at close quarters with other students who may do them harm. Experience shows that schools can be places of special danger.

In most settings, the First Amendment strongly limits the government's ability to suppress speech on the ground that it presents a threat of violence. See *Brandenburg v. Ohio,* 395 U.S. 444 (1969) *(per curiam).* But due to the special features of the school environment, school officials must have greater authority to intervene before speech leads to violence. And, in most cases, *Tinker's* "substantial disruption" standard permits school officials to step in before actual violence erupts....

Speech advocating illegal drug use poses a threat to student safety that is just as serious, if not always as immediately obvious. [I]llegal drug use presents a grave and in many ways unique threat to the physical safety of students. I therefore conclude that the public schools may ban speech advocating illegal drug use. But I regard such regulation as standing at the far reaches of what the First Amendment permits. I join the opinion of the Court with the understanding that the opinion does not endorse any further extension.

Justice Breyer, concurring in the judgment in part and dissenting in part.

This Court need not and should not decide this difficult First Amendment issue on the merits. [I]t should simply hold that qualified immunity bar's the student's claim for monetary damages and say no more.

. . .

... To say that school officials might reasonably prohibit students during school-related events from unfurling 14–foot banners (with any kind of irrelevant or inappropriate message) designed to attract attention from television cameras seems unlikely to undermine basic First Amendment principles. But to hold, as the Court does, that "schools may take steps to safeguard those entrusted to their care from speech that can reasonably be regarded as encouraging illegal drug use" (and that "schools" may "restrict student expression that they reasonably regard as promoting illegal drug use") is quite a different matter. This holding, based ... on viewpoint restrictions, raises a host of serious concerns.

One concern is that, while the holding is theoretically limited to speech promoting the use of illegal drugs, it could in fact authorize further viewpoint-based restrictions. Illegal drugs, after all, are not the only illegal substances. What about encouraging the underage consumption of alcohol? Moreover, it is unclear how far the Court's rule regarding drug advocacy extends. What about a conversation during the lunch period where one student suggests that glaucoma sufferers should smoke marijuana to relieve the pain? What about deprecating commentary about an antidrug film shown in school? And what about drug messages mixed with other, more expressly political, content? If, for example, Frederick's banner had read "LEGALIZE BONG HiTS," he might be thought to receive protection from the majority's rule, which goes to speech "encouraging *illegal* drug use." (emphasis added). But speech advocating change in drug laws might also be perceived of as promoting the disregard of existing drug laws.

. . . To say that illegal drug use is harmful to students, while surely true, does not itself constitute a satisfying explanation because there are many such harms. . . .

Although the dissent avoids some of the majority's pitfalls, I fear that, if adopted as law, it would risk significant interference with reasonable school efforts to maintain discipline. What is a principal to do when a student unfurls a 14–foot banner (carrying an irrelevant or inappropriate message) during a school-related event in an effort to capture the attention of television cameras? Nothing? In my view, a principal or a teacher might reasonably view Frederick's conduct, in this setting, as simply beyond the pale. And a school official, knowing that adolescents often test the outer boundaries of acceptable behavior, may believe it is important (for the offending student and his classmates) to establish when a student has gone too far.

Neither can I simply say that Morse may have taken the right action (confiscating Frederick's banner) but for the wrong reason ("drug speech"). Teachers are neither lawyers nor police officers; and the law should not demand that they fully understand the intricacies of our First Amendment jurisprudence. As the majority rightly points out, the circumstances here called for a quick decision. . . .

All of this is to say that, regardless of the outcome of the constitutional determination, a decision on the underlying First Amendment issue is both difficult and unusually portentous. And that is a reason for us *not to decide* the issue unless we must.

In some instances, it is appropriate to decide a constitutional issue in order to provide "guidance" for the future. But I cannot find much guidance in today's decision. The Court makes clear that school officials may "restrict" student speech that promotes "illegal drug use" and that they may "take steps" to "safeguard" students from speech that encourages "illegal drug use." Beyond "steps" that prohibit the unfurling of banners at school outings, the Court does not explain just what those "restrict[ions]" or those "steps" might be.

Nor, if we are to avoid the risk of interpretations that are too broad or too narrow, is it easy to offer practically valuable guidance. Students will test the limits of acceptable behavior in myriad ways better known to schoolteachers than to judges; school officials need a degree of flexible authority to respond to disciplinary challenges; and the law has always considered the relationship between teachers and students special. Under these circumstances, the more detailed the Court's supervision becomes, the more likely its law will engender further disputes among teachers and students. Consequently, larger numbers of those disputes will likely make their way from the schoolhouse to the courthouse. Yet no one wishes to substitute courts for school boards, or to turn the judge's chambers into the principal's office.

. . .

Justice Stevens, with whom Justice Souter and Justice Ginsburg join, dissenting.

. . .

In my judgment, the First Amendment protects student speech if the message itself neither violates a permissible rule nor expressly advocates conduct that is illegal and harmful to students. This nonsense banner does neither, and the Court does serious violence to the First Amendment in upholding—indeed, lauding—a school's decision to punish Frederick for expressing a view with which it disagreed.

I

. . .

Two cardinal First Amendment principles animate both the Court's opinion in *Tinker* and Justice Harlan's dissent. First, censorship based on the content of speech, particularly censorship that depends on the viewpoint of the speaker, is subject to the most rigorous burden of justification. . . .

Second, punishing someone for advocating illegal conduct is constitutional only when the advocacy is likely to provoke the harm that the government seeks to avoid. See *Brandenburg v. Ohio,* 395 U.S. 444, 449 (1969) *(per curiam)*. . . .

However necessary it may be to modify those principles in the school setting, *Tinker* affirmed their continuing vitality. . . .

Yet today the Court fashions a test that trivializes the two cardinal principles upon which *Tinker* rests. . . . The Court's test invites stark viewpoint discrimination. In this case, for example, the principal has unabashedly acknowledged that she disciplined Frederick because she disagreed with the pro-drug viewpoint she ascribed to the message on the banner—a viewpoint, incidentally, that Frederick has disavowed. . . . [T]he Court's holding in this case strikes at "the heart of the First Amendment" because it upholds a punishment meted out on the basis of a listener's disagreement with her understanding (or, more likely, misunderstanding) of the speaker's viewpoint. . . .

It is also perfectly clear that "promoting illegal drug use" comes nowhere close to proscribable "incitement to imminent lawless action." *Brandenburg,* . . . .Encouraging drug use might well increase the likelihood that a listener will try an illegal drug, but that hardly justifies censorship. . . .

No one seriously maintains that drug advocacy (much less Frederick's ridiculous sign) comes within the vanishingly small category of speech that can be prohibited because of its feared consequences. . . .

II

. . .

... [I]t might well be appropriate to tolerate some targeted viewpoint discrimination in this unique setting. And ... it is possible that our rigid imminence requirement ought to be relaxed at schools. . . .

But it is one thing to restrict speech that *advocates* drug use. It is another thing entirely to prohibit an obscure message with a drug theme that a third party subjectively—and not very reasonably—thinks is tantamount to express advocacy. . . .

There is absolutely no evidence that Frederick's banner's reference to drug paraphernalia "willful[ly]" infringed on anyone's rights or interfered with any of the school's educational programs. . . . [J]ust as we insisted in *Tinker* that the school establish some likely connection between the armbands and their feared consequences, so too JDHS must show that Frederick's supposed advocacy stands a meaningful chance of making otherwise-abstemious students try marijuana.

. . .

To the extent the Court defers to the principal's ostensibly reasonable judgment, it abdicates its constitutional responsibility. The beliefs of third parties, reasonable or otherwise, have never dictated which messages amount to proscribable advocacy. Indeed, it would be a strange constitutional doctrine that would allow the prohibition of only the narrowest category of speech advocating unlawful conduct, ... yet would permit a listener's perceptions to determine which speech deserved constitutional protection.

Such a peculiar doctrine is alien to our case law. . . . Even in *Fraser,* we made no inquiry into whether the school administrators reasonably thought the student's speech was obscene or profane; we rather satisfied ourselves that "[t]he pervasive sexual innuendo in Fraser's speech was plainly offensive to both teachers and students—indeed, to any mature person." . . .[6]

To the extent the Court independently finds that "BONG HiTS 4 JESUS" *objectively* amounts to the advocacy of illegal drug use—in other words, that it can *most* reasonably be interpreted as such—that conclusion practically refutes itself. This is a nonsense message, not advocacy. The Court's feeble effort to divine its hidden meaning is strong evidence of that. . . . Frederick's credible and uncontradicted explanation for the message—he just wanted to get on television—is also relevant because a speaker who does not intend to persuade his audience can hardly be said to be advocating anything. But most importantly, it takes real imagination to read a "cryptic" message (the Court's characterization, not mine) with a slanting drug reference as an incitement to drug use. . . . The notion that the message on this banner would actually persuade either the average student or even the dumbest one to change his or her behavior is most implausible. That the Court believes such a silly message can be proscribed as advocacy underscores the novelty of its position, and suggests that the principle it articulates has no stopping point.

. . .

6. ... When legislatures are entitled to no deference as to whether particular speech amounts to a "clear and present danger," ... it is hard to understand why the Court would so blithely defer to the judgment of a single school principal.

Among other things, the Court's ham-handed, categorical approach is deaf to the constitutional imperative to permit unfettered debate, even among high-school students, about the wisdom of the war on drugs or of legalizing marijuana for medicinal use.... If Frederick's stupid reference to marijuana can ... justify censorship, then high school students everywhere could be forgiven for zipping their mouths about drugs at school lest some "reasonable" observer censor and then punish them for promoting drugs....

Consider, too, that the school district's rule draws no distinction between alcohol and marijuana, but applies evenhandedly to all "substances that are illegal to minors." ... Given the tragic consequences of teenage alcohol consumption—drinking causes far more fatal accidents than the misuse of marijuana—the school district's interest in deterring teenage alcohol use is at least comparable to its interest in preventing marijuana use. Under the Court's reasoning, must the First Amendment give way whenever a school seeks to punish a student for any speech mentioning beer, or indeed anything else that might be deemed risky to teenagers? While I find it hard to believe the Court would support punishing Frederick for flying a "WINE SiPS 4 JESUS" banner—which could quite reasonably be construed either as a protected religious message or as a pro-alcohol message—the breathtaking sweep of its opinion suggests it would.

III

Although this case began with a silly, nonsensical banner, it ends with the Court inventing out of whole cloth a special First Amendment rule permitting the censorship of any student speech that mentions drugs, at least so long as someone could perceive that speech to contain a latent pro-drug message....

. . .

Even in high school, a rule that permits only one point of view to be expressed is less likely to produce correct answers than the open discussion of countervailing views.... Whatever the better policy may be, a full and frank discussion of the costs and benefits of the attempt to prohibit the use of marijuana is far wiser than suppression of speech because it is unpopular.

I respectfully dissent.

CHAPTER 15

PROTECTION OF PENUMBRAL FIRST AMENDMENT RIGHTS

SECTION 3. FREEDOM OF ASSOCIATION

C. LIMITS ON ASSOCIATION MEMBERSHIP POLICIES

Page 1591. Add at end of subsection:

Rumsfeld v. Forum for Academic and Institutional Rights, Inc.

547 U.S. 47, 126 S.Ct. 1297, 164 L.Ed.2d 156 (2006).

Chief Justice Roberts delivered the opinion of the Court.

When law schools began restricting the access of military recruiters to their students because of disagreement with the Government's policy on homosexuals in the military, Congress responded by enacting the Solomon Amendment. See 10 U.S.C.A. § 983 (Supp. 2005). That provision specifies that if any part of an institution of higher education denies military recruiters access equal to that provided other recruiters, the entire institution would lose certain federal funds. The law schools responded by suing, alleging that the Solomon Amendment infringed their First Amendment freedoms of speech and association. The District Court disagreed but was reversed by a divided panel of the Court of Appeals for the Third Circuit....

I

... The Solomon Amendment ... forces institutions to choose between enforcing their nondiscrimination policy against military recruiters ... and continuing to receive specified federal funding.

. . .

.... According to FAIR, the Solomon Amendment was unconstitutional because it forced law schools to choose between exercising their First Amendment right to decide whether to disseminate or accommodate a military recruiter's message, and ensuring the availability of federal funding for their universities.

. . .

113

II

... The Government and FAIR agree on what this statute requires: In order for a law school and its university to receive federal funding, the law school must offer military recruiters the same access to its campus and students that it provides to the nonmilitary recruiter receiving the most favorable access.

Certain law professors participating as *amici*, however, argue that the Government and FAIR misinterpret the statute.... According to these *amici*, the Solomon Amendment's equal-access requirement is satisfied when an institution applies to military recruiters the same policy it applies to all other recruiters. On this reading, a school excluding military recruiters would comply with the Solomon Amendment so long as it also excluded any other employer that violates its nondiscrimination policy.

. . .

We conclude that ... the Government and FAIR correctly interpret the Solomon Amendment. The statute requires the Secretary of Defense to compare the military's "access to campuses" and "access to students" to "the access to campuses and to students that is provided to *any other employer*." ... The statute does not call for an inquiry into why or how the "other employer" secured its access. Under *amici*'s reading, a military recruiter has the same "access" to campuses and students as, say, a law firm when the law firm is permitted on campus to interview students and the military is not. We do not think that the military recruiter has received equal "access" in this situation—regardless of whether the disparate treatment is attributable to the military's failure to comply with the school's nondiscrimination policy.

. . .

Not only does the text support this view, but this interpretation is necessary to give effect to the Solomon Amendment's recent revision. Under the prior version, the statute required "entry" without specifying how military recruiters should be treated once on campus.... The District Court thought that the DOD policy, which required equal access to students once recruiters were on campus, was unwarranted based on the text of the statute.... Congress responded directly to this decision by codifying the DOD policy. Under *amici*'s interpretation, this legislative change had no effect—law schools could still restrict military access, so long as they do so under a generally applicable nondiscrimination policy.... That is rather clearly *not* what Congress had in mind in codifying the DOD policy. We refuse to interpret the Solomon Amendment in a way that negates its recent revision, and indeed would render it a largely meaningless exercise.

We therefore read the Solomon Amendment the way both the Government and FAIR interpret it. It is insufficient for a law school to treat the military as it treats all other employers who violate its nondiscrimination policy. Under the statute, military recruiters must be given the same access as recruiters who comply with the policy.

III

. . .

Although Congress has broad authority to legislate on matters of military recruiting, it nonetheless chose to secure campus access for military recruiters indirectly, through its Spending Clause power. . . .

Congress' power to regulate military recruiting under the Solomon Amendment is arguably greater because universities are free to decline the federal funds. In Grove City College v. Bell, 465 U.S. 555, 575–576 (1984), we rejected a private college's claim that conditioning federal funds on its compliance with Title IX of the Education Amendments of 1972 violated the First Amendment. . . .

Other decisions, however, recognize a limit on Congress' ability to place conditions on the receipt of funds. We recently held that " 'the government may not deny a benefit to a person on a basis that infringes his constitutionally protected . . . freedom of speech even if he has no entitlement to that benefit.' " United States v. American Library Assn., Inc., 539 U.S. 194, 210 (2003). . . . Under this principle, known as the unconstitutional conditions doctrine, the Solomon Amendment would be unconstitutional if Congress could not directly require universities to provide military recruiters equal access to their students.

This case does not require us to determine when a condition placed on university funding goes beyond the "reasonable" choice offered in *Grove City* and becomes an unconstitutional condition. It is clear that a funding condition cannot be unconstitutional if it could be constitutionally imposed directly. . . . Because the First Amendment would not prevent Congress from directly imposing the Solomon Amendment's access requirement, the statute does not place an unconstitutional condition on the receipt of federal funds.

A

The Solomon Amendment neither limits what law schools may say nor requires them to say anything. Law schools remain free under the statute to express whatever views they may have on the military's congressionally mandated employment policy, all the while retaining eligibility for federal funds. . . . As a general matter, the Solomon Amendment regulates conduct, not speech. It affects what law schools must *do*—afford equal access to military recruiters— not what they may or may not *say*.

. . .

1

Some of this Court's leading First Amendment precedents have established the principle that freedom of speech prohibits the government from telling people what they must say. In West Virginia Bd. of Ed. v. Barnette, 319 U.S. 624, 642 (1943), we held unconstitutional a state law requiring schoolchildren to recite the Pledge of Allegiance and to salute the flag. And in Wooley v. Maynard, 430 U.S. 705, 717 (1977), we held unconstitutional another that required New Hampshire motorists to display the state motto—"Live Free or Die"—on their license plates.

The Solomon Amendment does not require any similar expression by law schools. . . .

. . . . The Solomon Amendment, unlike the laws at issue in those cases, does not dictate the content of the speech at all, which is only "compelled" if, and to the extent, the school provides such speech for other recruiters. There is nothing in this case approaching a Government-mandated pledge or motto that the school must endorse.

The compelled speech to which the law schools point is plainly incidental to the Solomon Amendment's regulation of conduct. . . . Compelling a law school that sends scheduling e-mails for other recruiters to send one for a military recruiter is simply not the same as forcing a student to pledge allegiance, or forcing a Jehovah's Witness to display the motto "Live Free or Die," and it trivializes the freedom protected in *Barnette* and *Wooley* to suggest that it is.

2

Our compelled-speech cases are not limited to the situation in which an individual must personally speak the government's message. We have also in a number of instances limited the government's ability to force one speaker to host or accommodate another speaker's message. See Hurley v. Irish–American Gay, Lesbian and Bisexual Group of Boston, Inc., 515 U.S. 557, 566 (1995) (state law cannot require a parade to include a group whose message the parade's organizer does not wish to send); Pacific Gas & Elec. Co. v. Public Util. Comm'n of Cal., 475 U.S. 1, 20–21 (1986) . . . (state agency cannot require a utility company to include a third-party newsletter in its billing envelope); Miami Herald Publishing Co. v. Tornillo, 418 U.S. 241, 258 (1974) (right-of-reply statute violates editors' right to determine the content of their newspapers). . . .

. . .

In this case, accommodating the military's message does not affect the law schools' speech, because the schools are not speaking when they host interviews and recruiting receptions. Unlike a parade organizer's choice of parade contingents, a law school's decision to allow recruiters on campus is not inherently expressive. Law schools facilitate recruiting to assist their students in obtaining jobs. A law school's recruiting services lack the expressive quality of a parade, a newsletter, or the editorial page of a newspaper; its accommodation of a military recruiter's message is not compelled speech because the accommodation does not sufficiently interfere with any message of the school.

. . .

. . . Nothing about recruiting suggests that law schools agree with any speech by recruiters, and nothing in the Solomon Amendment restricts what the law schools may say about the military's policies. We have held that high school students can appreciate the difference between speech a school sponsors and speech the school permits because legally required to do so, pursuant to an equal access policy. Board of Ed. of Westside Community Schools (Dist. 66) v. Mergens, 496 U.S. 226, 250 (1990). . . . Surely students have not lost that ability by the time they get to law school.

3

Having rejected the view that the Solomon Amendment impermissibly regulates speech, we must still consider whether the expressive nature of the conduct regulated by the statute brings that conduct within the First Amendment's protection. In *O'Brien,* we recognized that some forms of " 'symbolic speech' " were deserving of First Amendment protection. . . . But we rejected the view that "conduct can be labeled 'speech' whenever the person engaging in the conduct intends thereby to express an idea." . . . Instead, we have extended First Amendment protection only to conduct that is inherently expressive. In Texas v. Johnson, 491 U.S. 397, 406 (1989), for example, we applied *O'Brien* and held that burning the American flag was sufficiently expressive to warrant First Amendment protection.

. . .

The expressive component of a law school's actions is not created by the conduct itself but by the speech that accompanies it. The fact that such explanatory speech is necessary is strong evidence that the conduct at issue here is not so inherently expressive that it warrants protection under *O'Brien.* If combining speech and conduct were enough to create expressive conduct, a regulated party could always transform conduct into "speech" simply by talking about it. For instance, if an individual announces that he intends to express his disapproval of the Internal Revenue Service by refusing to pay his income taxes, we would have to apply *O'Brien* to determine whether the Tax Code violates the First Amendment. Neither *O'Brien* nor its progeny supports such a result.

. . .

B

The Solomon Amendment does not violate law schools' freedom of speech, but the First Amendment's protection extends beyond the right to speak. We have recognized a First Amendment right to associate for the purpose of speaking, which we have termed a "right of expressive association." See, e.g., Boy Scouts of America v. Dale, 530 U.S. 640, 644 (2000). The reason we have extended First Amendment protection in this way is clear: The right to speak is often exercised most effectively by combining one's voice with the voices of others. See Roberts v. United States Jaycees, 468 U.S. 609, 622 (1984). If the government were free to restrict individuals' ability to join together and speak, it could essentially silence views that the First Amendment is intended to protect.

. . .

FAIR argues that the Solomon Amendment violates law schools' freedom of expressive association. According to FAIR, law schools' ability to express their message that discrimination on the basis of sexual orientation is wrong is significantly affected by the presence of military recruiters on campus and the schools' obligation to assist them. . . .

In *Dale,* we held that the Boy Scouts' freedom of expressive association was violated by New Jersey's public accommodations law, which required the organization to accept a homosexual as a scoutmaster. After determining that the Boy Scouts was an expressive association, that "the forced inclusion of Dale would significantly affect its expression," and that the State's interests did not justify this intrusion, we concluded that the Boy Scout's First Amendment rights were violated. . . .

The Solomon Amendment, however, does not similarly affect a law school's associational rights. To comply with the statute, law schools must allow military recruiters on campus and assist them in whatever way the school chooses to assist other employers. Law schools therefore "associate" with military recruiters in the sense that they interact with them. But recruiters are not part of the law school. Recruiters are, by definition, outsiders who come onto campus for the limited purpose of trying to hire students—not to become members of the school's expressive association. This distinction is critical. Unlike the public accommodations law in *Dale*, the Solomon Amendment does not force a law school " 'to accept members it does not desire.' " . . . The law schools *say* that allowing military recruiters equal access impairs their own expression by requiring them to associate with the recruiters, but just as saying conduct is undertaken for expressive purposes cannot make it symbolic speech, . . . so too a speaker cannot "erect a shield" against laws requiring access "simply by asserting" that mere association "would impair its message." . . . .

FAIR correctly notes that the freedom of expressive association protects more than just a group's membership decisions. For example, we have held laws unconstitutional that require disclosure of membership lists for groups seeking anonymity, Brown v. Socialist Workers '74 Campaign Comm. (Ohio), 459 U.S. 87, 101–102 (1982), or impose penalties or withhold benefits based on membership in a disfavored group, Healy v. James, 408 U.S. 169, 180–184 (1972). Although these laws did not directly interfere with an organization's composition, they made group membership less attractive, raising the same First Amendment concerns about affecting the group's ability to express its message.

The Solomon Amendment has no similar effect on a law school's associational rights. Students and faculty are free to associate to voice their disapproval of the military's message; nothing about the statute affects the composition of the group by making group membership less desirable. The Solomon Amendment therefore does not violate a law school's First Amendment rights. A military recruiter's mere presence on campus does not violate a law school's right to associate, regardless of how repugnant the law school considers the recruiter's message.

* * *

In this case, FAIR has attempted to stretch a number of First Amendment doctrines well beyond the sort of activities these doctrines protect. The law schools object to having to treat military recruiters like other recruiters, but that regulation of conduct does not violate the First Amendment. To the extent that the Solomon Amendment incidentally affects expression, the law schools' effort to cast themselves as just like the schoolchildren in *Barnette*, the parade organizers in *Hurley,* and the Boy Scouts in *Dale* plainly overstates the expressive nature of their activity and the impact of the Solomon Amendment on it, while exaggerating the reach of our First Amendment precedents.

Because Congress could require law schools to provide equal access to military recruiters without violating the schools' freedoms of speech or association, the Court of Appeals erred in holding that the Solomon Amendment likely violates the First Amendment. We therefore reverse the judgment of the Third

Circuit and remand the case for further proceedings consistent with this opinion.

It is so ordered.

Justice Alito took no part in the consideration or decision of this case.

D. COMPULSORY ASSOCIATION MEMBERSHIP

Page 1594. Add after Keller v. State Bar of California:

DAVENPORT v. WASHINGTON EDUCATION ASSOCIATION, ___ U.S. ___, 127 S.Ct. 2372, ___ L.Ed.2d ___ (2007). Like many States, Washington authorizes public-sector unions to negotiate agency-shop agreements permitting the unions to charge nonmembers an agency fee equivalent to the full membership dues of the union and to have this fee collected by the employer through payroll deductions. A voter-approved initiative called the Fair Campaign Practices Act later provided, in § 760, as follows, however: "A labor organization may not use agency shop fees paid by an individual who is not a member of the organization to make contributions or expenditures to influence an election or to operate a political committee, unless affirmatively authorized by the individual." In a suit against a public employees' union for noncompliance, the Court rejected the union's constitutional defense and held "that it does not violate the First Amendment for a State to require that its public-sector unions receive affirmative authorization from a nonmember before spending that nonmember's agency fees for election-related purposes."

Justice Scalia's opinion for the majority noted that "unions have no constitutional entitlement to the fees of nonmember-employees" at all, so the imposition of a "modest limitation" on the "extraordinary benefit" the State granted the union to be able to "levy fees on government employees who do not wish to join the union" was of no great constitutional concern. This was not a restriction "on how a regulated entity may spend money that has come into its possession without the assistance of governmental coercion of its employees.... As applied to public-sector unions, § 760 is ... a condition placed upon the union's extraordinary *state* entitlement to acquire and spend *other people's* money." The Court also rejected the union's contention that § 760 "unconstitutionally draws distinctions based on the content of the union's speech, requiring affirmative consent only for election-related expenditures...." It said in part, and explicitly as applied to public-sector unions only:

> "... We do not believe that the voters of Washington impermissibly distorted the marketplace of ideas when they placed a reasonable, viewpoint-neutral limitation on the State's general authorization allowing public-sector unions to acquire and spend the money of government employees.... [T]he voters of Washington sought to protect the integrity of the election process, ... which the voters evidently thought was being impaired by the infusion of money extracted from nonmembers of unions without their consent. The restriction on the state-bestowed entitlement was thus limited to the state-created harm that the voters sought to remedy. The voters did not have to enact an across-the-board limitation on the use of nonmembers' agency fees by public-sector unions in order to vindicate their more narrow concern with the integrity of the election process.... [W]hen totally proscribable speech is at issue, content-based

regulation is permissible so long as 'there is no realistic possibility that official suppression of ideas is afoot.' . . . [T]he same is true when, as here, an extraordinary and totally repealable authorization to coerce payment from government employees is at issue. Even if it be thought necessary that the content limitation be reasonable and viewpoint neutral, the statute satisfies that requirement. Quite obviously, no suppression of ideas is afoot, since the union remains as free as any other entity to participate in the electoral process with all available funds other than the state-coerced agency fees lacking affirmative permission. In sum, given the unique context of public-sector agency-shop arrangements, the content-based nature of § 760 does not violate the First Amendment.''

Page 1599.   Replace Board of Regents of University of Wisconsin System v. Southworth:

Johanns v. Livestock Marketing Association

544 U.S. 550, 125 S.Ct. 2055, 161 L.Ed.2d 896 (2005).

Justice Scalia delivered the opinion of the Court.

For the third time in eight years, we consider whether a federal program that finances generic advertising to promote an agricultural product violates the First Amendment. In these cases, unlike the previous two, the dispositive question is whether the generic advertising at issue is the Government's own speech and therefore is exempt from First Amendment scrutiny.

I

A

The Beef Promotion and Research Act of 1985 (Beef Act or Act) . . . announces a federal policy of promoting the marketing and consumption of "beef and beef products," using funds raised by an assessment on cattle sales and importation. . . . The statute directs the Secretary of Agriculture to implement this policy by issuing a Beef Promotion and Research Order (Beef Order or Order) . . . and specifies four key terms it must contain: The Secretary is to appoint a Cattlemen's Beef Promotion and Research Board (Beef Board or Board), whose members are to be a geographically representative group of beef producers and importers, nominated by trade associations. . . . The Beef Board is to convene an Operating Committee, composed of 10 Beef Board members and 10 representatives named by a federation of state beef councils . . . The Secretary is to impose a $1-per-head assessment (or "checkoff") on all sales or importation of cattle and a comparable assessment on imported beef products. . . . And the assessment is to be used to fund beef-related projects, including promotional campaigns, designed by the Operating Committee and approved by the Secretary. . . .

. . .

B

Respondents are two associations whose members collect and pay the checkoff, and several individuals who raise and sell cattle subject to the checkoff. . . . They sued the Secretary, the Department of Agriculture, and the

Board in Federal District Court on a number of constitutional and statutory grounds not before us—in particular, that the Board impermissibly used checkoff funds to send communications supportive of the beef program to beef producers. . . .

While the litigation was pending, we held in United States v. United Foods, Inc., . . . that a mandatory checkoff for generic mushroom advertising violated the First Amendment. Noting that the mushroom program closely resembles the beef program, respondents amended their complaint to assert a First Amendment challenge to the use of the beef checkoff for promotional activity. . . .

After a bench trial, the District Court ruled for respondents on their First Amendment claim. . . .

The Court of Appeals for the Eighth Circuit affirmed. . . .

. . .

II

We have sustained First Amendment challenges to allegedly compelled expression in two categories of cases: true "compelled speech" cases, in which an individual is obliged personally to express a message he disagrees with, imposed by the government; and "compelled subsidy" cases, in which an individual is required by the government to subsidize a message he disagrees with, expressed by a private entity. We have not heretofore considered the First Amendment consequences of government-compelled subsidy of the government's own speech.

We first invalidated an outright compulsion of speech in West Virginia Bd. of Ed. v. Barnette, 319 U.S. 624 (1943). . . . We held that the First Amendment does not "le[ave] it open to public authorities to compel [a person] to utter" a message with which he does not agree. . . . Likewise, in Wooley v. Maynard, 430 U.S. 705 (1977), we held that requiring a New Hampshire couple to bear the State's motto, "Live Free or Die," on their cars' license plates was an impermissible compulsion of expression. Obliging people to "use their private property as a 'mobile billboard' for the State's ideological message" amounted to impermissible compelled expression. . . .

The reasoning of these compelled-speech cases has been carried over to certain instances in which individuals are compelled not to speak, but to subsidize a private message with which they disagree. Thus, although we have upheld state-imposed requirements that lawyers be members of the state bar and pay its annual dues, and that public-school teachers either join the labor union representing their "shop" or pay "service fees" equal to the union dues, we have invalidated the use of the compulsory fees to fund speech on political matters. See Keller v. State Bar of Cal., 496 U.S. 1, (1990); Abood v. Detroit Bd. of Ed., 431 U.S. 209 (1977). Bar or union speech with such content, we held, was not germane to the regulatory interests that justified compelled membership, and accordingly, making those who disagreed with it pay for it violated the First Amendment. . . .

These latter cases led us to sustain a compelled-subsidy challenge to an assessment very similar to the beef checkoff, imposed to fund mushroom advertising. *United Foods*, supra. . . . Deciding the case on the assumption that the advertising was private speech, not government speech, . . . we concluded that *Abood* and *Keller* were controlling. . . .

III

Respondents . . . assert that the challenged promotional campaigns differ dispositively from the type of government speech that, our cases suggest, is not susceptible to First Amendment challenge. They point to the role of the Beef Board and its Operating Committee in designing the promotional campaigns, and to the use of a mandatory assessment on beef producers to fund the advertising. We consider each in turn.

A

The Secretary of Agriculture does not write ad copy himself. Rather, the Beef Board's promotional campaigns are designed by the Beef Board's Operating Committee, only half of whose members are Beef Board members appointed by the Secretary. . . . Respondents contend that speech whose content is effectively controlled by a nongovernmental entity—the Operating Committee—cannot be considered "government speech." We need not address this contention, because we reject its premise. The message of the promotional campaigns is effectively controlled by the Federal Government itself.

. . .

B

Respondents also contend that the beef program does not qualify as "government speech" because it is funded by a targeted assessment on beef producers, rather than by general revenues. This funding mechanism, they argue, has two relevant effects: it gives control over the beef program not to politically accountable legislators, but to a narrow interest group that will pay no heed to respondents' dissenting views, and it creates the perception that the advertisements speak for beef producers such as respondents.

We reject the first point. The compelled-*subsidy* analysis is altogether unaffected by whether the funds for the promotions are raised by general taxes or through a targeted assessment. Citizens may challenge compelled support of private speech, but have no First Amendment right not to fund government speech. And that is no less true when the funding is achieved through targeted assessments devoted exclusively to the program to which the assessed citizens object. . . .

. . . The Secretary of Agriculture, a politically accountable official, oversees the program, appoints and dismisses the key personnel, and retains absolute veto power over the advertisements' content, right down to the wording. . . .

. . .

* * *

Respondents' complaint asserted a number of other grounds for declaring the Beef Act, the Beef Order, or both invalid in their entirety. The District Court, having enjoined the Act and the Order on the basis of the First Amendment, had no occasion to address these other grounds. Respondents may now proceed on these other claims. . . .

. . .

Justice Thomas, concurring.

I join the Court's opinion. I continue to believe that "[a]ny regulation that compels the funding of advertising must be subjected to the most stringent First Amendment scrutiny." . . . At the same time, I recognize that this principle must be qualified where the regulation compels the funding of speech that is the government's own. It cannot be that all taxpayers have a First Amendment objection to taxpayer-funded government speech, even if the funded speech is not "germane" to some broader regulatory program. . . .

. . .

Justice Breyer, concurring.

The beef checkoff program in these cases is virtually identical to the mushroom checkoff program in United States v. United Foods, Inc., which the Court struck down on First Amendment grounds. The "government speech" theory the Court adopts today was not before us in United Foods, and we declined to consider it when it was raised at the eleventh hour. . . .

I remain of the view that the assessments in these cases are best described as a form of economic regulation. However, I recognize that a majority of the Court does not share that view. Now that we have had an opportunity to consider the "government speech" theory, I accept it as a solution to the problem presented by these cases. With the caveat that I continue to believe that my dissent in *United Foods* offers a preferable approach, I join the Court's opinion.

Justice Ginsburg, concurring in the judgment.

I resist ranking the promotional messages . . . as government speech. . . . I remain persuaded, however, that the assessments in these cases qualify as permissible economic regulation. . . . For that reason, I concur in the judgment.

Justice Kennedy, dissenting.

I join Justice Souter's dissenting opinion, which demonstrates with persuasive analysis why the speech at issue here cannot meaningfully be considered government speech at all. I would reserve for another day the difficult First Amendment questions that would arise if the government were to target a discrete group of citizens to pay even for speech that the government does "embrace as publicly as it speaks."

Justice Souter, with whom Justice Stevens and Justice Kennedy join, dissenting.

. . .

. . . [I]n *United Foods* . . . we left open the possibility that a compelled subsidy would be justifiable not only as one element of an otherwise valid regulatory scheme, but also as speech of the Government itself, which the Government may pay for with revenue (usually from taxes) exacted from those who dissent from the message as well as from those who agree with it or do not care about it. Not surprisingly, the Government argues here that the beef advertising is its own speech, exempting it from the First Amendment bar against extracting special subsidies from those unwilling to underwrite an objectionable message.

The Court accepts the defense unwisely. The error is not that government speech can never justify compelling a subsidy, but that a compelled subsidy should not be justifiable by speech unless the government must put that speech forward as its own. Otherwise there is no check whatever on government's power to compel special speech subsidies, and the rule of *United Foods* is a dead letter. I take the view that if government relies on the government-speech doctrine to compel specific groups to fund speech with targeted taxes, it must make itself politically accountable by indicating that the content actually is a government message, not just the statement of one self-interested group the government is currently willing to invest with power. Sometimes, as in these very cases, government can make an effective disclosure only by explicitly labeling the speech as its own. Because the Beef Act fails to require the Government to show its hand, I would affirm the judgment of the Court of Appeals holding the Act unconstitutional, and I respectfully dissent from the Court's decision to condone this compelled subsidy.

. . .

The adequacy of the democratic process to render the subsidization of government speech tolerable is, naturally, tied to the character of the subsidy. For when government funds its speech with general tax revenue, as it usually does, no individual taxpayer or group of taxpayers can lay claim to a special, or even a particularly strong, connection to the money spent (and hence to the speech funded).... Outrage is likely to be rare, and disagreement tends to stay temperate. But the relative palatability of a remote subsidy shared by every taxpayer is not to be found when the speech is funded with targeted taxes. For then, as here, the particular interests of those singled out to pay the tax are closely linked with the expression, and taxpayers who disagree with it suffer a more acute limitation on their presumptive autonomy as speakers to decide what to say and what to pay for others to say....

. . .

In sum, the First Amendment cannot be implemented by sanctioning government deception by omission (or by misleading statement) of the sort the Court today condones, and expression that is not ostensibly governmental, which government is not required to embrace as publicly as it speaks, cannot constitute government speech sufficient to justify enforcement of a targeted subsidy to broadcast it. The Court of Appeals thus correctly held that *United Foods* renders the Beef Act's mandatory-assessment provisions unconstitutional.

SECTION 4. APPLICATION OF THE FIRST AMENDMENT TO GOVERNMENT REGULATION OF ELECTIONS

A. CHOOSING AND ELECTING CANDIDATES FOR PUBLIC OFFICE

Page 1616. Add at end of subsection:

Clingman v. Beaver

544 U.S. 581, 125 S.Ct. 2029, 161 L.Ed.2d 920 (2005).

Justice Thomas delivered the opinion of the Court, except as to Part II–A.

Oklahoma has a semiclosed primary system, in which a political party may invite only its own party members and voters registered as Independents to vote in the party's primary. The Court of Appeals held that this system violates the right to freedom of association of the Libertarian Party of Oklahoma (LPO) and several Oklahomans who are registered members of the Republican and Democratic parties. We hold that it does not.

I

Oklahoma's election laws provide that only registered members of a political party may vote in the party's primary . . . unless the party opens its primary to registered Independents as well. . . . In May 2000, the LPO notified the secretary of the Oklahoma State Election Board that it wanted to open its upcoming primary to all registered Oklahoma voters, without regard to their party affiliation. . . . [T]he secretary agreed as to Independent voters, but not as to voters registered with other political parties. The LPO and several Republican and Democratic voters then sued for declaratory and injunctive relief in the United States District Court for the Western District of Oklahoma, alleging that Oklahoma's semiclosed primary law unconstitutionally burdens their First Amendment right to freedom of political association. . . .

. . . The District Court . . . upheld the semiclosed primary statute as constitutional. . . .

On appeal, the Court of Appeals for the Tenth Circuit reversed. . . . [It] concluded that the State's semiclosed primary statute imposed a severe burden on respondents' associational rights. . . . Finding none of Oklahoma's interests compelling, the Court of Appeals enjoined Oklahoma from using its semiclosed primary law. Because the Court of Appeals' decision not only prohibits Oklahoma from using its primary system but also casts doubt on the semiclosed primary laws of 23 other States, we granted certiorari. . . .

II

The Constitution grants States "broad power to prescribe the 'Time, Places and Manner of holding Elections for Senators and Representatives,' Art 1, § 4, cl. 1, which power is matched by state control over the election process for state offices." . . . We have held that the First Amendment, among other things, protects the right of citizens "to band together in promoting among the electorate candidates who espouse their political views." California Democratic Party v. Jones, 530 U.S. 567. Regulations that impose severe burdens on associational rights must be narrowly tailored to serve a compelling state interest. . . . However, when regulations impose lesser burdens, "a State's important regulatory interests will usually be enough to justify reasonable, nondiscriminatory restrictions." . . . This case presents a question . . . whether a State may prevent a political party from inviting registered voters of other parties to vote in its primary . . . We are persuaded that any burden Oklahoma's semiclosed primary imposes is minor and justified by legitimate state interests. . . .

A

At the outset, we note that Oklahoma's semiclosed primary system is unlike other laws this Court has held to infringe associational rights. Oklahoma has not sought through its electoral system to . . . compel the LPO's association with unwanted members or voters, see *Jones*, supra, ... The LPO is free to canvass the electorate, enroll or exclude potential members, nominate the candidate of its choice, and engage in the same electoral activities as every other political party in Oklahoma. Oklahoma merely prohibits the LPO from leaving the selection of its candidates to people who are members of another political party. . . .

In other words, the Republican and Democratic voters who have brought this action do not want to associate with the LPO, at least not in any formal sense. They wish to remain registered with the Republican, Democratic, or Reform parties, and yet to assist in selecting the Libertarian Party's candidates for the general election. Their interest is in casting a vote for a Libertarian candidate in a particular primary election, rather than in banding together with fellow citizens committed to the LPO's political goals and ideas. . . . And the LPO is happy to have their votes, if not their membership on the party rolls.

However, a voter who is unwilling to disaffiliate from another party to vote in the LPO's primary forms little "association" with the LPO—nor the LPO with him. . . .

      . . .

. . . Oklahoma's law does not regulate the LPO's internal processes, its authority to exclude unwanted members, or its capacity to communicate with the public. . . . Oklahoma conditions the party's ability to welcome a voter into its primary on the voter's willingness to dissociate from his current party of choice. If anything, it is "[t]he moment of choosing the party's nominee" that matters far more, . . . for that is " 'the crucial juncture at which the appeal to common principles may be translated into concerted action, and hence to political power in the community,' ". . . . If a party may be prevented from associating with the candidate of its choice . . . because that candidate refuses to disaffiliate from another political party, a party may also be prevented from associating with a voter who refuses to do the same. . . .

      . . .

B

      . . .

. . . To deem ordinary and widespread burdens like these severe would subject virtually every electoral regulation to strict scrutiny, hamper the ability of States to run efficient and equitable elections, and compel federal courts to rewrite state electoral codes. The Constitution does not require that result, for it is beyond question "that States may, and inevitably must, enact reasonable regulations of parties, elections, and ballots to reduce election-and campaign-related disorder." . . .

C

When a state electoral provision places no heavy burden on associational rights, "a State's important regulatory interests will usually be enough to justify reasonable, nondiscriminatory restrictions." . . . Here, Oklahoma's semi-closed primary advances a number of regulatory interests that this Court recognizes as important: It "preserv[es] [political] parties as viable and identifiable interest groups," . . . enhances parties' electioneering and party-building efforts, . . . and guards against party raiding and "sore loser" candidacies by spurned primary contenders. . . . It does not matter that the LPO is willing to risk the surrender of its identity in exchange for electoral success. Oklahoma's interest is independent and concerns the integrity of its primary system. The State wants to "avoid primary election outcomes which would tend to confuse or mislead the general voting population to the extent [it] relies on party labels as representative of certain ideologies." . . . Oklahoma reasonably has concluded that opening the LPO's primary to all voters regardless of party affiliation would undermine the crucial role of political parties in the primary process. Cf. *Jones*, 530 U.S., at 574.

. . .

* * *

Oklahoma remains free to allow the LPO to invite registered voters of other parties to vote in its primary. But the Constitution leaves that choice to the democratic process, not to the courts. . . .

Justice O'Connor, with whom Justice Breyer joins except as to Part III, concurring in part and concurring in the judgment.

I join the Court's opinion except for Part II–A. Although I agree with most of the Court's reasoning, I write separately to emphasize two points. First, I think respondents' claim implicates important associational interests, and I see no reason to minimize those interests to dispose of this case. Second, I agree with the Court that only Oklahoma's semiclosed primary law is properly before us, that standing alone it imposes only a modest, nondiscriminatory burden on respondents' associational rights, and that this burden is justified by the State's legitimate regulatory interests. I note, however, that there are some grounds for concern that other state laws may unreasonably restrict voters' ability to change party registration so as to participate in the Libertarian Party of Oklahoma's (LPO) primary. A realistic assessment of regulatory burdens on associational rights would, in an appropriate case, require examination of the cumulative effects of the State's overall scheme governing primary elections; and any finding of a more severe burden would trigger more probing review of the justifications offered by the State.

. . .

. . . [W]here a party invites a voter to participate in its primary and the voter seeks to do so, we should begin with the premise that there are significant associational interests at stake. From this starting point, we can then ask to what extent and in what manner the State may justifiably restrict those interests.

. . .

Justice Stevens, with whom Justice Ginsburg joins, and with whom Justice Souter joins as to Parts I, II, and III, dissenting.

The Court's decision today diminishes the value of two important rights protected by the First Amendment: the individual citizen's right to vote for the candidate of her choice and a political party's right to define its own mission.

No one would contend that a citizen's membership in either the Republican or the Democratic Party could disqualify her from attending political functions sponsored by another party, or from voting for a third party's candidate in a general election. If a third party invites her to participate in its primary election, her right to support the candidate of her choice merits constitutional protection, whether she elects to make a speech, to donate funds, or to cast a ballot. The importance of vindicating that individual right far outweighs any public interest in punishing registered Republicans or Democrats for acts of disloyalty. The balance becomes even more lopsided when the individual right is reinforced by the right of the Libertarian Party of Oklahoma (LPO) to associate with willing voters.

In concluding that the State's interests override those important values, the Court focuses on interests that are not legitimate. States do not have a valid interest in manipulating the outcome of elections, in protecting the major parties from competition, or in stunting the growth of new parties. While States do have a valid interest in conducting orderly elections and in encouraging the maximum participation of voters, neither of these interests overrides (or, indeed, even conflicts with) the valid interests of both the LPO and the voters who wish to participate in its primary.

In the final analysis, this case is simple.... Oklahoma ... denies a party the right to invite willing voters to participate in its primary elections. I would therefore affirm the Court of Appeals' judgment.

B. POLITICAL FUNDRAISING AND EXPENDITURES

Page 1654. Add at end of subsection:

Federal Election Commission v. Wisconsin Right to Life, Inc.

___ U.S. ___, 127 S.Ct. 2652, ___ L.Ed.2d ___ (2007).

Chief Justice Roberts announced the judgment of the Court and delivered the opinion of the Court with respect to Parts I and II, and an opinion with respect to Parts III and IV, in which Justice Alito joins.

Section 203 of the Bipartisan Campaign Reform Act of 2002 (BCRA) ... makes it a federal crime for any corporation to broadcast, shortly before an election, any communication that names a federal candidate for elected office and is targeted to the electorate. In *McConnell v. Federal Election Comm'n*, 540 U.S. 93 (2003), this Court considered whether § 203 was facially overbroad under the First Amendment because it captured within its reach not only campaign speech, or "express advocacy," but also speech about public issues more generally, or "issue advocacy," that mentions a candidate for federal office. The Court concluded that there was no overbreadth concern to the extent the speech in question was the "functional equivalent" of express campaign speech.... On the other hand, the Court "assume[d]" that the interests it had found to "justify the regulation of campaign speech might not apply to the regulation of genuine issue ads." ... The Court nonetheless determined that § 203 was not facially overbroad. Even assuming § 203 "inhibit[ed] some constitutionally protected corporate and union speech," the Court concluded that those challenging the law on its face had failed to carry their "heavy burden" of establishing that all enforcement of the law should therefore be prohibited. . . .

. . .

We now confront . . . an as-applied challenge. Resolving it requires us first to determine whether the speech at issue is the "functional equivalent" of speech expressly advocating the election or defeat of a candidate for federal office, or instead a "genuine issue a[d]." *McConnell*, 540 U.S. at 206, and n. 88. We have long recognized that the distinction between campaign advocacy and issue advocacy "may often dissolve in practical application. Candidates, especially incumbents, are intimately tied to public issues involving legislative proposals and governmental actions." *Buckley v. Valeo*, 424 U.S. 1, 42 (1976) (per curiam). Our development of the law in this area requires us, however, to draw such a line, because we have recognized that the interests held to justify the regulation of campaign speech and its "functional equivalent" "might not apply" to the regulation of issue advocacy. . . .

In drawing that line, the First Amendment requires us to err on the side of protecting political speech rather than suppressing it. We conclude that the speech at issue in this as-applied challenge is not the "functional equivalent" of express campaign speech. We further conclude that the interests held to justify restricting corporate campaign speech or its functional equivalent do not justify restricting issue advocacy, and accordingly we hold that BCRA § 203 is unconstitutional as applied to the advertisements at issue in these cases.

I

Prior to BCRA, corporations were free under federal law to use independent expenditures to engage in political speech so long as that speech did not expressly advocate the election or defeat of a clearly identified federal candidate. . . .

BCRA significantly cut back on corporations' ability to engage in political speech. BCRA § 203, at issue in these cases, makes it a crime for any labor union or incorporated entity-whether the United Steelworkers, the American Civil Liberties Union, or General Motors-to use its general treasury funds to pay for any "electioneering communication." . . . BCRA's definition of "electioneering communication" is clear and expansive. It encompasses any broadcast, cable, or satellite communication that refers to a candidate for federal office and that is aired within 30 days of a federal primary election or 60 days of a federal general election in the jurisdiction in which that candidate is running for office. § 434(f)(3)(A).

Appellee Wisconsin Right to Life, Inc. (WRTL), is a nonprofit, nonstock, ideological advocacy corporation recognized by the Internal Revenue Service as tax exempt under § 501(c)(4) of the Internal Revenue Code. On July 26, 2004, as part of what it calls a "grassroots lobbying campaign," . . . WRTL began broadcasting a radio advertisement entitled "Wedding." The transcript of "Wedding" reads as follows:

" 'PASTOR: And who gives this woman to be married to this man?

" 'BRIDE'S FATHER: Well, as father of the bride, I certainly could. But instead, I'd like to share a few tips on how to properly install drywall. Now you put the drywall up . . .

" 'VOICE–OVER: Sometimes it's just not fair to delay an important decision.

" 'But in Washington it's happening. A group of Senators is using the filibuster delay tactic to block federal judicial nominees from a simple "yes" or "no" vote. So qualified candidates don't get a chance to serve.

" 'It's politics at work, causing gridlock and backing up some of our courts to a state of emergency.

" 'Contact Senators Feingold and Kohl and tell them to oppose the filibuster.

" 'Visit: BeFair.org

" 'Paid for by Wisconsin Right to Life (befair.org), which is responsible for the content of this advertising and not authorized by any candidate or candidate's committee.' " . . .

On the same day, WRTL aired a similar radio ad entitled "Loan." It had also invested treasury funds in producing a television ad entitled "Waiting," which is similar in substance and format to "Wedding" and "Loan."

WRTL planned on running "Wedding," "Waiting," and "Loan" throughout August 2004 and financing the ads with funds from its general treasury. It recognized, however, that as of August 15, 30 days prior to the Wisconsin primary, the ads would be illegal "electioneering communication[s]" under BCRA § 203.

Believing that it nonetheless possessed a First Amendment right to broadcast these ads, WRTL filed suit against the Federal Election Commission (FEC) on July 28, 2004, seeking declaratory and injunctive relief. . . . [The three-judge district court ruled in favor of WRTL and the FEC sought sought review in the Supreme Court.]

. . .

II

Article III's "case-or-controversy requirement subsists through all stages of federal judicial proceedings. . . . [I]t is not enough that a dispute was very much alive when suit was filed." . . . Based on these principles, the FEC argues (though the intervenors do not) that these cases are moot because the 2004 election has passed and WRTL "does not assert any continuing interest in running [its three] advertisements, nor does it identify any reason to believe that a significant dispute over Senate filibusters of judicial nominees will occur in the foreseeable future." . . .

As the [lower court] concluded, however, these cases fit comfortably within the established exception to mootness for disputes capable of repetition, yet evading review. . . .

III

WRTL rightly concedes that its ads are prohibited by BCRA § 203. Each ad clearly identifies Senator Feingold, who was running (unopposed) in the Wisconsin Democratic primary on September 14, 2004, and each ad would have been "targeted to the relevant electorate," . . . during the BCRA blackout period. WRTL further concedes that its ads do not fit under any of BCRA's exceptions to the term "electioneering communication." See § 434(f)(3)(B). The only question, then, is whether it is consistent with the First Amendment for BCRA § 203 to prohibit WRTL from running these three ads.

A

Appellants contend that WRTL should be required to demonstrate that BCRA is unconstitutional as applied to the ads. . . . After all, appellants reason, *McConnell* already held that BCRA § 203 was facially valid. These cases, however, present the separate question whether § 203 may constitutionally be applied to these specific ads. Because BCRA § 203 burdens political speech, it is subject to strict scrutiny. . . . Under strict scrutiny, the Government must prove that applying BCRA to WRTL's ads furthers a compelling interest and is narrowly tailored to achieve that interest. . . .

The strict scrutiny analysis is, of course, informed by our precedents. This Court has already ruled [in *McConnell*] that BCRA survives strict scrutiny to the extent it regulates express advocacy or its functional equivalent. . . . So to the extent the ads in these cases fit this description, the FEC's burden is not onerous; all it need do is point to *McConnell* and explain why it applies here. If, on the other hand, WRTL's ads are not express advocacy or its equivalent, the Government's task is more formidable. It must then demonstrate that banning such ads during the blackout periods is narrowly tailored to serve a compelling interest. No precedent of this Court [including *McConnell*] has yet reached that conclusion.

B

. . .

WRTL and the District Court majority . . . claim that *McConnell* did not adopt any test as the standard for future as-applied challenges. We agree. *McConnell*'s analysis was grounded in the evidentiary record before the Court. Two key studies in the *McConnell* record constituted "the central piece of evidence marshaled by defenders of BCRA's electioneering communication provisions in support of their constitutional validity." . . . Those studies asked "student coders" to separate ads based on whether the students thought the "purpose" of the ad was "to provide information about or urge action on a bill or issue," or "to generate support or opposition for a particular candidate." . . . The studies concluded " 'that BCRA's definition of Electioneering Communications accurately captures those ads that have the purpose or effect of supporting candidates for election to office.' " . . .

When the *McConnell* Court considered the possible facial overbreadth of § 203, it looked to the studies in the record analyzing ads broadcast during the blackout periods, and those studies had classified the ads in terms of intent and effect. The Court's assessment was accordingly phrased in the same terms, which the Court regarded as sufficient to conclude, on the record before it, that the plaintiffs had not "carried their heavy burden of proving" that § 203 was facially overbroad and could not be enforced in any circumstances.... The Court did not explain that it was adopting a particular test for determining what constituted the "functional equivalent" of express advocacy. The fact that the student coders who helped develop the evidentiary record before the Court in *McConnell* looked to intent and effect in doing so, and that the Court dealt with the record on that basis in deciding the facial overbreadth claim, neither compels nor warrants accepting that same standard as the constitutional test for separating, in an as-applied challenge, political speech protected under the First Amendment from that which may be banned.

More importantly, this Court in *Buckley* had already rejected an intent-and-effect test for distinguishing between discussions of issues and candidates.... After noting the difficulty of distinguishing between discussion of issues on the one hand and advocacy of election or defeat of candidates on the other, the *Buckley* Court explained that analyzing the question in terms " 'of intent and of effect' " would afford " 'no security for free discussion.' " ... It therefore rejected such an approach, and *McConnell* did not purport to overrule *Buckley* on this point-or even address what *Buckley* had to say on the subject.

For the reasons regarded as sufficient in Buckley, we decline to adopt a test for as-applied challenges turning on the speaker's intent to affect an election. The test to distinguish constitutionally protected political speech from speech that BCRA may proscribe should provide a safe harbor for those who wish to exercise First Amendment rights. The test should also "reflec[t] our 'profound national commitment to the principle that debate on public issues should be uninhibited, robust, and wide-open.' " ...

Far from serving the values the First Amendment is meant to protect, an intent-based test would chill core political speech by opening the door to a trial on every ad within the terms of § 203, on the theory that the speaker actually intended to affect an election, no matter how compelling the indications that the ad concerned a pending legislative or policy issue. No reasonable speaker would choose to run an ad covered by BCRA if its only defense to a criminal prosecution would be that its motives were pure. An intent-based standard "blankets with uncertainty whatever may be said," and "offers no security for free discussion." ...

. . .

Buckley also explains the flaws of a test based on the actual effect speech will have on an election or on a particular segment of the target audience. Such a test " 'puts the speaker ... wholly at the mercy of the varied understanding of his hearers.' " ... It would also typically lead to a burdensome, expert-driven inquiry, with an indeterminate result. Litigation on such a standard may or may not accurately predict electoral effects, but it will unquestionably chill a substantial amount of political speech.

C

"The freedom of speech ... guaranteed by the Constitution embraces at the least the liberty to discuss publicly and truthfully all matters of public concern without previous restraint or fear of subsequent punishment." ... To safeguard this liberty, the proper standard for an as-applied challenge to BCRA § 203 must be objective, focusing on the substance of the communication rather than amorphous considerations of intent and effect.... It must entail minimal if any discovery, to allow parties to resolve disputes quickly without chilling speech through the threat of burdensome litigation.... And it must eschew "the open-ended rough-and-tumble of factors," which "invit[es] complex argument in a trial court and a virtually inevitable appeal." ...

In light of these considerations, a court should find that an ad is the functional equivalent of express advocacy only if the ad is susceptible of no reasonable interpretation other than as an appeal to vote for or against a specific candidate. Under this test, WRTL's three ads are plainly not the functional equivalent of express advocacy. First, their content is consistent with that of a genuine issue ad: The ads focus on a legislative issue, take a position on the issue, exhort the public to adopt that position, and urge the public to contact public officials with respect to the matter. Second, their content lacks indicia of express advocacy: The ads do not mention an election, candidacy, political party, or challenger; and they do not take a position on a candidate's character, qualifications, or fitness for office.

. . .

Looking beyond the content of WRTL's ads, the FEC and intervenors argue that several "contextual" factors prove that the ads are the equivalent of express advocacy. First, appellants cite evidence that during the same election cycle, WRTL and its Political Action Committee (PAC) actively opposed Senator Feingold's reelection and identified filibusters as a campaign issue. This evidence goes to WRTL's subjective intent in running the ads, and we have already explained that WRTL's intent is irrelevant in an as-applied challenge. Evidence of this sort is therefore beside the point, as it should be-WRTL does not forfeit its right to speak on issues simply because in other aspects of its work it also opposes candidates who are involved with those issues.

Next, the FEC and intervenors seize on the timing of WRTL's ads. They observe that the ads were to be aired near elections but not near actual Senate votes on judicial nominees, and that WRTL did not run the ads after the elections. To the extent this evidence goes to WRTL's subjective intent, it is again irrelevant. To the extent it nonetheless suggests that the ads should be interpreted as express advocacy, it falls short. That the ads were run close to an election is unremarkable in a challenge like this. Every ad covered by BCRA § 203 will by definition air just before a primary or general election. If this were enough to prove that an ad is the functional equivalent of express advocacy, then BCRA would be constitutional in all of its applications....

That the ads were run shortly after the Senate had recessed is likewise unpersuasive. Members of Congress often return to their districts during recess, precisely to determine the views of their constituents; an ad run at that time may succeed in getting more constituents to contact the Representative while he or she is back home. In any event, a group can certainly choose to run an issue ad to coincide with public interest rather than a floor vote. Finally, WRTL did not resume running its ads after the BCRA blackout period because, as it explains, the debate had changed....

The last piece of contextual evidence the FEC and intervenors highlight is the ads' "specific and repeated cross-reference" to a website.... In the middle of the website's homepage, in large type, were the addresses, phone numbers, fax numbers, and email addresses of Senators Feingold and Kohl. Wisconsinites who viewed "Wedding," "Loan," or "Waiting" and wished to contact their Senators-as the ads requested-would be able to obtain the pertinent contact information immediately upon visiting the website. This is fully consistent with viewing WRTL's ads as genuine issue ads. The website also stated both Wisconsin Senators' positions on judicial filibusters, and allowed visitors to sign up for "e-alerts," some of which contained exhortations to vote against Senator Feingold. These details lend the electioneering interpretation of the ads more credence, but again, WRTL's participation in express advocacy in other aspects of its work is not a justification for censoring its issue-related speech. Any express advocacy on the website, already one step removed from the text of the ads themselves, certainly does not render an interpretation of the ads as genuine issue ads unreasonable.

. . .

Because WRTL's ads may reasonably be interpreted as something other than as an appeal to vote for or against a specific candidate, we hold they are not the functional equivalent of express advocacy, and therefore fall outside the scope of McConnell's holding....

IV

BCRA § 203 can be constitutionally applied to WRTL's ads only if it is narrowly tailored to further a compelling interest.... This Court has never recognized a compelling interest in regulating ads, like WRTL's, that are neither express advocacy nor its functional equivalent. The District Court below considered interests that might justify regulating WRTL's ads here, and found none sufficiently compelling.... We reach the same conclusion.

At the outset, we reject the contention that issue advocacy may be regulated because express election advocacy may be, and "the speech involved in so-called issue advocacy is [not] any more core political speech than are words of express advocacy." ... This greater-includes-the-lesser approach is not how strict scrutiny works. A corporate ad expressing support for the local football team could not be regulated on the ground that such speech is less "core" than corporate speech about an election, which we have held may be restricted. A court applying strict scrutiny must ensure that a compelling interest supports each application of a statute restricting speech. That a compelling interest justifies restrictions on express advocacy tells us little about whether a compelling interest justifies restrictions on issue advocacy; the *McConnell* Court itself made just that point.... Such a greater-includes-the-lesser argument would dictate that virtually all corporate speech can be suppressed, since few kinds of speech can lay claim to being as central to the First Amendment as campaign speech. That conclusion is clearly foreclosed by our precedent....

This Court has long recognized "the governmental interest in preventing corruption and the appearance of corruption" in election campaigns.... This interest has been invoked as a reason for upholding contribution limits. As

Buckley explained, "[t]o the extent that large contributions are given to secure a political quid pro quo from current and potential office holders, the integrity of our system of representative democracy is undermined." . . . We have suggested that this interest might also justify limits on electioneering expenditures because it may be that, in some circumstances, "large independent expenditures pose the same dangers of actual or apparent quid pro quo arrangements as do large contributions." . . .

McConnell arguably applied this interest-which this Court had only assumed could justify regulation of express advocacy-to ads that were the "functional equivalent" of express advocacy. . . . But to justify regulation of WRTL's ads, this interest must be stretched yet another step to ads that are not the functional equivalent of express advocacy. Enough is enough. Issue ads like WRTL's are by no means equivalent to contributions, and the quid-pro-quo corruption interest cannot justify regulating them. To equate WRTL's ads with contributions is to ignore their value as political speech.

. . .

Because WRTL's ads are not express advocacy or its functional equivalent, and because appellants identify no interest sufficiently compelling to justify burdening WRTL's speech, we hold that BCRA § 203 is unconstitutional as applied to WRTL's "Wedding," "Loan," and "Waiting" ads.

* * *

These cases are about political speech. The importance of the cases to speech and debate on public policy issues is reflected in the number of diverse organizations that have joined in supporting WRTL before this Court: the American Civil Liberties Union, the National Rifle Association, the American Federation of Labor and Congress of Industrial Organizations, the Chamber of Commerce of the United States of America, Focus on the Family, the Coalition of Public Charities, the Cato Institute, and many others.

Yet, as is often the case in this Court's First Amendment opinions, we have gotten this far in the analysis without quoting the Amendment itself: "Congress shall make no law . . . abridging the freedom of speech." The Framers' actual words put these cases in proper perspective. Our jurisprudence over the past 216 years has rejected an absolutist interpretation of those words, but when it comes to drawing difficult lines in the area of pure political speech-between what is protected and what the Government may ban-it is worth recalling the language we are applying. McConnell held that express advocacy of a candidate or his opponent by a corporation shortly before an election may be prohibited, along with the functional equivalent of such express advocacy. We have no occasion to revisit that determination today. But when it comes to defining what speech qualifies as the functional equivalent of express advocacy subject to such a ban-the issue we do have to decide-we give the benefit of the doubt to speech, not censorship. The First Amendment's command that "Congress shall make no law . . . abridging the freedom of speech" demands at least that.

The judgment of the United States District Court for the District of Columbia is affirmed.

It is so ordered.

Justice Alito, concurring.

I join the principal opinion because I conclude (a) that § 203 of the Bipartisan Campaign Reform Act of 2002 . . . as applied, cannot constitutionally ban any advertisement that may reasonably be interpreted as anything other than an appeal to vote for or against a candidate, (b) that the ads at issue here may reasonably be interpreted as something other than such an appeal, and (c) that because § 203 is unconstitutional as applied to the advertisements before us, it is unnecessary to go further and decide whether § 203 is unconstitutional on its face. If it turns out that the implementation of the as-applied standard set out in the principal opinion impermissibly chills political speech . . . we will presumably be asked in a future case to reconsider the holding in McConnell v. Federal Election Comm'n . . . that § 203 is facially constitutional.

Justice Scalia, with whom Justice Kennedy and Justice Thomas join, concurring in part and concurring in the judgment.

A Moroccan cartoonist once defended his criticism of the Moroccan monarch (lèse majesté being a serious crime in Morocco) as follows: " 'I'm not a revolutionary, I'm just defending freedom of speech. . . . I never said we had to change the king-no, no, no, no! But I said that some things the king is doing, I do not like. Is that a crime?' " Well, in the United States (making due allowance for the fact that we have elected representatives instead of a king) it is a crime, at least if the speaker is a union or a corporation (including not-for-profit public-interest corporations) and if the representative is identified by name within a certain period before a primary or congressional election in which he is running. That is the import of § 203 of the Bipartisan Campaign Reform Act of 2002 (BCRA), the constitutionality of which we upheld three Terms ago in *McConnell v. Federal Election Comm'n,* . . . . As an element essential to that determination of constitutionality, our opinion left open the possibility that a corporation or union could establish that, in the particular circumstances of its case, the ban was unconstitutional because it was (to pursue the analogy) only the king's policies and not his tenure in office that was criticized. Today's cases present the question of what sort of showing is necessary for that purpose. [It] is my view that no test for such a showing can both (1) comport with the requirement of clarity that unchilled freedom of political speech demands, and (2) be compatible with the facial validity of § 203 (as pronounced in *McConnell*). I would therefore reconsider the decision that sets us the unsavory task of separating issue-speech from election-speech with no clear criterion.

. . .

I would overrule that part of the Court's decision in McConnell upholding § 203(a) of BCRA. Accordingly, I join Parts I and II of today's principal opinion and otherwise concur only in the judgment.

Justice Souter with whom Justice Stevens, Justice Ginsburg, and Justice Breyer join, dissenting.

. . .

The indispensable ingredient of a political candidacy is money for advertising. In the 2004 campaign, more than half of the combined expenditures by the two principal presidential candidates (excluding fundraising) went for media time and space. . . . By the end of March 2007, almost a year before the first primary and more than 18 months before the general election, presidential candidates had already raised over $150 million. See Balz, Fundraising Totals Challenge Early Campaign Assumptions, Washington Post, Apr. 17, 2007, p. A1 (citing figures and noting that "[t]he campaign is living up to its reputation as the most expensive in U.S. history"). To reach this total, the leading fundraisers collected over $250,000 per day in the first quarter of 2007, Mullins, Clinton Leads the Money Race, Wall Street Journal, Apr. 16, 2007, p. A8, and the eventual nominees are expected to raise $500 million apiece (about $680,000 per day over a 2–year election cycle), Kirkpatrick and Pilhofer, McCain Lags in Income But Excels in Spending, Report Shows, N.Y. Times, Apr. 15, 2007, p. 20.

The indispensability of these huge sums has two significant consequences for American Government that are particularly on point here. The enormous demands, first, assign power to deep pockets. . . . Candidates occasionally boast about the number of contributors they have, but the headlines speaking in dollars reflect political reality. . . .

Some major contributors get satisfaction from pitching in for their candidates, but political preference fails to account for the frequency of giving "substantial sums to both major national parties," . . . a practice driven "by stark political pragmatism, not by ideological support for either party or their candidates," . . . What the high-dollar pragmatists of either variety get is special access to the officials they help elect, and with it a disproportionate influence on those in power. . . .

Voters know this. Hence, the second important consequence of the demand for big money to finance publicity: pervasive public cynicism. A 2002 poll found that 71 percent of Americans think Members of Congress cast votes based on the views of their big contributors, even when those views differ from the Member's own beliefs about what is best for the country. . . . The same percentage believes that the will of contributors tempts Members to vote against the majority view of their constituents. . . . Almost half of Americans believe that Members often decide how to vote based on what big contributors to their party want, while only a quarter think Members often base their votes on perceptions of what is best for the country or their constituents. . . .

Devoting concentrations of money in self-interested hands to the support of political campaigning therefore threatens the capacity of this democracy to represent its constituents and the confidence of its citizens in their capacity to govern themselves. These are the elements summed up in the notion of political integrity, giving it a value second to none in a free society.

II

If the threat to this value flowing from concentrations of money in politics has reached an unprecedented enormity, it has been gathering force for generations. . . .

. . . .

In sum, Congress in 1907 prohibited corporate contributions to candidates and in 1943 applied the same ban to unions. In 1947, Congress extended the complete ban from contributions to expenditures "in connection with" an election, a phrase so vague that in 1986 we held it must be confined to instances of express advocacy using magic words. Congress determined, in 2002, that corporate and union expenditures for fake issue ads devoid of magic words should be regulated using a narrow definition of "electioneering communication" to reach only broadcast ads that were the practical equivalents of express advocacy. In 2003, this Court found the provision free from vagueness and justified by the concern that drove its enactment.

This century-long tradition of legislation and judicial precedent rests on facing undeniable facts and testifies to an equally undeniable value. Campaign finance reform has been a series of reactions to documented threats to electoral integrity obvious to any voter, posed by large sums of money from corporate or union treasuries, with no redolence of "grassroots" about them. Neither Congress's decisions nor our own have understood the corrupting influence of money in politics as being limited to outright bribery or discrete quid pro quo; campaign finance reform has instead consistently focused on the more pervasive distortion of electoral institutions by concentrated wealth, on the special access and guaranteed favor that sap the representative integrity of American government and defy public confidence in its institutions. From early in the 20th century through the decision in McConnell, we have acknowledged that the value of democratic integrity justifies a realistic response when corporations and labor organizations commit the concentrated moneys in their treasuries to electioneering.

IV

The corporate appellee in these cases, Wisconsin Right to Life (WRTL), is a nonprofit corporation funded to a significant extent by contributions from other corporations. In 2004, WRTL accepted over $315,000 in corporate donations, ... and of its six general fund contributions of $50,000 or more between 2002 and 2005, three, including the largest (for $140,000), came from corporate donors, ...

Throughout the 2004 senatorial campaign, WRTL made no secret of its views about who should win the election and explicitly tied its position to the filibuster issue. Its PAC issued at least two press releases saying that its "Top Election Priorities" were to "Re-elect George W. Bush" and "Send Feingold Packing!" ...

It was under these circumstances that WRTL ran the three television and radio ads in question. The bills for them were not paid by WRTL's PAC, but out of the general treasury with its substantial proportion of corporate contributions; in fact, corporations earmarked more than $50,000 specifically to pay for the ads ...

WRTL's planned airing of the ads had no apparent relation to any Senate filibuster vote but was keyed to the timing of the senatorial election. WRTL began broadcasting the ads on July 26, 2004, four days after the Senate recessed for the summer, and although the filibuster controversy raged on through 2005, WRTL did not resume running the ads after the election.... During the campaign period that the ads did cover, Senator Feingold's support of the filibusters was a prominent issue. His position was well known, and his Republican opponents, who vocally opposed the filibusters, made the issue a major talking point in their campaigns against him.

In sum, any Wisconsin voter who paid attention would have known that Democratic Senator Feingold supported filibusters against Republican presidential judicial nominees, that the propriety of the filibusters was a major issue in the senatorial campaign, and that WRTL along with the Senator's Republican challengers opposed his reelection because of his position on filibusters. Any alert voters who heard or saw WRTL's ads would have understood that WRTL was telling them that the Senator's position on the filibusters should be grounds to vote against him.

Given these facts, it is beyond all reasonable debate that the ads are constitutionally subject to regulation under *McConnell*. There, we noted that BCRA was meant to remedy the problem of "[s]o-called issue ads" being used "to advocate the election or defeat of clearly identified federal candidates." . . . We then gave a paradigmatic example of these electioneering ads subject to regulation, saying that "[l]ittle difference existed . . . between an ad that urged viewers to 'vote against Jane Doe' and one that condemned Jane Doe's record on a particular issue before exhorting viewers to 'call Jane Doe and tell her what you think.'" . . .

The WRTL ads were indistinguishable from the Jane Doe ad; they "condemned [Senator Feingold's] record on a particular issue" and exhorted the public to contact him and "tell [him] what you think." And just as anyone who heard the Jane Doe ad would understand that the point was to defeat Doe, anyone who heard the Feingold ads (let alone anyone who went to the website they named) would know that WRTL's message was to vote against Feingold. If it is now unconstitutional to restrict WRTL's Feingold ads, then it follows that § 203 can no longer be applied constitutionally to McConnell's Jane Doe paradigm.

McConnell's holding that § 203 is facially constitutional is overruled. By what steps does the principal opinion reach this unacknowledged result less than four years after *McConnell* was decided?

A

First, it lays down a new test to identify a severely limited class of ads that may constitutionally be regulated as electioneering communications, a test that is flatly contrary to *McConnell*. An ad is the equivalent of express advocacy and subject to regulation, the opinion says, only if it is "susceptible of no reasonable interpretation other than as an appeal to vote for or against a specific candidate." . . . Since the Feingold ads could, in isolation, be read as at least including calls to communicate views on filibusters to the two Senators, those ads cannot be treated as the functional equivalent of express advocacy to elect or defeat anyone, and therefore may not constitutionally be regulated at all.

But the same could have been said of the hypothetical Jane Doe ad. Its spoken message ended with the instruction to tell Doe what the voter thinks. The same could also have been said of the actual Yellowtail ad. Yet in *McConnell*, we gave the Jane Doe ad as the paradigm of a broadcast message that could be constitutionally regulated as election conduct, and we explicitly described the Yellowtail ad as a "striking example" of one that was "clearly intended to influence the election," . . .

The principal opinion, in other words, simply inverts what we said in *McConnell*. While we left open the possibility of a "genuine" or "pure" issue ad that might not be open to regulation under § 203, . . . we meant that an issue ad without campaign advocacy could escape the restriction. The implication of the adjectives "genuine" and "pure" is unmistakable: if an ad is reasonably understood as going beyond a discussion of issues (that is, if it can be understood as electoral advocacy), then by definition it is not "genuine" or "pure." But the principal opinion inexplicably wrings the opposite conclusion from those words: if an ad is susceptible to any "reasonable interpretation other than as an appeal to vote for or against a specific candidate," then it must be a "pure" or "genuine" issue ad. . . . This stands *McConnell* on its head, and on this reasoning it is possible that even some ads with magic words could not be regulated.

. . .

E

The price of McConnell's demise as authority on § 203 seems to me to be a high one. The Court (and, I think, the country) loses when important precedent is overruled without good reason, and there is no justification for departing from our usual rule of stare decisis here. The same combination of alternatives that was available to corporations affected by *McConnell* in 2003 is available today: WRTL could have run a newspaper ad, could have paid for the broadcast ads through its PAC, could have established itself as an MCFL organization free of corporate money, and could have said "call your Senators" instead of naming Senator Feingold in its ads broadcasted just before the election. Nothing in the related law surrounding § 203 has changed in any way, let alone in any way that undermines *McConnell's* rationale. See *Planned Parenthood of Southeastern Pa. v. Casey*, 505 U.S. 833, 854–855 (1992).

Nor can any serious argument be made that McConnell's holding has been "unworkable in practice." . . . *McConnell* validated a clear rule resting on mostly bright-line conditions, and there is no indication that the statute has been difficult to apply . . .

Finally, it goes without saying that nothing has changed about the facts. In Justice Frankfurter's words, they demonstrate a threat to "the integrity of our electoral process," . . . which for a century now Congress has repeatedly found to be imperiled by corporate, and later union, money . . . *McConnell* was our latest decision vindicating clear and reasonable boundaries that Congress has drawn to limit " 'the corrosive and distorting effects of immense aggregations of wealth,' " . . . and the decision could claim the justification of ongoing fact as well as decisional history in recognizing Congress's authority to protect the integrity of elections from the distortion of corporate and union funds.

After today, the ban on contributions by corporations and unions and the limitation on their corrosive spending when they enter the political arena are open to easy circumvention, and the possibilities for regulating corporate and union campaign money are unclear. The ban on contributions will mean nothing much, now that companies and unions can save candidates the expense of advertising directly, simply by running "issue ads" without express advocacy, or by funneling the money through an independent corporation like WRTL.

But the understanding of the voters and the Congress that this kind of corporate and union spending seriously jeopardizes the integrity of democratic government will remain. The facts are too powerful to be ignored, and further efforts at campaign finance reform will come. It is only the legal landscape that now is altered, and it may be that today's departure from precedent will drive further reexamination of the constitutional analysis: of the distinction between contributions and expenditures, or the relation between spending and speech, which have given structure to our thinking since *Buckley* itself was decided.

I cannot tell what the future will force upon us, but I respectfully dissent from this judgment today.

Randall v. Sorrell

___ U.S. ___, 126 S.Ct. 2479, 165 L.Ed.2d 482 (2006).

Justice Breyer announced the judgment of the Court, and delivered an opinion in which the Chief Justice joins, and in which Justice Alito joins except as to Parts II–B–1 and II–B–2.

We here consider the constitutionality of a Vermont campaign finance statute that limits both (1) the amounts that candidates for state office may spend on their campaigns (expenditure limitations) and (2) the amounts that individuals, organizations, and political parties may contribute to those campaigns (contribution limitations). . . . We hold that both sets of limitations are inconsistent with the First Amendment. Well-established precedent makes clear that the expenditure limits violate the First Amendment. Buckley v. Valeo. . . . The contribution limits are unconstitutional because in their specific details (involving low maximum levels and other restrictions) they fail to satisfy the First Amendment's requirement of careful tailoring. . . . That is to say, they impose burdens upon First Amendment interests that (when viewed in light of the statute's legitimate objectives) are disproportionately severe.

I

A

Prior to 1997, Vermont's campaign finance law imposed no limit upon the amount a candidate for state office could spend. It did, however, impose limits upon the amounts that individuals, corporations, and political committees could contribute to the campaign of such a candidate. Individuals and corporations could contribute no more than $1,000 to any candidate for state office. § 2805(a) (1996). Political committees, excluding political parties, could contribute no more than $3,000. § 2805(b). The statute imposed no limit on the amount that political parties could contribute to candidates.

In 1997, Vermont enacted a more stringent campaign finance law. . . . Act 64 . . . took effect immediately after the 1998 elections[. It] imposes mandatory expenditure limits on the total amount a candidate for state office can spend during a two-year general election cycle, i.e., the primary plus the general election, in approximately the following amounts: governor, $300,000; lieutenant governor, $100,000; other statewide offices, $45,000; state senator, $4,000 (plus an additional $2,500 for each additional seat in the district); state representative (two-member district), $3,000; and state representative (single member district), $2,000. . . . Incumbents seeking reelection to statewide office may spend no more than 85% of the above amounts, and incumbents seeking reelection to the State Senate or House may spend no more than 90% of the above amounts. . . . With certain minor exceptions, expenditures over $50 made on a candidate's behalf by others count against the candidate's expenditure limit if those expenditures are "intentionally facilitated by, solicited by or approved by" the candidate's campaign. These provisions apply so as to count against a campaign's expenditure limit any spending by political parties or committees that is coordinated with the campaign and benefits the candidate. . . . And any party expenditure that "primarily benefits six or fewer candidates who are associated with the political party" is "presumed" to be coordinated with the campaign and therefore to count against the campaign's expenditure limit. . . .

Act 64 also imposes strict contribution limits. The amount any single individual can contribute to the campaign of a candidate for state office during a "two-year general election cycle" is limited as follows: governor, lieutenant governor, and other statewide offices, $400; state senator, $300; and state representative, $200. . . . Unlike its expenditure limits, Act 64's contribution limits are not indexed for inflation.

A political committee is subject to these same limits. . . . So is a political party . . . as well as "national or regional affiliates" of a party (taken separately or together). . . . Thus, for example, the statute treats the local, state, and national affiliates of the Democratic Party as if they were a single entity and limits their total contribution to a single candidate's campaign for governor (during the primary and the general election together) to $400.

The Act also imposes a limit of $2,000 upon the amount any individual can give to a political party during a 2–year general election cycle. . . .

. . .

There are a few exceptions. A candidate's own contributions to the campaign and those of the candidate's family fall outside the contribution limits. . . . Volunteer services do not count as contributions. . . . Nor does the cost of a meet-the-candidate function, provided that the total cost for the function amounts to $100 or less. . . .

In addition to these expenditure and contribution limits, the Act sets forth disclosure and reporting requirements and creates a voluntary public financing system for gubernatorial elections. . . .

B

The petitioners are individuals who have run for state office in Vermont, citizens who vote in Vermont elections and contribute to Vermont campaigns, and political parties and committees that participate in Vermont politics. Soon after Act 64 became law, they brought this lawsuit in Federal District Court against the respondents, state officials charged with enforcement of the Act. Several other private groups and individual citizens intervened in the District Court proceedings in support of the Act and are joined here as respondents as well.

The District Court agreed with the petitioners that the Act's expenditure limits violate the First Amendment. See *Buckley*.... The court also held unconstitutional the Act's limits on the contributions of political parties to candidates. At the same time, the court found the Act's other contribution limits constitutional....

... A divided panel of the Court of Appeals for the Second Circuit held that *all* of the Act's contribution limits are constitutional. It also held that the Act's expenditure limits may be constitutional.... It found those limits supported by two compelling interests, namely, an interest in preventing corruption or the appearance of corruption and an interest in limiting the amount of time state officials must spend raising campaign funds. The Circuit then remanded the case to the District Court with instructions to determine whether the Act's expenditure limits were narrowly tailored to those interests.

.   .   .

II

We turn first to the Act's expenditure limits. Do those limits violate the First Amendment's free speech guarantees?

A

.   .   .

Over the last 30 years, in considering the constitutionality of a host of different campaign finance statutes, this Court has repeatedly adhered to *Buckley*'s constraints, including those on expenditure limits....

B

1

The respondents recognize that, in respect to expenditure limits, *Buckley* appears to be a controlling—and unfavorable—precedent. They seek to overcome that precedent in two ways. First, they ask us in effect to overrule *Buckley*....

Second, in the alternative, they ask us to ... distinguish[] ... *Buckley* from the present case. They advance as a ground for distinction a justification for expenditure limitations that, they say, *Buckley* did not consider, namely that such limits help to protect candidates from spending too much time raising money rather than devoting that time to campaigning among ordinary voters. We find neither argument persuasive.

2

The Court has often recognized the "fundamental importance" of *stare decisis*....

We can find here no such special justification that would require us to overrule *Buckley*. Subsequent case law has not made *Buckley* a legal anomaly or otherwise undermined its basic legal principles.... We cannot find in the respondents' claims any demonstration that circumstances have changed so radically as to undermine *Buckley*'s critical factual assumptions. The respondents have not shown, for example, any dramatic increase in corruption or its appearance in Vermont; nor have they shown that expenditure limits are the only way to attack that problem.... *Buckley* has promoted considerable reliance. Congress and state legislatures have used *Buckley* when drafting campaign finance laws. And, as we have said, this Court has followed *Buckley*, upholding and applying its reasoning in later cases. Overruling *Buckley* now would dramatically undermine this reliance on our settled precedent.

. . .

3

The respondents also ask us to distinguish these cases from *Buckley*. But we can find no significant basis for that distinction. Act 64's expenditure limits are not substantially different from those at issue in *Buckley*. In both instances the limits consist of a dollar cap imposed upon a candidate's expenditures. Nor is Vermont's primary justification for imposing its expenditure limits significantly different from Congress' rationale for the *Buckley* limits: preventing corruption and its appearance.

. . .

... [T]he respondents' argument amounts to no more than an invitation so to limit *Buckley*'s holding as effectively to overrule it. For the reasons set forth above, we decline that invitation as well. And, given *Buckley*'s continued authority, we must conclude that Act 64's expenditure limits violate the First Amendment.

III

We turn now to a more complex question, namely the constitutionality of Act 64's contribution limits. The parties, while accepting *Buckley*'s approach, dispute whether, despite *Buckley*'s general approval of statutes that limit campaign contributions, Act 64's contribution limits are so severe that in the circumstances its particular limits violate the First Amendment.

A

As with the Act's expenditure limits, we begin with *Buckley*. . . .

... [C]ontribution limitations are permissible as long as the Government demonstrates that the limits are "closely drawn" to match a "sufficiently important interest." ... It found that the interest advanced in the case, "prevent[ing] corruption" and its "appearance," was "sufficiently important" to justify the statute's contribution limits. . . .

. . .

Since *Buckley*, the Court has consistently upheld contribution limits in other statutes. ... The Court has recognized, however, that contribution limits might *sometimes* work more harm to protected First Amendment interests than their anticorruption objectives could justify. ... And individual Members of the Court have expressed concern lest too low a limit magnify the reputation-related or media-related advantages of incumbency and thereby "insulat[e] legislators from effective electoral challenge."

B

Following *Buckley*, we must determine whether Act 64's contribution limits prevent candidates from "amassing the resources necessary for effective [campaign] advocacy," . . .; whether they magnify the advantages of incumbency to the point where they put challengers to a significant disadvantage; in a word, whether they are too low and too strict to survive First Amendment scrutiny. . . . In practice, the legislature is better equipped to make such empirical judgments. . . . Thus ordinarily we have deferred to the legislature's determination of such matters.

Nonetheless, as *Buckley* acknowledged, we must recognize the existence of some lower bound. At some point the constitutional risks to the democratic electoral process become too great. . . .

We find those danger signs present here. As compared with the contribution limits upheld by the Court in the past, and with those in force in other States, Act 64's limits are sufficiently low as to generate suspicion that they are not closely drawn. . . .

These limits are well below the limits this Court upheld in *Buckley*. Indeed, . . . adjusting for inflation . . . the Act's $200 per election limit on individual contributions to a campaign for governor is slightly more than one-twentieth of the limit on contributions to campaigns for federal office before the Court in *Buckley*. Adjusted to reflect its value in 1976 (the year Buckley was decided), Vermont's contribution limit on campaigns for statewide office (including governor) amounts to $113.91 per 2–year election cycle, or roughly $57 per election, as compared to the $1,000 per election limit on individual contributions at issue in *Buckley*. (The adjusted value of Act 64's limit on contributions from political parties to candidates for statewide office, again $200 per candidate per election, is just over one one-hundredth of the comparable limit before the Court in *Buckley*, $5,000 per election.) Yet Vermont's gubernatorial district—the entire State—is no smaller than the House districts to which *Buckley*'s limits applied. . . .

Moreover, considered as a whole, Vermont's contribution limits are the lowest in the Nation. . . . And we are aware of no State that has a lower limit on contributions from political parties to state legislative candidates. . . .

Finally, Vermont's limit is well below the lowest limit this Court has previously upheld. . . .

. . .

In sum, Act 64's contribution limits are substantially lower than both the limits we have previously upheld and comparable limits in other States. These are danger signs that Act 64's contribution limits may fall outside tolerable First Amendment limits. We consequently must examine the record independently and carefully to determine whether Act 64's contribution limits are "closely drawn" to match the State's interests.

C

Our examination of the record convinces us that, from a constitutional perspective, Act 64's contribution limits are too restrictive. We reach this conclusion based not merely on the low dollar amounts of the limits themselves, but also on the statute's effect on political parties and on volunteer activity in Vermont elections. *Taken together*, Act 64's substantial restrictions on the ability of candidates to raise the funds necessary to run a competitive election, on the ability of political parties to help their candidates get elected, and on the ability of individual citizens to volunteer their time to campaigns show that the Act is not closely drawn to meet its objectives. . . .

.   .   .

. . . Act 64's contribution limits are not narrowly tailored. Rather, the Act burdens First Amendment interests by threatening to inhibit effective advocacy by those who seek election, particularly challengers; its contribution limits mute the voice of political parties; they hamper participation in campaigns through volunteer activities; and they are not indexed for inflation. Vermont does not point to a legitimate statutory objective that might justify these special burdens. We understand that many, though not all, campaign finance regulations impose certain of these burdens to some degree. We also understand the legitimate need for constitutional leeway in respect to legislative line-drawing. But our discussion indicates why we conclude that Act 64 in this respect nonetheless goes too far. It disproportionately burdens numerous First Amendment interests, and consequently, in our view, violates the First Amendment.

.   .   .

IV

. . . [T]he judgment of the Court of Appeals is reversed, and the cases are remanded for further proceedings.

It is so ordered.

Justice Alito, concurring in part and concurring in the judgment.

I concur in the judgment and join in Justice Breyer's opinion except for Parts II–B–1 and II–B–2. Contrary to the suggestion of those sections, respondents' primary defense of Vermont's expenditure limits is that those limits are consistent with Buckley v. Valeo. . . . Only as a backup argument, an afterthought almost, do respondents make a naked plea for us to "revisit *Buckley*." . . . More to the point, respondents fail to discuss the doctrine of *stare decisis* or the Court's cases elaborating on the circumstances in which it is appropriate to reconsider a prior constitutional decision. . . .

Whether or not a case can be made for reexamining *Buckley* in whole or in part, what matters is that respondents do not do so here, and so I think it unnecessary to reach the issue.

Justice Kennedy, concurring in the judgment.

The Court decides the constitutionality of the limitations Vermont places on campaign expenditures and contributions. I agree that both limitations violate the First Amendment.

.   .   .

The universe of campaign finance regulation is one this Court has in part created and in part permitted by its course of decisions. That new order may cause more problems than it solves. On a routine, operational level the present system requires us to explain why $200 is too restrictive a limit while $1,500 is not. Our own experience gives us little basis to make these judgments, and certainly no traditional or well-established body of law exists to offer guidance. On a broader, systemic level political parties have been denied basic First Amendment rights....

Viewed within the legal universe we have ratified and helped create, the result the plurality reaches is correct; given my own skepticism regarding that system and its operation, however, it seems to me appropriate to concur only in the judgment.

Justice Thomas, with whom Justice Scalia joins, concurring in the judgment.

Although I agree with the plurality that ... Act 64 ... is unconstitutional, I disagree with its rationale for striking down that statute.... Accordingly, I concur only in the judgment.

I

I adhere to my view that this Court erred in *Buckley* when it distinguished between contribution and expenditure limits, finding the former to be a less severe infringement on First Amendment rights.... I would overrule *Buckley* and subject both the contribution and expenditure restrictions of Act 64 to strict scrutiny, which they would fail....

II

. . .

... *Buckley*, as the plurality has applied it, gives us license to simply strike down any limits that just *seem* to be too stringent, and to uphold the rest. The First Amendment does not grant us this authority. *Buckley* provides no consistent protection to the core of the First Amendment, and must be overruled.

. . .

Justice Stevens, dissenting.

... I am convinced that *Buckley*'s holding on expenditure limits is wrong, and that the time has come to overrule it.

... [S]*tare decisis* is a principle of " 'fundamental importance.' " But it is not an inexorable command, and several factors, taken together, provide special justification for revisiting the constitutionality of statutory limits on candidate expenditures.

... *Buckley*'s holding on expenditure limits itself upset a long-established practice. For the preceding 65 years, congressional races had been subject to statutory limits on both expenditures and contributions....

. . .

[W]hile we have explicitly recognized the importance of *stare decisis* in the context of *Buckley*'s holding on contribution limits, ... we have never before done so with regard to its rejection of expenditure limits....

. . .

... I am firmly persuaded that the Framers would have been appalled by the impact of modern fundraising practices on the ability of elected officials to perform their public responsibilities. I think they would have viewed federal statutes limiting the amount of money that congressional candidates might spend in future elections as well within Congress' authority. And they surely would not have expected judges to interfere with the enforcement of expenditure limits that merely require candidates to budget their activities without imposing any restrictions whatsoever on what they may say in their speeches, debates, and interviews....

... I agree with Justice Souter that it would be entirely appropriate to allow further proceedings on expenditure limits to go forward in these cases.... I also agree that Vermont's contribution limits and presumption of coordinated expenditures by political parties are constitutional, and so join those portions of his opinion.

Justice Souter, with whom Justice Ginsburg joins, and with whom Justice Stevens joins as to Parts II and III, dissenting.

... I would adhere to the Court of Appeals's decision to remand for further enquiry bearing on the limitations on candidates' expenditures, and I think the contribution limits satisfy controlling precedent. I respectfully dissent.

I

Rejecting Act 64's expenditure limits as directly contravening Buckley v. Valeo ... is at least premature....

... Whatever the observations made to the *Buckley* Court about the effect of fundraising on candidates' time, the Court did not squarely address a time-protection interest as support for the expenditure limits, much less one buttressed by as thorough a record as we have here.

Vermont's argument therefore does not ask us to overrule *Buckley*; it asks us to apply *Buckley*'s framework to determine whether its evidence here on a need to slow the fundraising treadmill suffices to support the enacted limitations....

The legislature's findings are surely significant enough to justify the Court of Appeals's remand to the District Court to decide whether Vermont's spending limits are the least restrictive means of accomplishing what the court unexceptionably found to be worthy objectives.... [W]e are left with an unresolved question of narrow tailoring and with consequent doubt about the justifiability of the spending limits as necessary and appropriate correctives.... I would not, therefore, disturb the Court of Appeals's stated intention to remand.

II

Although I would defer judgment on the merits of the expenditure limitations, I believe the Court of Appeals correctly rejected the challenge to the contribution limits. Low though they are, one cannot say that "the contribution limitation[s are] so radical in effect as to render political association ineffective, drive the sound of a candidate's voice below the level of notice, and render contributions pointless." . . .

. . .

. . . The Legislature of Vermont evidently tried to account for the realities of campaigning in Vermont, and I see no evidence of constitutional miscalculation sufficient to dispense with respect for its judgments.

. . .

SECTION 5. SPEECH AND ASSOCIATION RIGHTS OF GOVERNMENT EMPLOYEES

Page 1661.   Add after Rankin v. McPherson:

Garcetti v. Ceballos

___ U.S. ___, 126 S.Ct. 1951, 164 L.Ed.2d 689 (2006).

Justice Kennedy delivered the opinion of the Court.

It is well settled that "a State cannot condition public employment on a basis that infringes the employee's constitutionally protected interest in freedom of expression." Connick v. Myers, 461 U.S. 138, 142 (1983). The question presented by the instant case is whether the First Amendment protects a government employee from discipline based on speech made pursuant to the employee's official duties.

I

Respondent Richard Ceballos has been employed since 1989 as a deputy district attorney for the Los Angeles County District Attorney's Office. During the period relevant to this case, Ceballos was a calendar deputy in the office's Pomona branch, and in this capacity he exercised certain supervisory responsibilities over other lawyers. In February 2000, a defense attorney contacted Ceballos about a pending criminal case. The defense attorney said there were inaccuracies in an affidavit used to obtain a critical search warrant. . . .

After examining the affidavit and visiting the location it described, Ceballos determined the affidavit contained serious misrepresentations. . . .

. . . He relayed his findings to his supervisors, petitioners Carol Najera and Frank Sundstedt, and followed up by preparing a disposition memorandum. The memo explained Ceballos' concerns and recommended dismissal of the case. On March 2, 2000, Ceballos submitted the memo to Sundstedt for his review. . . .

Based on Ceballos' statements, a meeting was held to discuss the affidavit. Attendees included Ceballos, Sundstedt, and Najera, as well as the warrant affiant and other employees from the sheriff's department. The meeting allegedly became heated, with one lieutenant sharply criticizing Ceballos for his handling of the case.

Despite Ceballos' concerns, Sundstedt decided to proceed with the prosecution, pending disposition of the defense motion to traverse. The trial court held a hearing on the motion. Ceballos was called by the defense and recounted his observations about the affidavit, but the trial court rejected the challenge to the warrant.

Ceballos claims that in the aftermath of these events he was subjected to a series of retaliatory employment actions. The actions included reassignment from his calendar deputy position to a trial deputy position, transfer to another courthouse, and denial of a promotion.... Ceballos sued in the United States District Court ... alleg[ing that] petitioners violated the First and Fourteenth Amendments by retaliating against him based on his memo of March 2.

... Petitioners moved for summary judgment, and the District Court granted their motion....

The Court of Appeals for the Ninth Circuit reversed, holding that "Ceballos's allegations of wrongdoing in the memorandum constitute protected speech under the First Amendment." ...

. . .

We granted certiorari, and we now reverse.

II

As the Court's decisions have noted, for many years "the unchallenged dogma was that a public employee had no right to object to conditions placed upon the terms of employment—including those which restricted the exercise of constitutional rights." Connick, 461 U.S., at 143. That dogma has been qualified in important respects....

Pickering provides a useful starting point in explaining the Court's doctrine. There the relevant speech was a teacher's letter to a local newspaper addressing issues including the funding policies of his school board.... "The problem in any case," the Court stated, "is to arrive at a balance between the interests of the teacher, as a citizen, in commenting upon matters of public concern and the interest of the State, as an employer, in promoting the efficiency of the public services it performs through its employees." ... [T]he Court concluded that "the interest of the school administration in limiting teachers' opportunities to contribute to public debate is not significantly greater than its interest in limiting a similar contribution by any member of the general public." ...

Pickering and the cases decided in its wake identify two inquiries to guide interpretation of the constitutional protections accorded to public employee speech. The first requires determining whether the employee spoke as a citizen on a matter of public concern.... If the answer is no, the employee has no First Amendment cause of action based on his or her employer's reaction to the speech.... If the answer is yes, then the possibility of a First Amendment claim arises. The question becomes whether the relevant government entity had an adequate justification for treating the employee differently from any other member of the general public.... This consideration reflects the importance of the relationship between the speaker's expressions and employment. A government entity has broader discretion to restrict speech when it acts in its role as employer, but the restrictions it imposes must be directed at speech that has some potential to affect the entity's operations.

To be sure, conducting these inquiries sometimes has proved difficult. This is the necessary product of "the enormous variety of fact situations in which critical statements by teachers and other public employees may be thought by their superiors to furnish grounds for dismissal." . . . The Court's overarching objectives, though, are evident.

When a citizen enters government service, the citizen by necessity must accept certain limitations on his or her freedom. . . . ("[T]he government as employer indeed has far broader powers than does the government as sovereign"). Government employers, like private employers, need a significant degree of control over their employees' words and actions; without it, there would be little chance for the efficient provision of public services. . . . "([G]overnment offices could not function if every employment decision became a constitutional matter"). Public employees, moreover, often occupy trusted positions in society. When they speak out, they can express views that contravene governmental policies or impair the proper performance of governmental functions.

At the same time, the Court has recognized that a citizen who works for the government is nonetheless a citizen. The First Amendment limits the ability of a public employer to leverage the employment relationship to restrict, incidentally or intentionally, the liberties employees enjoy in their capacities as private citizens. . . . So long as employees are speaking as citizens about matters of public concern, they must face only those speech restrictions that are necessary for their employers to operate efficiently and effectively. . . .

The Court's employee-speech jurisprudence protects, of course, the constitutional rights of public employees. Yet the First Amendment interests at stake extend beyond the individual speaker. The Court has acknowledged the importance of promoting the public's interest in receiving the well-informed views of government employees engaging in civic discussion. *Pickering* again provides an instructive example. The Court characterized its holding as rejecting the attempt of school administrators to "limi[t] teachers' opportunities to contribute to public debate." . . .

The Court's decisions, then, have sought both to promote the individual and societal interests that are served when employees speak as citizens on matters of public concern and to respect the needs of government employers attempting to perform their important public functions. . . .

III

With these principles in mind we turn to the instant case. Respondent Ceballos . . . conveyed his opinion and recommendation in a memo to his supervisor. That Ceballos expressed his views inside his office, rather than publicly, is not dispositive. Employees in some cases may receive First Amendment protection for expressions made at work. . . . Many citizens do much of their talking inside their respective workplaces, and it would not serve the goal of treating public employees like "any member of the general public," . . . to hold that all speech within the office is automatically exposed to restriction.

The memo concerned the subject matter of Ceballos' employment, but this, too, is nondispositive. The First Amendment protects some expressions related to the speaker's job.... "[I]t is essential that they be able to speak out freely on such questions without fear of retaliatory dismissal." ...

The controlling factor in Ceballos' case is that his expressions were made pursuant to his duties as a calendar deputy.... That consideration—the fact that Ceballos spoke as a prosecutor fulfilling a responsibility to advise his supervisor about how best to proceed with a pending case—distinguishes Ceballos' case from those in which the First Amendment provides protection against discipline. We hold that when public employees make statements pursuant to their official duties, the employees are not speaking as citizens for First Amendment purposes, and the Constitution does not insulate their communications from employer discipline.

. . .

Ceballos did not act as a citizen when he went about conducting his daily professional activities, such as supervising attorneys, investigating charges, and preparing filings. In the same way he did not speak as a citizen by writing a memo that addressed the proper disposition of a pending criminal case. When he went to work and performed the tasks he was paid to perform, Ceballos acted as a government employee. The fact that his duties sometimes required him to speak or write does not mean his supervisors were prohibited from evaluating his performance.

. . .

Our holding likewise is supported by the emphasis of our precedents on affording government employers sufficient discretion to manage their operations. Employers have heightened interests in controlling speech made by an employee in his or her professional capacity. Official communications have official consequences, creating a need for substantive consistency and clarity. Supervisors must ensure that their employees' official communications are accurate, demonstrate sound judgment, and promote the employer's mission. Ceballos' memo is illustrative. It demanded the attention of his supervisors and led to a heated meeting with employees from the sheriff's department. If Ceballos' superiors thought his memo was inflammatory or misguided, they had the authority to take proper corrective action.

Ceballos' proposed contrary rule, adopted by the Court of Appeals, would commit state and federal courts to a new, permanent, and intrusive role, mandating judicial oversight of communications between and among government employees and their superiors in the course of official business. This displacement of managerial discretion by judicial supervision finds no support in our precedents. When an employee speaks as a citizen addressing a matter of public concern, the First Amendment requires a delicate balancing of the competing interests surrounding the speech and its consequences. When, however, the employee is simply performing his or her job duties, there is no warrant for a similar degree of scrutiny. To hold otherwise would be to demand permanent judicial intervention in the conduct of governmental operations to a degree inconsistent with sound principles of federalism and the separation of powers.

The Court of Appeals based its holding in part on what it perceived as a doctrinal anomaly. The court suggested it would be inconsistent to compel public employers to tolerate certain employee speech made publicly but not speech made pursuant to an employee's assigned duties. This objection misconceives the theoretical underpinnings of our decisions. Employees who make public statements outside the course of performing their official duties retain some possibility of First Amendment protection because that is the kind of activity engaged in by citizens who do not work for the government. The same goes for writing a letter to a local newspaper, see *Pickering*, . . . or discussing politics with a co-worker, see *Rankin*. . . . When a public employee speaks pursuant to employment responsibilities, however, there is no relevant analogue to speech by citizens who are not government employees.

The Court of Appeals' concern also is unfounded as a practical matter. The perceived anomaly, it should be noted, is limited in scope: It relates only to the expressions an employee makes pursuant to his or her official responsibilities, not to statements or complaints (such as those at issue in cases like *Pickering* and *Connick*) that are made outside the duties of employment. If, moreover, a government employer is troubled by the perceived anomaly, it has the means at hand to avoid it. A public employer that wishes to encourage its employees to voice concerns privately retains the option of instituting internal policies and procedures that are receptive to employee criticism. Giving employees an internal forum for their speech will discourage them from concluding that the safest avenue of expression is to state their views in public.

Proper application of our precedents thus leads to the conclusion that the First Amendment does not prohibit managerial discipline based on an employee's expressions made pursuant to official responsibilities. Because Ceballos' memo falls into this category, his allegation of unconstitutional retaliation must fail.

. . .

IV

. . .

We reject . . . the notion that the First Amendment shields from discipline the expressions employees make pursuant to their professional duties. Our precedents do not support the existence of a constitutional cause of action behind every statement a public employee makes in the course of doing his or her job.

The judgment of the Court of Appeals is reversed, and the case is remanded for proceedings consistent with this opinion.

. . .

Justice Stevens, dissenting.

The proper answer to the question "whether the First Amendment protects a government employee from discipline based on speech made pursuant to the employee's official duties," is "Sometimes," not "Never." Of course a supervisor may take corrective action when such speech is "inflammatory or misguided." But what if it is just unwelcome speech because it reveals facts that the supervisor would rather not have anyone else discover?

As Justice Souter explains, public employees are still citizens while they are in the office. The notion that there is a categorical difference between speaking as a citizen and speaking in the course of one's employment is quite wrong. Over a quarter of a century has passed since then-Justice Rehnquist, writing for a unanimous Court, rejected "the conclusion that a public employee forfeits his protection against governmental abridgment of freedom of speech if he decides to express his views privately rather than publicly." [In] *Givhan* ... [w]e had no difficulty recognizing that the First Amendment applied when Bessie Givhan, an English teacher, raised concerns about the school's racist employment practices to the principal. Our silence as to whether or not her speech was made pursuant to her job duties demonstrates that the point was immaterial. That is equally true today, for it is senseless to let constitutional protection for exactly the same words hinge on whether they fall within a job description. Moreover, it seems perverse to fashion a new rule that provides employees with an incentive to voice their concerns publicly before talking frankly to their superiors.

. . .

Justice Souter, with whom Justice Stevens and Justice Ginsburg join, dissenting.

... I would hold that private and public interests in addressing official wrongdoing and threats to health and safety can outweigh the government's stake in the efficient implementation of policy, and when they do public employees who speak on these matters in the course of their duties should be eligible to claim First Amendment protection.

I

Open speech by a private citizen on a matter of public importance lies at the heart of expression subject to protection by the First Amendment.... At the other extreme, a statement by a government employee complaining about nothing beyond treatment under personnel rules raises no greater claim to constitutional protection against retaliatory response than the remarks of a private employee.... In between these points lies a public employee's speech unwelcome to the government but on a significant public issue. Such an employee speaking as a citizen, that is, with a citizen's interest, is protected from reprisal unless the statements are too damaging to the government's capacity to conduct public business to be justified by any individual or public benefit thought to flow from the statements.... Entitlement to protection is thus not absolute.

This significant, albeit qualified, protection of public employees who irritate the government is understood to flow from the First Amendment, in part, because a government paycheck does nothing to eliminate the value to an individual of speaking on public matters, and there is no good reason for categorically discounting a speaker's interest in commenting on a matter of public concern just because the government employs him. Still, the First Amendment safeguard rests on something more, being the value to the public of receiving the opinions and information that a public employee may disclose.
. . .

. . .

The difference between a case like *Givhan* and this one is that the subject of Ceballos's speech fell within the scope of his job responsibilities, whereas choosing personnel was not what the teacher was hired to do. The effect of the majority's constitutional line between these two cases, then, is that a *Givhan* schoolteacher is protected when complaining to the principal about hiring policy, but a school personnel officer would not be if he protested that the principal disapproved of hiring minority job applicants. This is an odd place to draw a distinction. . . .

As all agree, the qualified speech protection embodied in *Pickering* balancing resolves the tension between individual and public interests in the speech, on the one hand, and the government's interest in operating efficiently without distraction or embarrassment by talkative or headline-grabbing employees. The need for a balance hardly disappears when an employee speaks on matters his job requires him to address; rather, it seems obvious that the individual and public value of such speech is no less, and may well be greater, when the employee speaks pursuant to his duties in addressing a subject he knows intimately for the very reason that it falls within his duties.

. . . Would anyone deny that a prosecutor like Richard Ceballos may claim the interest of any citizen in speaking out against a rogue law enforcement officer, simply because his job requires him to express a judgment about the officer's performance? . . .

. . .

Nothing, then, accountable on the individual and public side of the *Pickering* balance changes when an employee speaks "pursuant" to public duties. On the side of the government employer, however, something is different, and to this extent, I agree with the majority of the Court. The majority is rightly concerned that the employee who speaks out on matters subject to comment in doing his own work has the greater leverage to create office uproars and fracture the government's authority to set policy to be carried out coherently through the ranks. "Official communications have official consequences, creating a need for substantive consistency and clarity. Supervisors must ensure that their employees' official communications are accurate, demonstrate sound judgment, and promote the employer's mission." Up to a point, then, the majority makes good points: government needs civility in the workplace, consistency in policy, and honesty and competence in public service.

But why do the majority's concerns, which we all share, require categorical exclusion of First Amendment protection against any official retaliation for things said on the job? . . .

. . . [A]n adjustment using the basic *Pickering* balancing scheme is perfectly feasible here. [T]he extent of the government's legitimate authority over subjects of speech required by a public job can be recognized in advance by setting in effect a minimum heft for comments with any claim to outweigh it. Thus, the risks to the government are great enough for us to hold from the outset that an employee commenting on subjects in the course of duties should not prevail on balance unless he speaks on a matter of unusual importance and satisfies high standards of responsibility in the way he does it. . . .

. . .

II

. . .

. . . This ostensible domain beyond the pale of the First Amendment is spacious enough to include even the teaching of a public university professor, and I have to hope that today's majority does not mean to imperil First Amendment protection of academic freedom in public colleges and universities, whose teachers necessarily speak and write "pursuant to official duties."

. . .

Justice Breyer dissenting.

. . .

. . . I believe that courts should apply the *Pickering* standard, even though the government employee speaks upon matters of public concern in the course of his ordinary duties.

This is such a case. The respondent, a government lawyer, complained of retaliation, in part, on the basis of speech contained in his disposition memorandum that he says fell within the scope of his obligations under Brady v. Maryland, 373 U.S. 83 (1963). . . .

. . .

Where professional and special constitutional obligations are both present, the need to protect the employee's speech is augmented, the need for broad government authority to control that speech is likely diminished, and administrable standards are quite likely available. Hence, I would find that the Constitution mandates special protection of employee speech in such circumstances. Thus I would apply the *Pickering* balancing test here.

. . .

While I agree with much of Justice Souter's analysis, I believe that the constitutional standard he enunciates fails to give sufficient weight to the serious managerial and administrative concerns that the majority describes. . . .

There are, however, far too many issues of public concern, even if defined as "matters of unusual importance," for the screen to screen out very much. Government administration typically involves matters of public concern. Why else would government be involved? . . .

Moreover, the speech of vast numbers of public employees deals with wrongdoing, health, safety, and honesty. . . .

The underlying problem with this breadth of coverage is that the standard . . . does not avoid the judicial need to *undertake the balance* in the first place. And this form of judicial activity—the ability of a dissatisfied employee to file a complaint, engage in discovery, and insist that the court undertake a balancing of interests—itself may interfere unreasonably with both the managerial function (the ability of the employer to control the way in which an employee performs his basic job) and with the use of other grievance-resolution mechanisms, such as arbitration, civil service review boards, and whistle-blower remedies, for which employees and employers may have bargained or which legislatures may have enacted.

   . . .

I conclude that the First Amendment sometimes does authorize judicial actions based upon a government employee's speech that both (1) involves a matter of public concern and also (2) takes place in the course of ordinary job-related duties. But it does so only in the presence of augmented need for constitutional protection and diminished risk of undue judicial interference with governmental management of the public's affairs. In my view, these conditions are met in this case and *Pickering* balancing is consequently appropriate.

With respect, I dissent.

CHAPTER 17

RELIGION AND THE CONSTITUTION

SECTION 1. THE ESTABLISHMENT CLAUSE

B. GOVERNMENT RELIGIOUS EXERCISES, CEREMONIES, DISPLAYS, AND PRACTICES

2. RELIGIOUS SPEECH AND DISPLAYS ON PUBLIC PROPERTY

Page 1748. Replace County of Allegheny v. American Civil Liberties Union:

McCreary County, Kentucky v. American Civil Liberties Union of Kentucky

545 U.S. 844, 125 S.Ct. 2722, 162 L.Ed.2d 729 (2005).

Justice Souter delivered the opinion of the Court.

Executives of two counties posted a version of the Ten Commandments on the walls of their courthouses. After suits were filed charging violations of the Establishment Clause, the legislative body of each county adopted a resolution calling for a more extensive exhibit meant to show that the Commandments are Kentucky's "precedent legal code." The result in each instance was a modified display of the Commandments surrounded by texts containing religious references as their sole common element. After changing counsel, the counties revised the exhibits again by eliminating some documents, expanding the text set out in another, and adding some new ones.

The issues are whether a determination of the counties' purpose is a sound basis for ruling on the Establishment Clause complaints, and whether evaluation of the counties' claim of secular purpose for the ultimate displays may take their evolution into account. We hold that the counties' manifest objective may be dispositive of the constitutional enquiry, and that the development of the presentation should be considered when determining its purpose.

I

. . .

In November 1999, respondents . . . sued the Counties in Federal District Court . . . and sought a preliminary injunction against maintaining the displays, which the ACLU charged were violations of the prohibition of religious establishment included in the First Amendment of the Constitution. Within a month, and before the District Court had responded to the request for injunction, the legislative body of each County authorized a second, expanded display, by nearly identical resolutions reciting that the Ten Commandments are "the precedent legal code upon which the civil and criminal codes of ... Kentucky are founded," and stating several grounds for taking that position: that "the Ten Commandments are codified in Kentucky's civil and criminal laws"; that the Kentucky House of Representatives had in 1993 "voted unanimously ... to adjourn ... 'in remembrance and honor of Jesus Christ, the Prince of Ethics' "; that the "County Judge and ... magistrates agree with the arguments set out by Judge [Roy] Moore" in defense of his "display [of] the Ten Commandments in his courtroom"; and that the "Founding Father[s] [had an] explicit understanding of the duty of elected officials to publicly acknowledge God as the source of America's strength and direction."

As directed by the resolutions, the Counties expanded the displays of the Ten Commandments in their locations, presumably along with copies of the resolution, which instructed that it, too, be posted. In addition to the first display's large framed copy of the edited King James version of the Commandments, the second included eight other documents in smaller frames, each either having a religious theme or excerpted to highlight a religious element. The documents were the "endowed by their Creator" passage from the Declaration of Independence; the Preamble to the Constitution of Kentucky; the national motto, "In God We Trust"; a page from the Congressional Record of February 2, 1983, proclaiming the Year of the Bible and including a statement of the Ten Commandments; a proclamation by President Abraham Lincoln designating April 30, 1863, a National Day of Prayer and Humiliation; an excerpt from President Lincoln's "Reply to Loyal Colored People of Baltimore upon Presentation of a Bible," reading that "[t]he Bible is the best gift God has ever given to man"; a proclamation by President Reagan marking 1983 the Year of the Bible; and the Mayflower Compact.

After argument, the District Court entered a preliminary injunction on May 5, 2000, ordering that the "display ... be removed from [each] County Courthouse IMMEDIATELY" and that no county official "erect or cause to be erected similar displays." ... As to governmental purpose, it concluded that the original display "lack[ed] any secular purpose" because the Commandments "are a distinctly religious document...." The court found that the second version also "clearly lack[ed] a secular purpose" because the "Count[ies] narrowly tailored [their] selection of foundational documents to incorporate only those with specific references to Christianity."

The Counties ... voluntarily dismissed [their appeal] after hiring new lawyers. They then installed another display in each courthouse, the third within a year. No new resolution authorized this one, nor did the Counties repeal the resolutions that preceded the second. The posting consists of nine framed documents of equal size, one of them setting out the Ten Commandments explicitly identified as the "King James Version" at Exodus 20:3–17 and quoted at greater length than before.... Assembled with the Commandments are framed copies of the Magna Carta, the Declaration of Independence, the Bill of Rights, the lyrics of the Star Spangled Banner, the Mayflower Compact, the National Motto, the Preamble to the Kentucky Constitution, and a picture of Lady Justice. The collection is entitled "The Foundations of American Law and Government Display" and each document comes with a statement about its historical and legal significance. The comment on the Ten Commandments reads:

> "The Ten Commandments have profoundly influenced the formation of Western legal thought and the formation of our country. That influence is clearly seen in the Declaration of Independence, which declared that 'We hold these truths to be self-evident, that all men are created equal, that they are endowed by their Creator with certain unalienable Rights, that among these are Life, Liberty, and the pursuit of Happiness.' The Ten Commandments provide the moral background of the Declaration of Independence and the foundation of our legal tradition."

The ACLU moved to supplement the preliminary injunction to enjoin the Counties' third display, and the Counties responded with several explanations for the new version, including desires "to demonstrate that the Ten Commandments were part of the foundation of American Law and Government" and "to educate the citizens of the county regarding some of the documents that played a significant role in the foundation of our system of law and government." . . . The court, however, took the objective of proclaiming the Commandments' foundational value as "a religious, rather than secular, purpose" . . . and found that the assertion that the Counties' broader educational goals are secular "crumble[s] . . . upon an examination of the history of this litigation,"

   . . . As requested, the trial court supplemented the injunction, and a divided panel of the Court of Appeals for the Sixth Circuit affirmed. . . .

We . . . now affirm.

II

Twenty-five years ago in a case prompted by posting the Ten Commandments in Kentucky's public schools, this Court recognized that the Commandments "are undeniably a sacred text in the Jewish and Christian faiths" and held that their display in public classrooms violated the First Amendment's bar against establishment of religion. Stone [v. Graham] 449 U.S., at 41. *Stone* found a predominantly religious purpose in the government's posting of the Commandments, given their prominence as " 'an instrument of religion,' " . . . The Counties ask for a different approach here by arguing that official purpose is unknowable and the search for it inherently vain. In the alternative, the Counties would avoid the District Court's conclusion by having us limit the scope of the purpose enquiry so severely that any trivial rationalization would suffice, under a standard oblivious to the history of religious government action like the progression of exhibits in this case.

A

Ever since Lemon v. Kurtzman summarized the three familiar considerations for evaluating Establishment Clause claims, looking to whether government action has "a secular legislative purpose" has been a common, albeit seldom dispositive, element of our cases. . . . Though we have found government action motivated by an illegitimate purpose only four times since *Lemon*, and "the secular purpose requirement alone may rarely be determinative . . . , it nevertheless serves an important function." . . .

The touchstone for our analysis is the principle that the "First Amendment mandates governmental neutrality between religion and religion, and between religion and nonreligion." . . . When the government acts with the ostensible and predominant purpose of advancing religion, it violates that central Establishment Clause value of official religious neutrality, there being no neutrality when the government's ostensible object is to take sides. . . . By showing a purpose to favor religion, the government "sends the . . . message to . . . nonadherents 'that they are outsiders, not full members of the political community, and an accompanying message to adherents that they are insiders, favored members' " . . . .

. . .

B

Despite the intuitive importance of official purpose to the realization of Establishment Clause values, the Counties ask us to abandon *Lemon*'s purpose test, or at least to truncate any enquiry into purpose here. Their first argument is that the very consideration of purpose is deceptive: according to them, true "purpose" is unknowable, and its search merely an excuse for courts to act selectively and unpredictably in picking out evidence of subjective intent. The assertions are as seismic as they are unconvincing.

Examination of purpose is a staple of statutory interpretation that makes up the daily fare of every appellate court in the country, . . . and governmental purpose is a key element of a good deal of constitutional doctrine, e.g., Washington v. Davis, 426 U.S. 229. . . . With enquiries into purpose this common, if they were nothing but hunts for mares' nests deflecting attention from bare judicial will, the whole notion of purpose in law would have dropped into disrepute long ago.

But scrutinizing purpose does make practical sense, as in Establishment Clause analysis, where an understanding of official objective emerges from readily discoverable fact, without any judicial psychoanalysis of a drafter's heart of hearts. . . . There is, then, nothing hinting at an unpredictable or disingenuous exercise when a court enquires into purpose after a claim is raised under the Establishment Clause.

The cases with findings of a predominantly religious purpose point to the straightforward nature of the test. . . . [I]n *Stone*, the Court held that the "[p]osting of religious texts on the wall serve[d] no . . . educational function," and found that if "the posted copies of the Ten Commandments [were] to have any effect at all, it [would] be to induce the schoolchildren to read, meditate upon, perhaps to venerate and obey, the Commandments." . . .

Nor is there any indication that the enquiry is rigged in practice to finding a religious purpose dominant every time a case is filed. In the past, the test has not been fatal very often, presumably because government does not generally act unconstitutionally, with the predominant purpose of advancing religion. That said, one consequence of the corollary that Establishment Clause analysis does not look to the veiled psyche of government officers could be that in some of the cases in which establishment complaints failed, savvy officials had disguised their religious intent so cleverly that the objective observer just missed it. But that is no reason for great constitutional concern. If someone in the government hides religious motive so well that the " 'objective observer, acquainted with the text, legislative history, and implementation of the statute,' " . . . cannot see it, then without something more the government does not make a divisive announcement that in itself amounts to taking religious sides. A secret motive stirs up no strife and does nothing to make outsiders of nonadherents, and it suffices to wait and see whether such government action turns out to have (as it may even be likely to have) the illegitimate effect of advancing religion.

C

After declining the invitation to abandon concern with purpose wholesale, we also have to avoid the Counties' alternative tack of trivializing the enquiry into it. The Counties would read the cases as if the purpose enquiry were so naive that any transparent claim to secularity would satisfy it, and they would cut context out of the enquiry, to the point of ignoring history, no matter what bearing it actually had on the significance of current circumstances. There is no precedent for the Counties' arguments, or reason supporting them.

1

. . .

. . . [W]e have not made the purpose test a pushover for any secular claim. . . . [I]n those unusual cases where the claim was an apparent sham, or the secular purpose secondary, the unsurprising results have been findings of no adequate secular object, as against a predominantly religious one.

2

The Counties' second proffered limitation can be dispatched quickly. They argue that purpose in a case like this one should be inferred, if at all, only from the latest news about the last in a series of governmental actions, however close they may all be in time and subject. But the world is not made brand new every morning, and the Counties are simply asking us to ignore perfectly probative evidence; they want an absentminded objective observer, not one presumed to be familiar with the history of the government's actions and competent to learn what history has to show. . . .

III

. . .

We take *Stone* as the initial legal benchmark, our only case dealing with the constitutionality of displaying the Commandments. *Stone* recognized that the Commandments are an "instrument of religion" and that, at least on the facts before it, the display of their text could presumptively be understood as meant to advance religion: although state law specifically required their posting in public school classrooms, their isolated exhibition did not leave room even for an argument that secular education explained their being there. . . . But *Stone* did not purport to decide the constitutionality of every possible way the Commandments might be set out by the government, and under the Establishment Clause detail is key. . . .

A

The display rejected in *Stone* had two obvious similarities to the first one in the sequence here: both set out a text of the Commandments as distinct from any traditionally symbolic representation, and each stood alone, not part of an arguably secular display. *Stone* stressed the significance of integrating the Commandments into a secular scheme to forestall the broadcast of an otherwise clearly religious message, ... and for good reason, the Commandments being a central point of reference in the religious and moral history of Jews and Christians. They proclaim the existence of a monotheistic god (no other gods). They regulate details of religious obligation (no graven images, no sabbath breaking, no vain oath swearing). And they unmistakably rest even the universally accepted prohibitions (as against murder, theft, and the like) on the sanction of the divinity proclaimed at the beginning of the text. Displaying that text is thus different from a symbolic depiction, like tablets with 10 roman numerals, which could be seen as alluding to a general notion of law, not a sectarian conception of faith.... Actually, the posting by the Counties lacked even the *Stone* display's implausible disclaimer that the Commandments were set out to show their effect on the civil law. What is more, at the ceremony for posting the framed Commandments in Pulaski County, the county executive was accompanied by his pastor, who testified to the certainty of the existence of God. The reasonable observer could only think that the Counties meant to emphasize and celebrate the Commandments' religious message.

This is not to deny that the Commandments have had influence on civil or secular law; a major text of a majority religion is bound to be felt. The point is simply that the original text viewed in its entirety is an unmistakably religious statement dealing with religious obligations and with morality subject to religious sanction. When the government initiates an effort to place this statement alone in public view, a religious object is unmistakable.

B

Once the Counties were sued, they modified the exhibits and invited additional insight into their purpose in a display that hung for about six months. This new one was the product of forthright and nearly identical Pulaski and McCreary County resolutions listing a series of American historical documents with theistic and Christian references, which were to be posted in order to furnish a setting for displaying the Ten Commandments and any "other Kentucky and American historical documen[t]" without raising concern about "any Christian or religious references" in them.... [T]he resolutions expressed support for an Alabama judge who posted the Commandments in his courtroom, and cited the fact the Kentucky Legislature once adjourned a session in honor of "Jesus Christ, Prince of Ethics." ...

In this second display, unlike the first, the Commandments were not hung in isolation, merely leaving the Counties' purpose to emerge from the pervasively religious text of the Commandments themselves. Instead, the second version was required to include the statement of the government's purpose expressly set out in the county resolutions, and underscored it by juxtaposing the Commandments to other documents with highlighted references to God as their sole common element. The display's unstinting focus was on religious passages, showing that the Counties were posting the Commandments precisely because of their sectarian content. That demonstration of the government's objective was enhanced by serial religious references and the accompanying resolution's claim about the embodiment of ethics in Christ. Together, the display and resolution presented an indisputable, and undisputed, showing of an impermissible purpose.

. . .

C

1

After the Counties changed lawyers, they mounted a third display, without a new resolution or repeal of the old one. The result was the "Foundations of American Law and Government" exhibit, which placed the Commandments in the company of other documents the Counties thought especially significant in the historical foundation of American government. In trying to persuade the District Court to lift the preliminary injunction, the Counties cited several new purposes for the third version, including a desire "to educate the citizens of the county regarding some of the documents that played a significant role in the foundation of our system of law and government." The Counties' claims did not, however, persuade the court, intimately familiar with the details of this litigation, or the Court of Appeals, neither of which found a legitimizing secular purpose in this third version of the display. " 'When both courts [that have already passed on the case] are unable to discern an arguably valid secular purpose, this Court normally should hesitate to find one.' "

[N]ew statements of purpose were presented only as a litigating position, there being no further authorizing action by the Counties' governing boards. And although repeal of the earlier county authorizations would not have erased them from the record of evidence bearing on current purpose, the extraordinary resolutions for the second display passed just months earlier were not repealed or otherwise repudiated. Indeed, the sectarian spirit of the common resolution found enhanced expression in the third display, which quoted more of the purely religious language of the Commandments than the first two displays had done. . . .

. . .

2

In holding the preliminary injunction adequately supported by evidence that the Counties' purpose had not changed at the third stage, we do not decide that the Counties' past actions forever taint any effort on their part to deal with the subject matter. We hold only that purpose needs to be taken seriously under the Establishment Clause and needs to be understood in light of context; an implausible claim that governmental purpose has changed should not carry the day in a court of law any more than in a head with common sense. It is enough to say here that district courts are fully capable of adjusting preliminary relief to take account of genuine changes in constitutionally significant conditions. . . .

Nor do we have occasion here to hold that a sacred text can never be integrated constitutionally into a governmental display on the subject of law, or American history. We do not forget, and in this litigation have frequently been reminded, that our own courtroom frieze was deliberately designed in the exercise of governmental authority so as to include the figure of Moses holding tablets exhibiting a portion of the Hebrew text of the later, secularly phrased Commandments; in the company of 17 other lawgivers, most of them secular figures, there is no risk that Moses would strike an observer as evidence that the National Government was violating neutrality in religion.

IV

The importance of neutrality as an interpretive guide is no less true now than it was when the Court broached the principle in *Everson* ... and a word needs to be said about the different view taken in today's dissent. We all agree, of course, on the need for some interpretative help. The First Amendment contains no textual definition of "establishment," and the term is certainly not self-defining. No one contends that the prohibition of establishment stops at a designation of a national (or with Fourteenth Amendment incorporation, ... a state) church, but nothing in the text says just how much more it covers. There is no simple answer, for more than one reason.

The prohibition on establishment covers a variety of issues from prayer in widely varying government settings, to financial aid for religious individuals and institutions, to comment on religious questions. In these varied settings, issues about interpreting inexact Establishment Clause language, like difficult interpretative issues generally, arise from the tension of competing values, each constitutionally respectable, but none open to realization to the logical limit.

The First Amendment has not one but two clauses tied to "religion," the second forbidding any prohibition on the "the free exercise thereof," and sometimes, the two clauses compete: spending government money on the clergy looks like establishing religion, but if the government cannot pay for military chaplains a good many soldiers and sailors would be kept from the opportunity to exercise their chosen religions.... At other times, limits on governmental action that might make sense as a way to avoid establishment could arguably limit freedom of speech when the speaking is done under government auspices.... The dissent, then, is wrong to read cases like Walz v. Tax Comm'n of City of New York, 397 U.S. 664 (1970), as a rejection of neutrality on its own terms, for trade-offs are inevitable, and an elegant interpretative rule to draw the line in all the multifarious situations is not be had.

Given the variety of interpretative problems, the principle of neutrality has provided a good sense of direction: the government may not favor one religion over another, or religion over irreligion, religious choice being the prerogative of individuals under the Free Exercise Clause.... A sense of the past thus points to governmental neutrality as an objective of the Establishment Clause, and a sensible standard for applying it. To be sure, given its generality as a principle, an appeal to neutrality alone cannot possibly lay every issue to rest, or tell us what issues on the margins are substantial enough for constitutional significance, a point that has been clear from the Founding era to modern times....

The dissent, however, puts forward a limitation on the application of the neutrality principle, with citations to historical evidence said to show that the Framers understood the ban on establishment of religion as sufficiently narrow to allow the government to espouse submission to the divine will. The dissent identifies God as the God of monotheism, all of whose three principal strains (Jewish, Christian, and Muslim) acknowledge the religious importance of the Ten Commandments. On the dissent's view, it apparently follows that even rigorous espousal of a common element of this common monotheism, is consistent with the establishment ban.

But the dissent's argument for the original understanding is flawed from the outset by its failure to consider the full range of evidence showing what the Framers believed. The dissent is certainly correct in putting forward evidence that some of the Framers thought some endorsement of religion was compatible with the establishment ban; the dissent quotes the first President as stating that "national morality [cannot] prevail in exclusion of religious principle," for example, and it cites his first Thanksgiving proclamation giving thanks to God. . . . Surely if expressions like these from Washington and his contemporaries were all we had to go on, there would be a good case that the neutrality principle has the effect of broadening the ban on establishment beyond the Framers' understanding of it (although there would, of course, still be the question of whether the historical case could overcome some 60 years of precedent taking neutrality as its guiding principle).

But the fact is that we do have more to go on, for there is also evidence supporting the proposition that the Framers intended the Establishment Clause to require governmental neutrality in matters of religion, including neutrality in statements acknowledging religion. The very language of the Establishment Clause represented a significant departure from early drafts that merely prohibited a single national religion, and, the final language instead "extended [the] prohibition to state support for 'religion' in general." . . .

The historical record, moreover, is complicated beyond the dissent's account by the writings and practices of figures no less influential than Thomas Jefferson and James Madison. Jefferson, for example, refused to issue Thanksgiving Proclamations because he believed that they violated the Constitution. . . .

The fair inference is that there was no common understanding about the limits of the establishment prohibition, and the dissent's conclusion that its narrower view was the original understanding, stretches the evidence beyond tensile capacity. What the evidence does show is a group of statesmen, like others before and after them, who proposed a guarantee with contours not wholly worked out, leaving the Establishment Clause with edges still to be determined. And none the worse for that. Indeterminate edges are the kind to have in a constitution meant to endure, and to meet "exigencies which, if foreseen at all, must have been seen dimly, and which can be best provided for as they occur." . . .

While the dissent fails to show a consistent original understanding from which to argue that the neutrality principle should be rejected, it does manage to deliver a surprise. As mentioned, the dissent says that the deity the Framers had in mind was the God of monotheism, with the consequence that government may espouse a tenet of traditional monotheism. This is truly a remarkable view. Other members of the Court have dissented on the ground that the Establishment Clause bars nothing more than governmental preference for one religion over another . . ., but at least religion has previously been treated inclusively. Today's dissent, however, apparently means that government should be free to approve the core beliefs of a favored religion over the tenets of others, a view that should trouble anyone who prizes religious liberty. Certainly history cannot justify it; on the contrary, history shows that the religion of concern to the Framers was not that of the monotheistic faiths generally, but Christianity in particular, a fact that no member of this Court takes as a premise for construing the Religion Clauses.... [T]here is, it seems, no escape from interpretative consequences that would surprise the Framers. Thus, it appears to be common ground in the interpretation of a Constitution "intended to endure for ages to come," ... that applications unanticipated by the Framers are inevitable.

Historical evidence thus supports no solid argument for changing course ... [T]he divisiveness of religion in current public life is inescapable. This is no time to deny the prudence of understanding the Establishment Clause to require the Government to stay neutral on religious belief, which is reserved for the conscience of the individual.

V

Given the ample support for the District Court's finding of a predominantly religious purpose behind the Counties' third display, we affirm the Sixth Circuit in upholding the preliminary injunction.

. . .

Justice O'Connor, concurring.

I join in the Court's opinion....

Reasonable minds can disagree about how to apply the Religion Clauses in a given case. But the goal of the Clauses is clear: to carry out the Founders' plan of preserving religious liberty to the fullest extent possible in a pluralistic society. By enforcing the Clauses, we have kept religion a matter for the individual conscience, not for the prosecutor or bureaucrat. At a time when we see around the world the violent consequences of the assumption of religious authority by government, Americans may count themselves fortunate: Our regard for constitutional boundaries has protected us from similar travails, while allowing private religious exercise to flourish....

. . .

Given the history of this particular display of the Ten Commandments, the Court correctly finds an Establishment Clause violation. The purpose behind the counties' display is relevant because it conveys an unmistakable message of endorsement to the reasonable observer....

. . .

Justice Scalia, with whom the Chief Justice and Justice Thomas join, and with whom Justice Kennedy joins as to Parts II and III, dissenting.

I would uphold McCreary County and Pulaski County, Kentucky's (hereinafter Counties) displays of the Ten Commandments. I shall discuss first, why the Court's oft repeated assertion that the government cannot favor religious practice is false; second, why today's opinion extends the scope of that falsehood even beyond prior cases; and third, why even on the basis of the Court's false assumptions the judgment here is wrong.

I

. . .

. . . [Absolutely forbidding a Head of State to invoke God's blessing] is one model of the relationship between church and state—a model spread across Europe by the armies of Napoleon, and reflected in the Constitution of France, which begins "France is [a] . . . secular Republic." . . . This is not, and never was, the model adopted by America. . . .

. . .

Nor have the views of our people on this matter significantly changed. Presidents continue to conclude the Presidential oath with the words "so help me God." Our legislatures, state and national, continue to open their sessions with prayer led by official chaplains. The sessions of this Court continue to open with the prayer "God save the United States and this Honorable Court." Invocation of the Almighty by our public figures, at all levels of government, remains commonplace. Our coinage bears the motto "IN GOD WE TRUST." And our Pledge of Allegiance contains the acknowledgment that we are a Nation "under God." . . .

With all of this reality (and much more) staring it in the face, how can the Court *possibly* assert that " 'the First Amendment mandates governmental neutrality between . . . religion and nonreligion,' " and that "[m]anifesting a purpose to favor . . . adherence to religion generally," is unconstitutional? Who says so? Surely not the words of the Constitution. Surely not the history and traditions that reflect our society's constant understanding of those words. Surely not even the current sense of our society, recently reflected in an Act of Congress adopted *unanimously* by the Senate and with only 5 nays in the House of Representatives, . . . criticizing a Court of Appeals opinion that had held "under God" in the Pledge of Allegiance unconstitutional. . . . And it is, moreover, a thoroughly discredited say-so. It is discredited, to begin with, because a majority of the Justices on the current Court (including at least one Member of today's majority) have, in separate opinions, repudiated the brain-spun *"Lemon* test" that embodies the supposed principle of neutrality between religion and irreligion. . . . And it is discredited because the Court has not had the courage (or the foolhardiness) to apply the neutrality principle consistently.

What distinguishes the rule of law from the dictatorship of a shifting Supreme Court majority is the absolutely indispensable requirement that judicial opinions be grounded in consistently applied principle. That is what prevents judges from ruling now this way, now that—thumbs up or thumbs down—as their personal preferences dictate. Today's opinion forthrightly (or actually, somewhat less than forthrightly) admits that it does not rest upon consistently applied principle. . . . [T]he Court acknowledges that the "Establishment Clause doctrine" it purports to be applying "lacks the comfort of categorical absolutes." What the Court means by this lovely euphemism is that sometimes the Court chooses to decide cases on the principle that government cannot favor religion, and sometimes it does not. The footnote goes on to say that "[i]n special instances we have found good reason" to dispense with the principle, but "[n]o such reasons present themselves here." ... It does not identify all of those "special instances," much less identify the "good reason" for their existence.

. . .

Besides appealing to the demonstrably false principle that the government cannot favor religion over irreligion, today's opinion suggests that the posting of the Ten Commandments violates the principle that the government cannot favor one religion over another.... That is indeed a valid principle where public aid or assistance to religion is concerned, ... or where the free exercise of religion is at issue, but it necessarily applies in a more limited sense to public acknowledgment of the Creator. If religion in the public forum had to be entirely nondenominational, there could be no religion in the public forum at all. One cannot say the word "God," or "the Almighty," one cannot offer public supplication or thanksgiving, without contradicting the beliefs of some people that there are many gods, or that God or the gods pay no attention to human affairs. With respect to public acknowledgment of religious belief, it is entirely clear from our Nation's historical practices that the Establishment Clause permits this disregard of polytheists and believers in unconcerned deities, just as it permits the disregard of devout atheists....

Historical practices thus demonstrate that there is a distance between the acknowledgment of a single Creator and the establishment of a religion....

B

. . .

II

As bad as the *Lemon* test is, it is worse for the fact that, since its inception, its seemingly simple mandates have been manipulated to fit whatever result the Court aimed to achieve. Today's opinion is no different. In two respects it modifies *Lemon* to ratchet up the Court's hostility to religion. First, the Court justifies inquiry into legislative purpose, not as an end itself, but as a means to ascertain the appearance of the government action to an " 'objective observer.' " Because in the Court's view the true danger to be guarded against is that the objective observer would feel like an "outside[r]" or "not [a] full membe[r]" of the political community," its inquiry focuses not on the *actual purpose* of government action, but the "purpose apparent from government action." Under this approach, even if a government could show that its actual purpose was not to advance religion, it would presumably violate the Constitution as long as the Court's objective observer would think otherwise....

I have remarked before that it is an odd jurisprudence that bases the unconstitutionality of a government practice that does not *actually* advance religion on the hopes of the government that it *would* do so.... But that oddity pales in comparison to the one invited by today's analysis: the legitimacy of a government action with a wholly secular effect would turn on the *misperception* of an imaginary observer that the government officials behind the action had the intent to advance religion.

... *Lemon*'s more limited requirement ... finds no support in our cases. In all but one of the five cases in which this Court has invalidated a government practice on the basis of its purpose to benefit religion, it has first declared that the statute was motivated entirely by the desire to advance religion.... In Edwards [v. Aguillard, 482 U.S. 578 (1987)], the Court did say that the state action was invalid because its "primary" or "preeminent" purpose was to advance a particular religious belief, ... but that statement was unnecessary to the result, since the Court rejected the State's only proffered secular purpose as a sham....

. . .

III

Even accepting the Court's *Lemon*-based premises, the displays at issue here were constitutional.

A

To any person who happened to walk down the hallway of the McCreary or Pulaski County Courthouse during the roughly nine months when the Foundations Displays were exhibited, the displays must have seemed unremarkable—if indeed they were noticed at all. The walls of both courthouses were already lined with historical documents and other assorted portraits; each Foundations Display was exhibited in the same format as these other displays and nothing in the record suggests that either County took steps to give it greater prominence.

Entitled "The Foundations of American Law and Government Display," each display consisted of nine equally sized documents: the original version of the Magna Carta, the Declaration of Independence, the Bill of Rights, the Star Spangled Banner, the Mayflower Compact of 1620, a picture of Lady Justice, the National Motto of the United States ("In God We Trust"), the Preamble to the Kentucky Constitution, and the Ten Commandments. The displays did not emphasize any of the nine documents in any way: The frame holding the Ten Commandments was of the same size and had the same appearance as that which held each of the other documents....

Posted with the documents was a plaque, identifying the display, and explaining that it "contains documents that played a significant role in the foundation of our system of law and government." ... The explanation related to the Ten Commandments was third in the list of nine and did not serve to distinguish it from the other documents....

B

On its face, the Foundations Displays manifested the purely secular purpose that the Counties asserted before the District Court: "to display documents that played a significant role in the foundation of our system of law and government." ...

. . .

C

In any event, the Court's conclusion that the Counties exhibited the Foundations Displays with the purpose of promoting religion is doubtful. In the Court's view, the impermissible motive was apparent from the initial displays of the Ten Commandments all by themselves: When that occurs, the Court says, "a religious object is unmistakable." Surely that cannot be. If, as discussed above, the Commandments have a proper place in our civic history, even placing them by themselves can be civically motivated—especially when they are placed, not in a school (as they were in the *Stone* case upon which the Court places such reliance), but in a courthouse. . . .

. . . What Justice Kennedy said of the creche in *Allegheny County* is equally true of the Counties' original Ten Commandments displays:

"No one was compelled to observe or participate in any religious ceremony or activity. [T]he count[ies] [did not] contribut[e] significant amounts of tax money to serve the cause of one religious faith. [The Ten Commandments] are purely passive symbols of [the religious foundation for many of our laws and governmental institutions]. Passersby who disagree with the message conveyed by th[e] displays are free to ignore them, or even to turn their backs, just as they are free to do when they disagree with any other form of government speech." 492 U.S., at 664. . . .

Nor is it the case that a solo display of the Ten Commandments advances any one faith. They are assuredly a religious symbol, but they are not so closely associated with a single religious belief that their display can reasonably be understood as preferring one religious sect over another. The Ten Commandments are recognized by Judaism, Christianity, and Islam alike as divinely given. . . .

. . .

Turning at last to the displays actually at issue in this case, the Court faults the Counties for not *repealing* the resolution expressing what the Court believes to be an impermissible intent. Under these circumstances, the Court says, "no reasonable observer could swallow the claim that the Counties had cast off the objective so unmistakable in the earlier displays." Even were I to accept all that the Court has said before, I would not agree with that assessment. To begin with, of course, it is unlikely that a reasonable observer *would even have been aware* of the resolutions, so there would be nothing to "cast off." The Court implies that the Counties may have been able to remedy the "taint" from the old resolutions by enacting a new one. But that action would have been wholly unnecessary in light of the explanation that the Counties included *with the displays themselves:* A plaque next to the documents informed all who passed by that each display "contains documents that played a significant role in the foundation of our system of law and government." Additionally, there was no reason for the Counties to repeal or repudiate the resolutions adopted with the hanging of the second displays, since they related *only to the second displays.* After complying with the District Court's order to remove the second displays "immediately," and erecting new displays that in content and by express assertion reflected a different purpose from that identified in the resolutions, the Counties had no reason to believe that their previous resolutions would be deemed to be the basis for their actions. After the Counties discovered that the sentiments expressed in the resolutions could be attributed to their most recent displays (in oral argument before this Court), they repudiated them immediately.

In sum: The first displays did not necessarily evidence an intent to further religious practice; nor did the second displays, or the resolutions authorizing them; and there is in any event no basis for attributing whatever intent motivated the first and second displays to the third. Given the presumption of regularity that always accompanies our review of official action, the Court has identified no evidence of a purpose to advance religion in a way that is inconsistent with our cases. The Court may well be correct in identifying the third displays as the fruit of a desire to display the Ten Commandments but neither our cases nor our history support its assertion that such a desire renders the fruit poisonous.

* * *

For the foregoing reasons, I would reverse the judgment of the Court of Appeals.

Van Orden v. Perry

545 U.S. 677, 125 S.Ct. 2854, 162 L.Ed.2d 607 (2005).

Chief Justice Rehnquist announced the judgment of the Court and delivered an opinion, in which Justice Scalia, Justice Kennedy, and Justice Thomas join.

The question here is whether the Establishment Clause of the First Amendment allows the display of a monument inscribed with the Ten Commandments on the Texas State Capitol grounds. We hold that it does.

The 22 acres surrounding the Texas State Capitol contain 17 monuments and 21 historical markers commemorating the "people, ideals, and events that compose Texan identity." . . . The monolith challenged here stands 6–feet high and 3 1/2–feet wide. It is located to the north of the Capitol building, between the Capitol and the Supreme Court building. Its primary content is the text of the Ten Commandments. An eagle grasping the American flag, an eye inside of a pyramid, and two small tablets with what appears to be an ancient script are carved above the text of the Ten Commandments. Below the text are two Stars of David and the superimposed Greek letters Chi and Rho, which represent Christ. The bottom of the monument bears the inscription "PRESENTED TO THE PEOPLE AND YOUTH OF TEXAS BY THE FRATERNAL ORDER OF EAGLES OF TEXAS 1961." . . .

The legislative record surrounding the State's acceptance of the monument from the Eagles—a national social, civic, and patriotic organization—is limited to legislative journal entries. After the monument was accepted, the State selected a site for the monument based on the recommendation of the state organization responsible for maintaining the Capitol grounds. The Eagles paid the cost of erecting the monument, the dedication of which was presided over by two state legislators.

Petitioner Thomas Van Orden is a native Texan and a resident of Austin. At one time he was a licensed lawyer, having graduated from Southern Methodist Law School. . . .

Forty years after the monument's erection and six years after Van Orden began to encounter the monument frequently, he sued numerous state officials ... seeking both a declaration that the monument's placement violates the Establishment Clause and an injunction requiring its removal. After a bench trial, the District Court held that the monument did not contravene the Establishment Clause. It found that the State had a valid secular purpose in recognizing and commending the Eagles for their efforts to reduce juvenile delinquency. The District Court also determined that a reasonable observer, mindful of the history, purpose, and context, would not conclude that this passive monument conveyed the message that the State was seeking to endorse religion. The Court of Appeals affirmed the District Court's holdings with respect to the monument's purpose and effect. We ... affirm.

Our cases, Januslike, point in two directions in applying the Establishment Clause. One face looks toward the strong role played by religion and religious traditions throughout our Nation's history.... The other face looks toward the principle that governmental intervention in religious matters can itself endanger religious freedom.

This case, like all Establishment Clause challenges, presents us with the difficulty of respecting both faces. Our institutions presuppose a Supreme Being, yet these institutions must not press religious observances upon their citizens. One face looks to the past in acknowledgment of our Nation's heritage, while the other looks to the present in demanding a separation between church and state. Reconciling these two faces requires that we neither abdicate our responsibility to maintain a division between church and state nor evince a hostility to religion by disabling the government from in some ways recognizing our religious heritage....

These two faces are evident in representative cases both upholding and invalidating laws under the Establishment Clause. Over the last 25 years, we have sometimes pointed to Lemon v. Kurtzman, 403 U.S. 602, (1971), as providing the governing test in Establishment Clause challenges.... Others have applied it only after concluding that the challenged practice was invalid under a different Establishment Clause test.

Whatever may be the fate of the *Lemon* test in the larger scheme of Establishment Clause jurisprudence, we think it not useful in dealing with the sort of passive monument that Texas has erected on its Capitol grounds. Instead, our analysis is driven both by the nature of the monument and by our Nation's history.

As we explained in Lynch v. Donnelly, 465 U.S. 668 (1984): "There is an unbroken history of official acknowledgment by all three branches of government of the role of religion in American life from at least 1789"....

Recognition of the role of God in our Nation's heritage has also been reflected in our decisions....

In this case we are faced with a display of the Ten Commandments on government property outside the Texas State Capitol. Such acknowledgments of the role played by the Ten Commandments in our Nation's heritage are common throughout America. We need only look within our own Courtroom. Since 1935, Moses has stood, holding two tablets that reveal portions of the Ten Commandments written in Hebrew, among other lawgivers in the south frieze.

Representations of the Ten Commandments adorn the metal gates lining the north and south sides of the Courtroom as well as the doors leading into the Courtroom. Moses also sits on the exterior east facade of the building holding the Ten Commandments tablets.

Similar acknowledgments can be seen throughout a visitor's tour of our Nation's Capital. . . .

Our opinions, like our building, have recognized the role the Decalogue plays in America's heritage. . . . These displays and recognitions of the Ten Commandments bespeak the rich American tradition of religious acknowledgments.

Of course, the Ten Commandments are religious—they were so viewed at their inception and so remain. The monument, therefore, has religious significance. According to Judeo–Christian belief, the Ten Commandments were given to Moses by God on Mt. Sinai. But Moses was a lawgiver as well as a religious leader. And the Ten Commandments have an undeniable historical meaning, as the foregoing examples demonstrate. Simply having religious content or promoting a message consistent with a religious doctrine does not run afoul of the Establishment Clause. . . .

There are, of course, limits to the display of religious messages or symbols. For example, we held unconstitutional a Kentucky statute requiring the posting of the Ten Commandments in every public schoolroom. Stone v. Graham, 449 U.S. 39 (1980) *(per curiam)*. In the classroom context, we found that the Kentucky statute had an improper and plainly religious purpose. . . . As evidenced by *Stone*'s almost exclusive reliance upon two of our school prayer cases, it stands as an example of the fact that we have "been particularly vigilant in monitoring compliance with the Establishment Clause in elementary and secondary schools," . . . . Neither *Stone* itself nor subsequent opinions have indicated that *Stone*'s holding would extend to a legislative chamber, . . . or to capitol grounds.

The placement of the Ten Commandments monument on the Texas State Capitol grounds is a far more passive use of those texts than was the case in *Stone*, where the text confronted elementary school students every day. Indeed, Van Orden, the petitioner here, apparently walked by the monument for a number of years before bringing this lawsuit. . . . Texas has treated her Capitol grounds monuments as representing the several strands in the State's political and legal history. The inclusion of the Ten Commandments monument in this group has a dual significance, partaking of both religion and government. We cannot say that Texas' display of this monument violates the Establishment Clause of the First Amendment.

The judgment of the Court of Appeals is affirmed.

. . .

Justice Scalia, concurring.

I join the opinion of the Chief Justice because I think it accurately reflects our current Establishment Clause jurisprudence—or at least the Establishment Clause jurisprudence we currently apply some of the time. I would prefer to reach the same result by adopting an Establishment Clause jurisprudence that is in accord with our Nation's past and present practices, and that can be consistently applied—the central relevant feature of which is that there is nothing unconstitutional in a State's favoring religion generally, honoring God through public prayer and acknowledgment, or, in a nonproselytizing manner, venerating the Ten Commandments . . .

Justice Thomas, concurring.

. . . I join the Chief Justice's opinion in full.

This case would be easy if the Court were willing to abandon the inconsistent guideposts it has adopted for addressing Establishment Clause challenges, and return to the original meaning of the Clause. I have previously suggested that the Clause's text and history "resis[t] incorporation" against the States. . . . If the Establishment Clause does not restrain the States, then it has no application here, where only state action is at issue.

Even if the Clause is incorporated, or if the Free Exercise Clause limits the power of States to establish religions, . . . our task would be far simpler if we returned to the original meaning of the word "establishment" than it is under the various approaches this Court now uses. The Framers understood an establishment "necessarily [to] involve actual legal coercion." . . .

There is no question that, based on the original meaning of the Establishment Clause, the Ten Commandments display at issue here is constitutional. In no sense does Texas compel petitioner Van Orden to do anything. The only injury to him is that he takes offense at seeing the monument as he passes it on his way to the Texas Supreme Court Library. He need not stop to read it or even to look at it, let alone to express support for it or adopt the Commandments as guides for his life. The mere presence of the monument along his path involves no coercion and thus does not violate the Establishment Clause.

Returning to the original meaning would do more than simplify our task. It also would avoid the pitfalls present in the Court's current approach to such challenges. This Court's precedent elevates the trivial to the proverbial "federal case," by making benign signs and postings subject to challenge. Yet even as it does so, the Court's precedent attempts to avoid declaring all religious symbols and words of longstanding tradition unconstitutional, by counterfactually declaring them of little religious significance. . . .

. . .

[T]he very "flexibility" of this Court's Establishment Clause precedent leaves it incapable of consistent application. . . .

The unintelligibility of this Court's precedent raises the further concern that, either in appearance or in fact, adjudication of Establishment Clause challenges turns on judicial predilections. . . .

Much, if not all, of this would be avoided if the Court would return to the views of the Framers and adopt coercion as the touchstone for our Establishment Clause inquiry. Every acknowledgment of religion would not give rise to an Establishment Clause claim. Courts would not act as theological commissions, judging the meaning of religious matters. Most important, our precedent would be capable of consistent and coherent application. While the Court correctly rejects the challenge to the Ten Commandments monument on the

Texas Capitol grounds, a more fundamental rethinking of our Establishment Clause jurisprudence remains in order.

Justice Breyer, concurring in the judgment.

In School Dist. of Abington Township v. Schempp, 374 U.S. 203 (1963), Justice Goldberg, joined by Justice Harlan, wrote, in respect to the First Amendment's Religion Clauses, that there is "no simple and clear measure which by precise application can readily and invariably demark the permissible from the impermissible." . . . One must refer instead to the basic purposes of those Clauses. They seek to "assure the fullest possible scope of religious liberty and tolerance for all." They seek to avoid that divisiveness based upon religion that promotes social conflict, sapping the strength of government and religion alike. . . . They seek to maintain that "separation of church and state" that has long been critical to the "peaceful dominion that religion exercises in [this] country," . . . .

. . .

Thus, as Justices Goldberg and Harlan pointed out, the Court has found no single mechanical formula that can accurately draw the constitutional line in every case. . . . Where the Establishment Clause is at issue, tests designed to measure "neutrality" alone are insufficient, both because it is sometimes difficult to determine when a legal rule is "neutral," and because "untutored devotion to the concept of neutrality can lead to invocation or approval of results which partake not simply of that noninterference and noninvolvement with the religious which the Constitution commands, but of a brooding and pervasive devotion to the secular and a passive, or even active, hostility to the religious." . . .

Neither can this Court's other tests readily explain the Establishment Clause's tolerance, for example, of the prayers that open legislative meetings, . . . certain references to, and invocations of, the Deity in the public words of public officials; the public references to God on coins, decrees, and buildings; or the attention paid to the religious objectives of certain holidays, including Thanksgiving. . . .

If the relation between government and religion is one of separation, but not of mutual hostility and suspicion, one will inevitably find difficult borderline cases. And in such cases, I see no test-related substitute for the exercise of legal judgment. . . . That judgment is not a personal judgment. Rather, as in all constitutional cases, it must reflect and remain faithful to the underlying purposes of the Clauses, and it must take account of context and consequences measured in light of those purposes. While the Court's prior tests provide useful guideposts—and might well lead to the same result the Court reaches today. . . .—no exact formula can dictate a resolution to such fact-intensive cases.

The case before us is a borderline case. It concerns a large granite monument bearing the text of the Ten Commandments located on the grounds of the Texas State Capitol. On the one hand, the Commandments' text undeniably has a religious message, invoking, indeed emphasizing, the Deity. On the other hand, focusing on the text of the Commandments alone cannot conclusively resolve this case. Rather, to determine the message that the text here conveys, we must examine how the text is *used*. And that inquiry requires us to consider the context of the display.

In certain contexts, a display of the tablets of the Ten Commandments can convey not simply a religious message but also a secular moral message (about proper standards of social conduct). And in certain contexts, a display of the tablets can also convey a historical message (about a historic relation between those standards and the law)—a fact that helps to explain the display of those tablets in dozens of courthouses throughout the Nation, including the Supreme Court of the United States. . . .

Here the tablets have been used as part of a display that communicates not simply a religious message, but a secular message as well. The circumstances surrounding the display's placement on the capitol grounds and its physical setting suggest that the State itself intended the latter, nonreligious aspects of the tablets' message to predominate. And the monument's 40–year history on the Texas state grounds indicates that that has been its effect.

The group that donated the monument, the Fraternal Order of Eagles, a private civic (and primarily secular) organization, while interested in the religious aspect of the Ten Commandments, sought to highlight the Command-ments' role in shaping civic morality as part of that organization's efforts to combat juvenile delinquency. . . . The Eagles' consultation with a committee composed of members of several faiths in order to find a nonsectarian text underscores the group's ethics-based motives. The tablets, as displayed on the monument, prominently acknowledge that the Eagles donated the display, a factor which, though not sufficient, thereby further distances the State itself from the religious aspect of the Commandments' message.

. . .

. . . As far as I can tell, 40 years passed in which the presence of this monument, legally speaking, went unchallenged (until the single legal objection raised by petitioner). And I am not aware of any evidence suggesting that this was due to a climate of intimidation. Hence, those 40 years suggest more strongly than can any set of formulaic tests that few individuals, whatever their system of beliefs, are likely to have understood the monument as amounting, in any significantly detrimental way, to a government effort to favor a particular religious sect, primarily to promote religion over nonreligion, to "engage in" any "religious practic[e]," to "compel" any "religious practic[e]," or to "work deterrence" of any "religious belief." . . . Those 40 years suggest that the public visiting the capitol grounds has considered the religious aspect of the tablets' message as part of what is a broader moral and historical message reflective of a cultural heritage.

This case, moreover, is distinguishable from instances where the Court has found Ten Commandments displays impermissible. The display is not on the grounds of a public school, where, given the impressionability of the young, government must exercise particular care in separating church and state. . . . This case also differs from *McCreary County*, where the short (and stormy) history of the courthouse Commandments' displays demonstrates the substan-tially religious objectives of those who mounted them, and the effect of this readily apparent objective upon those who view them. . . . That history there indicates a governmental effort substantially to promote religion, not simply an effort primarily to reflect, historically, the secular impact of a religiously inspired document. And, in today's world, in a Nation of so many different religious and comparable nonreligious fundamental beliefs, a more contemporary state effort to focus attention upon a religious text is certainly likely to prove divisive in a way that this longstanding, pre-existing monument has not.

For these reasons, I believe that the Texas display—serving a mixed but primarily nonreligious purpose, not primarily "advanc[ing]" or "inhibit[ing] religion," and not creating an "excessive government entanglement with religion,"—might satisfy this Court's more formal Establishment Clause tests.... But, as I have said, in reaching the conclusion that the Texas display falls on the permissible side of the constitutional line, I rely less upon a literal application of any particular test than upon consideration of the basic purposes of the First Amendment's Religion Clauses themselves. This display has stood apparently uncontested for nearly two generations. That experience helps us understand that as a practical matter of *degree* this display is unlikely to prove divisive. And this matter of degree is, I believe, critical in a borderline case such as this one.

At the same time, to reach a contrary conclusion here, based primarily upon the religious nature of the tablets' text would, I fear, lead the law to exhibit a hostility toward religion that has no place in our Establishment Clause traditions. Such a holding might well encourage disputes concerning the removal of longstanding depictions of the Ten Commandments from public buildings across the Nation. And it could thereby create the very kind of religiously based divisiveness that the Establishment Clause seeks to avoid....

In light of these considerations, I cannot agree with today's plurality's analysis. Nor can I agree with Justice Scalia's dissent in ... *McCreary County*.... I do agree with Justice O'Connor's statement of principles in *McCreary County*, ... though I disagree with her evaluation of the evidence as it bears on the application of those principles to this case.

I concur in the judgment of the Court.

Justice Stevens, with whom Justice Ginsburg joins, dissenting.

The sole function of the monument on the grounds of Texas' State Capitol is to display the full text of one version of the Ten Commandments. The monument is not a work of art and does not refer to any event in the history of the State....

. . .

As the story goes, the program was initiated by the late Judge E.J. Ruegemer, a Minnesota juvenile court judge and then-Chairman of the Eagles National Commission on Youth Guidance. Inspired by a juvenile offender who had never heard of the Ten Commandments, the judge approached the Minnesota Eagles with the idea of distributing paper copies of the Commandments to be posted in courthouses nationwide. The State's Aerie undertook this project and its popularity spread. When Cecil B. DeMille, who at that time was filming the movie The Ten Commandments, heard of the judge's endeavor, he teamed up with the Eagles to produce the type of granite monolith now displayed in front of the Texas Capitol and at courthouse squares, city halls, and public parks throughout the Nation. Granite was reportedly chosen over DeMille's original suggestion of bronze plaques to better replicate the original Ten Commandments.

The donors were motivated by a desire to "inspire the youth" and curb juvenile delinquency by providing children with a "code of conduct or standards by which to govern their actions." It is the Eagles' belief that disseminating the message conveyed by the Ten Commandments will help to persuade young men and women to observe civilized standards of behavior, and will lead to more productive lives. . . .

The desire to combat juvenile delinquency by providing guidance to youths is both admirable and unquestionably secular. But achieving that goal through biblical teachings injects a religious purpose into an otherwise secular endeavor. By spreading the word of God and converting heathens to Christianity, missionaries expect to enlighten their converts, enhance their satisfaction with life, and improve their behavior. Similarly, by disseminating the "law of God"—directing fidelity to God and proscribing murder, theft, and adultery—the Eagles hope that this divine guidance will help wayward youths conform their behavior and improve their lives. In my judgment, the significant secular by-products that are intended consequences of religious instruction—indeed, of the establishment of most religions—are not the type of "secular" purposes that justify government promulgation of sacred religious messages.

Though the State of Texas may genuinely wish to combat juvenile delinquency, and may rightly want to honor the Eagles for their efforts, it cannot effectuate these admirable purposes through an explicitly religious medium. . . . The State may admonish its citizens not to lie, cheat or steal, to honor their parents and to respect their neighbors' property; and it may do so by printed words, in television commercials, or on granite monuments in front of its public buildings. Moreover, the State may provide its schoolchildren and adult citizens with educational materials that explain the important role that our forebears' faith in God played in their decisions to select America as a refuge from religious persecution, to declare their independence from the British Crown, and to conceive a new Nation. . . . The message at issue in this case, however, is fundamentally different from either a bland admonition to observe generally accepted rules of behavior or a general history lesson.

The reason this message stands apart is that the Decalogue is a venerable religious text. . . . Thankfully, the plurality does not attempt to minimize the religious significance of the Ten Commandments. . . . Attempts to secularize what is unquestionably a sacred text defy credibility and disserve people of faith.

The profoundly sacred message embodied by the text inscribed on the Texas monument is emphasized by the especially large letters that identify its author: "**I AM the LORD thy God.**" . . . It commands present worship of Him and no other deity. It directs us to be guided by His teaching in the current and future conduct of all of our affairs. It instructs us to follow a code of divine law, some of which has informed and been integrated into our secular legal code ("Thou shalt not kill"), but much of which has not ("Thou shalt not make to thyself any graven images. . . . Thou shalt not covet").

Moreover, despite the Eagles' best efforts to choose a benign nondenominational text, the Ten Commandments display projects not just a religious, but an inherently sectarian message. There are many distinctive versions of the Decalogue, ascribed to by different religions and even different denominations within a particular faith; to a pious and learned observer, these differences may be of enormous religious significance. . . .

Even if, however, the message of the monument, despite the inscribed text, fairly could be said to represent the belief system of all Judeo–Christians, it would still run afoul of the Establishment Clause by prescribing a compelled code of conduct from one God, namely a Judeo–Christian God, that is rejected by prominent polytheistic sects, such as Hinduism, as well as nontheistic religions, such as Buddhism. . . . Any of those bases, in my judgment, would be sufficient to conclude that the message should not be proclaimed by the State of Texas on a permanent monument at the seat of its government.

. . .

Recognizing the diversity of religious and secular beliefs held by Texans and by all Americans, it seems beyond peradventure that allowing the seat of government to serve as a stage for the propagation of an unmistakably Judeo–Christian message of piety would have the tendency to make nonmonotheists and nonbelievers "feel like [outsiders] in matters of faith, and [strangers] in the political community." . . .

. . .

Critical examination of the Decalogue's prominent display at the seat of Texas government, rather than generic citation to the role of religion in American life, unmistakably reveals on which side of the "slippery slope" this display must fall. God, as the author of its message, the Eagles, as the donor of the monument, and the State of Texas, as its proud owner, speak with one voice for a common purpose—to encourage Texans to abide by the divine code of a "Judeo–Christian" God. If this message is permissible, then the shining principle of neutrality to which we have long adhered is nothing more than mere shadow.

III

The plurality relies heavily on the fact that our Republic was founded, and has been governed since its nascence, by leaders who spoke then (and speak still) in plainly religious rhetoric. . . .

The speeches and rhetoric characteristic of the founding era, however, do not answer the question before us. I have already explained why Texas' display of the full text of the Ten Commandments, given the content of the actual display and the context in which it is situated, sets this case apart from the countless examples of benign government recognitions of religion. But there is another crucial difference. Our leaders, when delivering public addresses, often express their blessings simultaneously in the service of God and their constituents. Thus, when public officials deliver public speeches, we recognize that their words are not exclusively a transmission from *the* government because those oratories have embedded within them the inherently personal views of the speaker as an individual member of the polity. The permanent placement of a textual religious display on state property is different in kind; it amalgamates otherwise discordant individual views into a collective statement of government approval. Moreover, the message never ceases to transmit itself to objecting viewers whose only choices are to accept the message or to ignore the offense by averting their gaze.

The plurality's reliance on early religious statements and proclamations made by the Founders is also problematic because those views were not espoused at the Constitutional Convention in 1787 nor enshrined in the Constitution's text. Thus, the presentation of these religious statements as a unified historical narrative is bound to paint a misleading picture. . . .

. . .

Ardent separationists aside, there is another critical nuance lost in the plurality's portrayal of history. Simply put, many of the Founders who are often cited as authoritative expositors of the Constitution's original meaning understood the Establishment Clause to stand for a *narrower* proposition than the plurality, for whatever reason, is willing to accept. Namely, many of the Framers understood the word "religion" in the Establishment Clause to encompass only the various sects of Christianity.

. . .

Unless one is willing to renounce over 65 years of Establishment Clause jurisprudence and cross back over the incorporation bridge, . . . appeals to the religiosity of the Framers ring hollow. But even if there were a coherent way to embrace incorporation with one hand while steadfastly abiding by the Founders' purported religious views on the other, the problem of the selective use of history remains. As the widely divergent views espoused by the leaders of our founding era plainly reveal, the historical record of the preincorporation Establishment Clause is too indeterminate to serve as an interpretive North Star.

It is our duty, therefore, to interpret the First Amendment's command that "Congress shall make no law respecting an establishment of religion" not by merely asking what those words meant to observers at the time of the founding, but instead by deriving from the Clause's text and history the broad principles that remain valid today. To reason from the broad principles contained in the Constitution does not, as Justice Scalia suggests, require us to abandon our heritage in favor of unprincipled expressions of personal preference. The task of applying the broad principles that the Framers wrote into the text of the First Amendment is, in any event, no more a matter of personal preference than is one's selection between two (or more) sides in a heated historical debate. We serve our constitutional mandate by expounding the meaning of constitutional provisions with one eye towards our Nation's history and the other fixed on its democratic aspirations. . . .

The principle that guides my analysis is neutrality. The basis for that principle is firmly rooted in our Nation's history and our Constitution's text. I recognize that the requirement that government must remain neutral between religion and irreligion would have seemed foreign to some of the Framers; so too would a requirement of neutrality between Jews and Christians. . . . The evil of discriminating today against atheists, "polytheists[,] and believers in unconcerned deities," *McCreary County*, . . . (Scalia, J., dissenting), is in my view a direct descendent of the evil of discriminating among Christian sects.

The Establishment Clause thus forbids it and, in turn, forbids Texas from displaying the Ten Commandments monument the plurality so casually affirms.

IV

The Eagles may donate as many monuments as they choose to be displayed in front of Protestant churches, benevolent organizations' meeting places, or on the front lawns of private citizens. The expurgated text of the King James version of the Ten Commandments that they have crafted is unlikely to be accepted by Catholic parishes, Jewish synagogues, or even some Protestant denominations, but the message they seek to convey is surely more compatible with church property than with property that is located on the government side of the metaphorical wall.

The judgment of the Court in this case stands for the proposition that the Constitution permits governmental displays of sacred religious texts. This makes a mockery of the constitutional ideal that government must remain neutral between religion and irreligion. If a State may endorse a particular deity's command to "have no other gods before me," it is difficult to conceive of any textual display that would run afoul of the Establishment Clause.

The disconnect between this Court's approval of Texas's monument and the constitutional prohibition against preferring religion to irreligion cannot be reduced to the exercise of plotting two adjacent locations on a slippery slope.... Rather, it is the difference between the shelter of a fortress and exposure to "the winds that would blow" if the wall were allowed to crumble.... That wall, however imperfect, remains worth preserving.

I respectfully dissent.

Justice O'Connor, dissenting.

For essentially the reasons given by Justice Souter, as well as the reasons given in my concurrence in McCreary County v. American Civil Liberties Union of Ky., I respectfully dissent.

Justice Souter, with whom Justice Stevens and Justice Ginsburg join, dissenting.

Although the First Amendment's Religion Clauses have not been read to mandate absolute governmental neutrality toward religion, ... the Establishment Clause requires neutrality as a general rule.... A governmental display of an obviously religious text cannot be squared with neutrality, except in a setting that plausibly indicates that the statement is not placed in view with a predominant purpose on the part of government either to adopt the religious message or to urge its acceptance by others.

Until today, only one of our cases addressed the constitutionality of posting the Ten Commandments, Stone v. Graham, 449 U.S. 39, 41–42 (1980) *(per curiam)*. A Kentucky statute required posting the Commandments on the walls of public school classrooms, and the Court described the State's purpose (relevant under the tripartite test laid out in Lemon v. Kurtzman ...) as being at odds with the obligation of religious neutrality.

. . .

What these observations underscore are the simple realities that the Ten Commandments constitute a religious statement, that their message is inherently religious, and that the purpose of singling them out in a display is clearly the same.

Thus, a pedestrian happening upon the monument at issue here needs no training in religious doctrine to realize that the statement of the Commandments, quoting God himself, proclaims that the will of the divine being is the source of obligation to obey the rules, including the facially secular ones. In this case, moreover, the text is presented to give particular prominence to the Commandments' first sectarian reference, "I am the Lord thy God." That proclamation is centered on the stone and written in slightly larger letters than the subsequent recitation. To ensure that the religious nature of the monument is clear to even the most casual passerby, the word "Lord" appears in all capital letters (as does the word "am"), so that the most eye-catching segment of the quotation is the declaration "I AM the LORD thy God." What follows, of course, are the rules against other gods, graven images, vain swearing, and Sabbath breaking. And the full text of the fifth Commandment puts forward filial respect as a condition of long life in the land "which the Lord they God giveth thee." . . .

To drive the religious point home, and identify the message as religious to any viewer who failed to read the text, the engraved quotation is framed by religious symbols: two tablets with what appears to be ancient script on them, two Stars of David, and the superimposed Greek letters Chi and Rho as the familiar monogram of Christ. Nothing on the monument, in fact, detracts from its religious nature. . . .

The monument's presentation of the Commandments with religious text emphasized and enhanced stands in contrast to any number of perfectly constitutional depictions of them, the frieze of our own Courtroom providing a good example, where the figure of Moses stands among history's great law-givers. While Moses holds the tablets of the Commandments showing some Hebrew text, no one looking at the lines of figures in marble relief is likely to see a religious purpose behind the assemblage or take away a religious message from it. Only one other depiction represents a religious leader, and the historical personages are mixed with symbols of moral and intellectual abstractions like Equity and Authority. . . .

Texas seeks to take advantage of the recognition that visual symbol and written text can manifest a secular purpose in secular company, when it argues that its monument (like Moses in the frieze) is not alone and ought to be viewed as only 1 among 17 placed on the 22 acres surrounding the state capitol. Texas, indeed, says that the Capitol grounds are like a museum for a collection of exhibits, the kind of setting that several Members of the Court have said can render the exhibition of religious artifacts permissible, even though in other circumstances their display would be seen as meant to convey a religious message forbidden to the State. . . . So, for example, the Government of the United States does not violate the Establishment Clause by hanging Giotto's Madonna on the wall of the National Gallery.

But 17 monuments with no common appearance, history, or esthetic role scattered over 22 acres is not a museum, and anyone strolling around the lawn would surely take each memorial on its own terms without any dawning sense that some purpose held the miscellany together more coherently than fortuity and the edge of the grass. One monument expresses admiration for pioneer women. One pays respect to the fighters of World War II. And one quotes the God of Abraham whose command is the sanction for moral law. The themes are individual grit, patriotic courage, and God as the source of Jewish and Christian morality; there is no common denominator....

. . .

Finally, though this too is a point on which judgment will vary, I do not see a persuasive argument for constitutionality in the plurality's observation that Van Orden's lawsuit comes "[f]orty years after the monument's erection ...," an observation that echoes the State's contention that one fact cutting in its favor is that "the monument stood ... in Austin ... for some forty years without generating any controversy or litigation,".... It is not that I think the passage of time is necessarily irrelevant in Establishment Clause analysis. We have approved framing-era practices because they must originally have been understood as constitutionally permissible, ... and we have recognized that Sunday laws have grown recognizably secular over time.... There is also an analogous argument, not yet evaluated, that ritualistic religious expression can become so numbing over time that its initial Establishment Clause violation becomes at some point too diminished for notice. But I do not understand any of these to be the State's argument, which rather seems to be that 40 years without a challenge shows that as a factual matter the religious expression is too tepid to provoke a serious reaction and constitute a violation. Perhaps, but the writer of Exodus chapter 20 was not lukewarm, and other explanations may do better in accounting for the late resort to the courts. Suing a State over religion puts nothing in a plaintiff's pocket and can take a great deal out, and even with volunteer litigators to supply time and energy, the risk of social ostracism can be powerfully deterrent. I doubt that a slow walk to the courthouse, even one that took 40 years, is much evidentiary help in applying the Establishment Clause.

I would reverse the judgment of the Court of Appeals.

SECTION 2.   The Free Exercise of Religion

C.   Financial Aid to Church–Related Schools and Church–Related Instruction

Page 1845.   Add at end of chapter:

Cutter v. Wilkinson

544 U.S. 709, 125 S.Ct. 2113, 161 L.Ed.2d 1020 (2005).

Justice Ginsburg delivered the opinion of the Court.

Section 3 of the Religious Land Use and Institutionalized Persons Act of 2000 (RLUIPA), 114 Stat. 804, provides in part: "No government shall impose a substantial burden on the religious exercise of a person residing in or confined to an institution," unless the burden furthers "a compelling governmental interest," and does so by "the least restrictive means." Plaintiffs below, petitioners here, are current and former inmates of institutions operated by the Ohio Department of Rehabilitation and Correction and assert that they are adherents of "nonmainstream" religions: the Satanist, Wicca, and Asatru religions, and the Church of Jesus Christ Christian. They complain that Ohio prison officials (respondents here), in violation of RLUIPA, have failed to accommodate their religious exercise "in a variety of different ways, including retaliating and discriminating against them for exercising their nontraditional faiths, denying them access to religious literature, denying them the same opportunities for group worship that are granted to adherents of mainstream religions, forbidding them to adhere to the dress and appearance mandates of their religions, withholding religious ceremonial items that are substantially identical to those that the adherents of mainstream religions are permitted, and failing to provide a chaplain trained in their faith." . . .

In response to petitioners' complaints, respondent prison officials have mounted a facial challenge to the institutionalized-persons provision of RLUIPA; respondents contend, *inter alia*, that the Act improperly advances religion in violation of the First Amendment's Establishment Clause. The District Court denied respondents' motion to dismiss petitioners' complaints, but the Court of Appeals reversed that determination. The appeals court held, as the prison officials urged, that the portion of RLUIPA applicable to institutionalized persons . . . violates the Establishment Clause. We reverse the Court of Appeals' judgment.

"This Court has long recognized that the government may . . . accommodate religious practices . . . without violating the Establishment Clause." . . . § 3 of RLUIPA, we hold, does not, on its face, exceed the limits of permissible government accommodation of religious practices.

I

A

RLUIPA is the latest of long-running congressional efforts to accord religious exercise heightened protection from government-imposed burdens, consistent with this Court's precedents. Ten years before RLUIPA's enactment, the Court held, in Employment Div., Dept. of Human Resources of Ore. v. Smith, . . . that the First Amendment's Free Exercise Clause does not inhibit enforcement of otherwise valid laws of general application that incidentally burden religious conduct. In particular, we ruled that the Free Exercise Clause did not bar Oregon from enforcing its blanket ban on peyote possession with no allowance for sacramental use of the drug. Accordingly, the State could deny unemployment benefits to persons dismissed from their jobs because of their religiously inspired peyote use. The Court recognized, however, that the political branches could shield religious exercise through legislative accommodation, for example, by making an exception to proscriptive drug laws for sacramental peyote use. . . .

Responding to *Smith*, Congress enacted the Religious Freedom Restoration Act of 1993 (RFRA). . . . In *City of Boerne*, this Court invalidated RFRA as applied to States and their subdivisions, holding that the Act exceeded Congress' remedial powers under the Fourteenth Amendment.[2] . . . Congress again responded, this time by enacting RLUIPA. Less sweeping than RFRA, and invoking federal authority under the Spending and Commerce Clauses, RLUIPA targets two areas: Section 2 of the Act concerns land-use regulation . . . ; § 3 relates to religious exercise by institutionalized persons. . . . Section 3, at issue here, provides that "[n]o [state or local] government shall impose a substantial burden on the religious exercise of a person residing in or confined to an institution," unless the government shows that the burden furthers "a compelling governmental interest" and does so by "the least restrictive means." . . . The Act defines "religious exercise" to include "any exercise of religion, whether or not compelled by, or central to, a system of religious belief." . . . Section 3 applies when "the substantial burden [on religious exercise] is imposed in a program or activity that receives Federal financial assistance," or "the substantial burden affects, or removal of that substantial burden would affect, commerce with foreign nations, among the several States, or with Indian tribes." . . . "A person may assert a violation of [RLUIPA] as a claim or defense in a judicial proceeding and obtain appropriate relief against a government." . . .

Before enacting § 3, Congress documented, in hearings spanning three years, that "frivolous or arbitrary" barriers impeded institutionalized persons' religious exercise. . . . To secure redress for inmates who encountered undue barriers to their religious observances, Congress carried over from RFRA the "compelling governmental interest"/"least restrictive means" standard. . . .

B

Petitioners initially filed suit against respondents asserting claims under the First and Fourteenth Amendments. After RLUIPA's enactment, petitioners amended their complaints to include claims under § 3. Respondents moved to dismiss the statutory claims. . . .

. . . [T]he District Court rejected the argument that § 3 conflicts with the Establishment Clause. . . .

. . . [T]he Court of Appeals for the Sixth Circuit reversed[, . . . holding] that § 3 of RLUIPA "impermissibly advanc[es] religion by giving greater protection to religious rights than to other constitutionally protected rights." . . . Affording "religious prisoners rights superior to those of nonreligious prisoners," the court suggested, might "encourag[e] prisoners to become religious in order to enjoy greater rights." . . .

We granted certiorari to resolve the conflict among Courts of Appeals on the question whether RLUIPA's institutionalized-persons provision, § 3 of the Act, is consistent with the Establishment Clause of the First Amendment. . . . We now reverse the judgment of the Court of Appeals for the Sixth Circuit.

II

A

. . . While the two [Religion] Clauses express complementary values, they often exert conflicting pressures. *See . . . Walz . . .* ("The Court has struggled to

---

2. RFRA, Courts of Appeals have held, remains operative as to the Federal Government and federal territories and posses- sions. . . . This Court, however, has not had occasion to rule on the matter.

find a neutral course between the two Religion Clauses, both of which are cast in absolute terms, and either of which, if expanded to a logical extreme, would tend to clash with the other.'').

Our decisions recognize that "there is room for play in the joints" between the Clauses, . . . some space for legislative action neither compelled by the Free Exercise Clause nor prohibited by the Establishment Clause. . . . On its face, the Act qualifies as a permissible legislative accommodation of religion that is not barred by the Establishment Clause.

Foremost, we find RLUIPA's institutionalized-persons provision compatible with the Establishment Clause because it alleviates exceptional government-created burdens on private religious exercise. . . . Furthermore, the Act on its face does not founder on shoals our prior decisions have identified: Properly applying RLUIPA, courts must take adequate account of the burdens a requested accommodation may impose on nonbeneficiaries . . . and they must be satisfied that the Act's prescriptions are and will be administered neutrally among different faiths. . . .

. . . Section 3 covers state-run institutions—mental hospitals, prisons, and the like—in which the government exerts a degree of control unparalleled in civilian society and severely disabling to private religious exercise. . . . RLUIPA thus protects institutionalized persons who are unable freely to attend to their religious needs and are therefore dependent on the government's permission and accommodation for exercise of their religion.

. . . In *Goldman v. Weinberger*, 475 U.S. 503, we held that the Free Exercise Clause did not require the Air Force to exempt an Orthodox Jewish officer from uniform dress regulations so that he could wear a yarmulke indoors. In a military community, the Court observed, "there is simply not the same [individual] autonomy as there is in the larger civilian community." . . . Congress responded to *Goldman* by prescribing that "a member of the armed forces may wear an item of religious apparel while wearing the uniform," unless "the wearing of the item would interfere with the performance [of] military duties [or] the item of apparel is not neat and conservative." . . .

We do not read RLUIPA to elevate accommodation of religious observances over an institution's need to maintain order and safety. Our decisions indicate that an accommodation must be measured so that it does not override other significant interests. In *Caldor*, the Court struck down a Connecticut law that "arm[ed] Sabbath observers with an absolute and unqualified right not to work on whatever day they designate[d] as their Sabbath." . . . We held the law invalid under the Establishment Clause because it "unyielding[ly] weigh[ted]" the interests of Sabbatarians "over all other interests." . . .

We have no cause to believe that RLUIPA would not be applied in an appropriately balanced way, with particular sensitivity to security concerns. While the Act adopts a "compelling governmental interest" standard, . . . [l]awmakers supporting RLUIPA were mindful of the urgency of discipline, order, safety, and security in penal institutions. . . .

. . . .

B

The Sixth Circuit misread our precedents to require invalidation of RLUI-PA as "impermissibly advancing religion by giving greater protection to religious rights than to other constitutionally protected rights." . . . Our decision in *Amos* counsels otherwise. There, we upheld against an Establishment Clause challenge a provision exempting "religious organizations from Title VII's prohibition against discrimination in employment on the basis of religion." . . . Religious accommodations, we held, need not "come packaged with benefits to secular entities." . . .

Were the Court of Appeals' view the correct reading of our decisions, all manner of religious accommodations would fall. Congressional permission for members of the military to wear religious apparel while in uniform would fail. . . . Ohio could not, as it now does, accommodate "traditionally recognized" religions . . .: The State provides inmates with chaplains "but not with publicists or political consultants," and allows "prisoners to assemble for worship, but not for political rallies."

In upholding RLUIPA's institutionalized-persons provision, we emphasize that respondents "have raised a facial challenge to [the Act's] constitutionality, and have not contended that under the facts of any of [petitioners'] specific cases . . . [that] applying RLUIPA would produce unconstitutional results." . . .

. . .

Justice Thomas, concurring.

I join the opinion of the Court. I agree with the Court that the Religious Land Use and Institutionalized Persons Act of 2000 (RLUIPA) is constitutional under our modern Establishment Clause case law. I write to explain why a proper historical understanding of the Clause as a federalism provision leads to the same conclusion.

. . .

†